Date Due

Campaign It!

Campaign It!
Achieving success through communication

Alan Barnard and Chris Parker

KoganPage

LONDON PHILADELPHIA NEW DELHI

First published in Great Britain and the United States in 2012 by Kogan Page Limited

120 Pentonville Road	1518 Walnut Street, Suite 1100	4737/23 Ansari Road
London N1 9JN	Philadelphia PA 19102	Daryaganj
United Kingdom	USA	New Delhi 110002
www.koganpage.com		India

© Alan Barnard and Chris Parker, 2012

The right of Alan Barnard and Chris Parker to be identified as the authors of this work has been asserted by them in accordance with the Copyright, Designs and Patents Act 1988.

ISBN   978 0 7494 6420 2
E-ISBN   978 0 7494 6421 9

British Library Cataloguing-in-Publication Data

A CIP record for this book is available from the British Library.

Library of Congress Cataloging-in-Publication Data

Barnard, Alan.
    Campaign it! : achieving success through communication / Alan Barnard, Chris Parker.
      p. cm.
    ISBN 978-0-7494-6420-2 (pbk.) – ISBN 978-0-7494-6421-9 ( )   1. Business communication.
2. Interpersonal communication.   3. Marketing.   I. Parker, Chris.   II. Title.
    HF5718.B367 2012
    650.101'4–dc23
                                                                                          2011043134

Typeset by Graphicraft Ltd, Hong Kong
Print production managed by Jellyfish
Printed and bound in Great Britain by CPI Group (UK) Ltd, Croydon, CR0 4YY

CONTENTS

ABOUT THE AUTHORS

This book is based on the ongoing work, practice, study and collaborations of Alan Barnard and Chris Parker. The *Campaign It!* model has been developed as a result of many years of practical campaigning at the highest levels. The authors use stories from campaigns and examples of their communications to illustrate some of the concepts and principles behind the *Campaign It!* model. This is a brief outline of their careers showing where they learned and plied their trade.

Alan Barnard began his professional career as a Project Leader at a hostel for homeless youngsters. The experience he gained there made him realize that sometimes society needs more than just a sticking plaster and so he went to work for his local Labour Party to campaign to get housing expert Chris Smith elected to Parliament. As a result of his successes there, Alan joined Labour's head office team in charge of the marginal seats, helping to change and modernize Labour's election campaigning ahead of the 1997 general election. Alan was given responsibility for planning and implementing the vital 'Last Five Days' of Tony Blair's general election landslide. With Labour in government he became its Director of Campaigns and Elections. In his time with Labour Alan learnt much from studying national and international elections and valued his secondment to work on Bill Clinton's 1992 Presidential Campaign in the USA.

Having effected change at Labour, Alan turned his mind to his other passion and joined The Football Association as their first ever Head of Campaigns and Research. Two years later he moved on to work as a freelance consultant. It was in 2003 that his approach to campaigning was first modelled for Chris Parker's book *Developing Management Skills for Leadership*. It is an approach he has continued to develop, leading to the *Campaign It!* model.

Alan set up his company, bbm campaigns, in 2005 to transfer the skills, techniques, attitudes and principles of campaigning to help businesses and organizations achieve success. bbm's clients have included Three UK, Asda, University College London and the Law Society.

Chris Parker began his study of interpersonal and intrapersonal communications in 1976. It became a lifelong study that has underpinned over three decades of work in a variety of professional roles and contexts. Chris is a highly experienced management trainer, business consultant, lecturer and writer. He has provided communications and creativity training for a wide range of clients including blue-chip organizations, LEAs, public and private leisure providers, sportsmen and women, politicians, actors and healthcare professionals. He has taught on undergraduate and postgraduate programmes throughout the UK and Europe, and has worked with many individuals to help create personal and/or professional change.

Chris is the author of several novels, a selection of short stories and a stage musical, as well as having written and contributed to a number of management texts. A martial artist since 1973, he has been a columnist and features writer for several of the worlds leading martial arts magazines and journals. He is particularly interested in the ways martial arts principles can be applied to enhance many aspects of our personal and professional lives, and provides training to individuals, groups and organizations in the physical, psychological and holistic benefits of martial arts practice.

Chris is currently Principal Lecturer in Sport and Leisure Management at Nottingham Trent University.

His personal website is **www.powerfromweakness.com**.

Introduction

Welcome to the beginning. We wrote it some time ago and, as Maria Robinson observed, we cannot change it now. We might, of course, if our publishers ask for a second or third edition. Books, like history, are only ever re-written by those who are successful. We will come back to this point later. Now, though, we are going to begin by making a bold claim:

> This book can improve the way you communicate, enabling you to achieve your desired personal, social and professional outcomes more effectively and efficiently.

In the following chapters we introduce, explain and demonstrate our new, unique and complete approach to communication. We call it the *Campaign It!* model. It is a model we have developed over several decades of working to create influence and change at the highest levels in different environments and contexts. It is tried and tested. We know it works.

Simply put, whenever we have an outcome we need to achieve we have to inform, persuade and gain agreement from at least some significant others. The *Campaign It!* model enables us to do this powerfully and positively.

Essentially, *Campaign It!* argues for a new paradigm:

> Taking a campaigning approach to all our communications is the best way to influence others powerfully and positively, and so gain permission to achieve our desired outcomes.

In short, we should all campaign our communications if we want to be successful. And we believe that the *Campaign It!* model is the best way to plan, structure and develop our communications.

The progression through this book is in four stages. We:

1 Provide a new definition of what it means to campaign, and show how the principles, skills and attitudes associated with a campaign of communications can be applied successfully to any area of our lives.

2 Explain and demonstrate the importance and power of having a cause, which we define as the emotional aspect of any outcome associated to any area of our life that is so significant we simply have to achieve it. We then show how the cause is the motivation for creating and sustaining a communication campaign.

3 Explain why, in our modern society, a communication campaign is the most powerful way to achieve any desired outcome or goal.

4 Show how to create and apply an irresistible communication campaign in any aspect of our lives, personal, social, professional, using the *Campaign It!* model.

Now, because we agree with Epiah Khan that there is always far less time between the beginning and the end than we expect, we are going to move things along quickly by asking and answering the questions that most people have posed when first introduced to the *Campaign It!* model.

Q&A

Q. What do you mean by campaign? Isn't it something to do with politics?
A. It is certainly the case that in the past the word campaign has been associated primarily with either politics or war; people referred to either a political campaign or a military campaign. More recently some people have made reference to a marketing campaign. For us, though, a campaign is far more of a holistic term that identifies a process and *a way of thinking and behaving* that is of value in all aspects of our lives.

For us a campaign is simply:

'A planned sequence of communications that makes use of all appropriate channels to achieve defined outcomes in a specific timeframe by influencing the decision-makers who will allow success.'

Q. And what is the *It*?
A. The *It* is any outcome a person chooses it to be. It can be anything in their personal, social, home or professional life that they would like to happen. Some of the stories throughout the book will help you understand how the model can be applied to anything. Any outcome can be campaigned, although, of course, some outcomes are easier to achieve than others and some can be achieved in fewer communications than others.

Q. Is it really necessary to campaign communications? Won't a 'word in the right direction' or a well-written email, or a great presentation work just as well?

A. It depends on the desired outcome. The three examples above can each be part of a campaign or they can be all that is required. Some outcomes can be achieved in one or two communications, whilst others might require far more. Some outcomes can be achieved in a matter of minutes or days, whilst others might need months or years. Our experience shows us that the more we campaign our communications the more likely we are to achieve our desired outcomes. In our modern world the ability to be influential in one-off interactions, is simply not enough. If we need to be heard above the ever-increasing communication clamour we have to make our communications achieve more for us and that means we have to become great campaigners.

Q. To what extent does the *Campaign It!* model include things that most people already know? After all, everyone communicates on a daily basis.
A. Depending on your background, there are probably some elements of the model you are consciously aware of and some you are only subconsciously aware of. However, the value of the model lies in its completeness. It can be applied to under-pin corporate strategy, support individual career development, enhance personal growth or create social change.

We realize, too, that the vast majority of us tend to regard ourselves as at least competent communicators and that we appreciate the importance of communication in both our private and professional lives.[1] Which is why we know the *Campaign It!* model is of value to everyone who needs to achieve a specific outcome.

Q. Can you really teach how to campaign your communications through a book?
A. Yes. The book provides learning points and sequenced activities. Do the activities and use these as a springboard for developing the required skills and associated attributes. Although this is just an introduction to campaigning communications, it is a practical text. Actually, we think of it as a workshop in a book. It is a practical tool that includes examples, stories and a range of activities. We think you'll enjoy it.

Q. Why is there an exclamation point?
A. Because, as we will discuss and demonstrate later, campaigns are sparked by an emotional compulsion to achieve a desired end outcome and they have to instil that same emotion in those whose support is needed for success. The exclamation point is a reminder of the fact that emotional commitment is the energy that fuels momentum. And as campaigners we need to create momentum in both ourselves and significant others.

---

[1] In Chapter 1 we share the results of our research that asked: 'How important is communication?' and 'How good at communicating are you?' We also share examples of the extensive costs we all pay for miscommunication.

> ## LEARNING POINTS
>
> - A campaign is: '*A planned sequence of communications that makes use of all appropriate channels to achieve defined outcomes in a specific timeframe by influencing the decision-makers who will allow success.*'
> - Any desired outcome in any and every aspect of our lives can be campaigned.
> - Some outcomes can be achieved through only one or two communications, some might take months or even years.

With that said, we will end our Introduction with the first of our stories. It is about a man and a problem with camels.

Camels

A wise man rode his camel into a desert village one evening and asked a villager for a drink of water.

'Of course,' the villager said and gave him a cup-full.

The man emptied the cup and said, 'Thank you for your kindness, can I help you in any way before I travel on?'

The villager said, 'Yes. We have a dispute in our family. Our father has just died and left us his herd of 17 camels. In his will he decreed that 1/2 of the herd should go to my eldest brother, 1/3 should go to the middle brother and 1/9 should go to me. How can we possibly divide a herd of 17 camels in that way without killing any, which we don't want to do?'

'Take me to your house,' the wise man said.

Inside the house he saw the other two brothers arguing violently.

'Wait,' the wise man said. 'I will help you now. Here, I give you my camel. Now you have 18 camels. 1/2 goes to the eldest son, that's 9 camels. 1/3 goes to the middle son, that's 6 camels, and 1/9 to the youngest, that's 2 camels.'

'That's only 17 altogether,' said the eldest son.

'Yes,' said the wise man. 'Luckily for me the camel left over is the one I gave to you. If you are willing to give it back to me, I will continue on my journey.'

And he did.

How is great communication – a *campaign* – like the 18th camel?

01 Our approach to campaigns and campaigning

" *I have always been a campaigner and over the years I have learnt to become better at it.* **ALAN BARNARD**

" *Communication works for those who work at it.* **JOHN POWELL**

The purpose of this chapter is to:

1 Share and explain our new definition of a campaign.
2 Explain and justify our approach to campaigning, including the purpose and philosophy of campaigning.
3 Outline the attitudes of a campaigner.
4 Introduce and provide an overview of our *Campaign It!* model.
5 Lay the foundation for everything that is to follow.

In this chapter we:

- Redefine campaigning.
- Explain the purpose of campaigning.
- Discuss the philosophy of campaigning and the attitudes of a campaigner.
- Justify the need for a campaigning approach in all aspects of our personal and professional lives.
- Share the results of our research that asked: 'How important is communication?' and 'How good at communicating are you?'

- Consider why we tend to rate ourselves highly as communicators and ask 'Are we really that good?'
- Discuss the inevitability of influence.
- Introduce the seven principles of campaigning.
- Introduce the *Campaign It!* model.

Learning to become better

The *Campaign It!* model is the result of many years of work that led us both through two very distinct learning curves. The first was based on the fact that Alan (AB) was totally focused on how to influence communities and societies and so to create social and/or global change and that Chris (CP) was totally focused on how to influence individuals and/or groups. Neither of us was fully aware of the skill sets of the other and neither of us had considered the value of these different skill sets to our own work.

Learning from each other required us both to embrace that most basic and challenging of all principles:

'We can only get better if we learn the things we need to know that we currently don't.'

Fortunately, we have had much fun learning from each other and we continue to do so.[1]

The second learning curve was in the creation of the *Campaign It!* model itself. Being able to do something well is one thing. Being able to structure and provide it for the benefit of others is something else altogether. There is a world of difference in being able to do something that helps others and being able to provide something that enables others to help themselves. We created the *Campaign It!* model to enable people to help themselves, their families, their businesses or their communities. It is the result of a process that began...

Well, to be honest, that depends to a certain extent on which one of us you ask. Here are our two answers to that same question:

CP: 'It began in 1976 when I met a man, a Malaysian martial artist, who could use words to change people in ways I had never imagined. I both observed and experienced personally how powerfully he could influence others. At that time I was studying to be a schoolteacher and it seemed to me that knowing how to use words to create powerful and positive change was a most appropriate capability (even though, for some reason, it wasn't part of the curriculum I was studying!). So I committed myself to learning from him. It was the start of a fascination with how to use words to empower ourselves and others that has continued for over three decades.

'In 2003, having worked as a schoolteacher and manager, an educational and corporate consultant and trainer, and a university lecturer, I asked Alan Barnard if I could model his approach to campaigning for a book I was writing about management skills and leadership. It was an insightful experience, interviewing and

---

[1] Which is not to say that we haven't challenged each other along the way!

observing the work of a man who was used to operating at the highest levels to create social and national change.

'Interestingly, like so many hugely talented individuals, Alan was not consciously aware of everything he did to achieve his outcomes. He demonstrated such a level of what Maslow termed "unconscious competence" that often he was only able to discuss the complexity of his work in the most simple of terms. Much of what he did, he said, was the "bleedin' obvious". But only to him, it certainly wasn't to me.

'The result of our time together was the creation of a basic model, a chapter based on his work and the start of a dialogue that led to us sharing and combining our different interests and skills in communication.

'I still believe that interpersonal communication, the words we use and the ways we interact with others, is crucial to enabling personal development and change. I understand now, though, that the approach that Alan uses to influence societies can also be applied and has enormous value when seeking to influence individuals, teams and groups. I also appreciate just how many of the principles and strategies that I apply in my work are also used by Alan in his.

'For example, having a desired, clearly defined end outcome is as important to me when I am working with an individual client or a lecture theatre filled with students, as it is for Alan when planning a corporate, social or political campaign. We both place great importance on the way we sequence our communications, on how we combine emotional language with persuasive facts and figures, and on how we share messages not just information. We both know that influential communication is based on an understanding of those we are communicating with and that you always have to begin from their starting point, not your own. As a result of the work we have done together, I realize now that even a single communication in a corridor can incorporate all of the elements of the *Campaign It!* model: as long as that conversation is driven by a cause.'

AB: 'I've always been a campaigner. It seems that throughout my life I have come across things that needed improving, and I've always seemed to have the desire to work to make those improvements happen. From my school days, through my degree and into work, I've always been trying to make changes happen and to influence others to give support and permission for those changes. I'd never wanted to write a book about it, though, until Chris got me thinking one day.

'Chris was writing a book about leadership aimed at the undergraduate market. He wanted to include some references to campaigning in it and needed an expert to interview. So he asked me.

'I remember being very uncomfortable. I rarely talked about my work as a campaigner, preferring to operate behind the scenes, and after all, why on earth would I give my secrets away? I was also acutely aware that the media were always looking for process stories about my work for Labour and I wasn't going to give them any opportunities. But we were talking generically, and Chris was modelling the approach for a book on theory, and wasn't going to include anything about the specifics of what I do – this was for a different audience – and I wanted to help him out.

'It took a few weeks, with many more conversations between us, but eventually Chris got back to me with the fruits of his labour. 'How's this for the "Barnard Campaign" model?' he asked.

'When I looked at it I realized that the model he had produced from what I thought was our sometimes rambling chats was really very clever. It was a little simplistic, in that each stage could have been explored in so much more detail: Chris had just produced the top line explanation for the section in his book, but that top line was spot on in its description of how I think about campaigning.

'Bloody hell,' I thought to myself. 'I wonder if we can write a book in which we simplify and explain the complexity of campaigning, and how it can be used in all walks of life?'

'Excitingly, at the same time, Chris introduced me to some of the ways in which he had been studying the power of words and how we all form the beliefs that govern our lives. That was the start of an exploration that is continuing. And it was the start of a new way for me to think about campaigning, incorporating the elements of micro-communications into my campaign thinking. It was the start of what became the *Campaign It!* model.'

Whenever the process actually began it has led us to:

- a clear, working definition of a campaign of communications;
- an evolved, functional model of the key elements of campaigning;
- a clear understanding of the philosophy, attitudes, behaviours and attributes of a campaigner.

It is also true to say that no matter when the process began it is far from over. The more we apply the *Campaign It!* approach in different professional, personal and social contexts, the more we learn. Whilst individual campaigns operate within specific timeframes, opportunities to campaign communications are endless depending, of course, on your definition of a campaign. Let's revisit ours:

Our new definition and our approach to campaigning

For us, a campaign is:

> 'A planned sequence of communications that makes use of all appropriate channels to achieve defined outcomes in a specific timeframe by influencing the decision-makers who will allow success.'

A campaign is a planned series of communications because there is a defined outcome to be achieved that is too important to leave to chance. It is planned because others are often seeking to influence our audience too and we need to be heard above them and to be more persuasive than them. It is planned because there is usually a limited timeframe within which to operate and because as campaigners we care about our audience and our desired outcome.

The notion of caring, of having an emotional compulsion to achieve something, is central to our philosophy and approach to campaigning communications. We believe that, to a great extent, the quality of our personal, social and professional lives is determined by the quality of our communications. Our ability to create change or defend an aspect of the status quo certainly is. Whilst, as we will discuss later, we influence others just through our very existence, in order to influence deliberately, positively and ethically we need an attitude, a skill set and a willingness to commit.

We live in an age in which it is easier than ever before to share your thoughts, ideas and stories with entire communities. Technology has enabled everyone with access to it to become a storyteller, a critic, a reviewer, an apparent online expert. We have the capability to change from one form of media and from one story to another in the blink of an eye. We can shift and share our attention from one thing to the next with incredible ease. In our modern world more individuals, groups, societies and organizations can be seen and heard and, therefore, influence, more easily than ever before.

It is because we live in a world of communication overload that we have to be able to back up our emotional desire to achieve a particular outcome with a comprehensive approach to communications if we are to improve our chances of success.

A campaign of communications incorporates a story, a structure and a sequence designed to create maximum influence. It provides a planned, deliberate sharing of messages that are supported by relevant information. It shares key themes, lines to take and is evocative, newsworthy and integrated fully. It combines big picture planning with absolute attention to detail and it is managed and measured throughout to ensure that it gains momentum as it builds towards the inevitable climax. Everything is based on an understanding of the current experiences, attitudes and starting knowledge of the target audiences and of their preferred communication styles and channels. The initial plan is mapped and developed before the campaign begins and can then be adapted in response to feedback.

In business a campaign of communications is far more than just marketing or public relations or organizing a wonderful launch event to mark the start of a new initiative. All of these might well be a part of the overall campaign, however the emphasis on integration throughout the *Campaign It!* model means that a campaign is actually the totality of the organization's communications, joined up and working together to tell the chosen narrative in the most influential way. It is far more than just using a common slogan and logo, or having printed media that provides accurate information.

A fully integrated communications campaign requires analysis, creativity and commitment to sustain the level of work that is required to ensure congruency and consistency of message, approach and purpose across all audience touch points, and to remind and reinforce the audience of the benefits on offer.

In our social life running a campaign of communications is far more than organizing one single fete or going on a march or just signing a petition. Whilst it is true that some campaigns are made up of just a handful of communications, which can be informal in nature, many are not. Our social world is also a part of the many complex and busy communication structures that influence us on every level. Therefore, if we truly care about any social issue the best way to communicate that is to campaign it by creating a fully integrated, timeframed, sequence of communications.

The same is true for the challenges of managing and developing personal relationships and family life. We can campaign our love for another person or teach our children how to become great citizens or friends just as we can campaign everything else that really matters to us. And, in our personal lives as in other every other aspect of our lives, it is rare that one single communication will achieve the desired end outcome.

Purpose, philosophy, attitude and attributes

The purpose of a campaign is either to make change happen or to reinforce the value of some aspect of the status quo. This purpose is underpinned by a philosophy, an attitude, a skill set and, for us, the *Campaign It!* model.

Campaigns are driven by a cause. It is our commitment to the cause, whatever it may be, that fires our emotional compulsion to act. The cause creates a need, a powerful desire to campaign. Whilst we are always able to offer a rational and logical argument for supporting the cause, we will also feel that it is absolutely the right thing to do. The philosophy behind campaigning is to grow support for the cause in an ethical way whilst being true to your own beliefs and values. It is much harder to campaign for something you do not believe in. Indeed, without that, you do not have a cause to campaign.

Campaigning is also based on the clear understanding that we need to gain the permission of others and that ultimately emotional compulsion always beats rational argument. To grow support campaigners need to seize the initiative wherever possible, be on the front foot and take a lead. The importance of being willing to go first, as with all of the other skills, attributes and essential processes, will be discussed more fully throughout the book.

Campaigns are fully integrated plans put into action and adapted if necessary in response to feedback. We recommend working from the desired end outcome backwards when creating the campaign plan. In our experience this increases the chances of identifying and incorporating all of the necessary steps and elements and also makes it easier to get the sequencing of the narrative and associated activities right. It also makes sure that we act in a timely manner and are ready for the end of the campaign.

AB discovered that this was an approach that was also used by many times paralympic gold medallist Baroness Tanni Grey-Thompson when planning her training. She explained: 'I always plan from the end point and then just start plotting backwards.'

We call this approach *reverse planning*.

For us, the attitude needed to take a campaigning approach to communications is one of curiosity, adaptability, courage and care. It grows out of a desire for seeking continual improvement for ourselves and others and of an acceptance of the inevitability of influence. Campaigners are willing to take the initiative and accept responsibility for the outcomes they create. They have to be able to manage uncertainty and their own emotional commitment. Caring can blinker perception and limit adaptability and we believe that campaigners have to be willing to change as they progress their campaign.

> *Campaigns are based on reverse planning and emotional commitment. They either create something new or defend something that is currently in place.*

The *Campaign It!* model incorporates all the elements, procedures and skills necessary to communicate and influence effectively and with practice these become an instinctive part of how we think and operate on a daily basis.

The *Campaign It!* model exists and is applied within this framework as shown below:

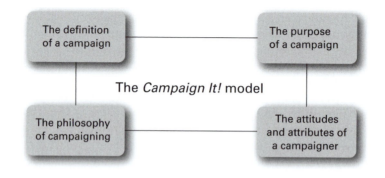

We call this:

'Thinking inside the box.'

LEARNING POINTS

- A campaign is a planned sequence of communications that makes use of all appropriate channels to achieve defined outcomes in a specific timeframe by influencing the decision-makers who will allow success.
- The purpose of a campaign is to change or maintain some aspect of the status quo.
- The campaigning philosophy is to grow support for your cause whilst being true to your values and beliefs.
- The campaigning attitude combines curiosity, adaptability, courage and care.
- Use reverse planning.
- Seize the initiative.
- Think inside the box.

Leaders, vacuums and campaigns

We don't live and operate in a communications vacuum. If we did there would never be any need to get the permission of others for things we want to accomplish. And, therefore, there would never be a need to campaign our communications. On the other hand, if we did live in that communications vacuum we would miss the vibrancy and complexity of our modern world and the challenges, benefits and joy of the many different types of relationship that we all experience.

Our philosophy and approach to campaigning has been developed precisely because we do not, and never will, operate in a vacuum. Archbishop Desmond Tutu said:

'I am a leader by default, because nature does not allow a vacuum.'

In one sense, then, campaigning is a necessary celebration of nature's rule. We campaign to build momentum in a crowded world, to create a shared energy moving in a common direction.

Our *Campaign It!* model is based on:

- an understanding of the nature, purpose and value of communication;
- the inevitability of influence;
- the likelihood of resistance;
- the need for an ethical approach;
- our seven principles of campaigning.

The nature and purpose of communication

Communication is our primary method of exchange. Through our communication we can exchange ideas, thoughts, feelings and data. We can exchange emotions and beliefs. We can exchange by talking, writing or simply demonstrating. We can exchange through a variety of media and through a single glance. We can exchange when we don't mean to and, incredibly, we can even exchange when we do *nothing*.

Our communication is based upon, reflects and also creates our levels of awareness and understanding. Through our communication we can broaden our horizons and yet we also develop filters that limit our perception. We communicate consciously and subconsciously, seeking patterns, creating meanings and coming to conclusions sometimes in the merest fraction of a second as we determine how best to communicate.

In many respects the quality of our communication determines the nature and quality of our life experiences. It is through communication that we create and develop relationships (with ourselves as well as with others), progress our careers, influence our communities, agree and reflect social norms and inform and develop future generations.

The value of communication

Given that communication is an integral part of what it means to be human just take a moment to do the following activity:

Please answer this simple question: 'How good are you at communicating?'

Trust your instinct and give yourself a score between 1 and 10 as indicated on the scale below:

0 Non-existent

1 Dreadful

2 Very poor

3 Poor

4 Fairly poor

5 Average

6 Fairly good

7 Good

8 Very good

9 Excellent

10 Faultless

Thank you. Was the score you gave yourself somewhere in the range of 7 to 9 out of 10? Do you regard yourself as a good, a very good, or even an excellent, communicator?

If you don't you are in the minority. We asked over 600 men and women of different ages to score themselves using the continuum offered to you. The results were fascinating. More than 70 per cent rated themselves as 'Good' or 'Very good' and over 8 per cent rated themselves as 'Excellent' communicators.

You might wonder who we asked. Did we focus only on people who are most likely to be expert communicators? People like teachers, business leaders, sales staff, counsellors? Actually, we didn't. Whilst our survey did include some individuals from these professions, it also included technicians, web designers, gardeners, volunteer workers, quantity surveyors, administrators and many more.

In other words we received feedback from a range of professionals with varied skill sets. The results indicate that most of us think that we are very useful at this communicating thing and that we recognize how important it is. We also asked our respondents to score the importance of communication in both their professional and personal lives.

Once again, the vast majority were in no doubt, with 80 per cent reporting that their ability to communicate well was either 'Very important' or 'Essential' in the workplace, and 78 per cent describing it as 'Very important' or 'Essential' in their personal lives.

This came as no surprise. A survey of 1,400 British employers carried out in 2006 by the integrated accounting firm KPMG and the Chartered Institute of Personal Development revealed that communication skills were regarded as more important to employers than academic skills or even basic literacy and numeracy. The report concludes that school leavers need to be able to demonstrate the ability to communicate well along with a strong work ethic if they want to be viewed positively in the job market.

These results were reflected in a survey of 1,500 MBA graduates in the USA. When the graduates were asked what they thought was the single most important business skill, guess what their top answer was? Communication, of course. (If it had been Accountancy the story would have belonged in a different book.) Interestingly, the graduates also rated listening skills and the ability to manage change very highly.

A different survey conducted at Pepperdine's George L. Graziadio School of Business and Management near Los Angeles also resulted in communication and interpersonal skills ranking first in a list of essential management skills for the twenty-first century. So it appears that, for business executives and leaders, the focus needs to be 'Communication! Communication! Communication!'[2]

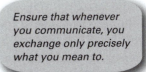

Ensure that whenever you communicate, you exchange only precisely what you mean to.

It is not just in the workplace where communication is perceived as vital. In the UK, the Department for Education and Skills produced a non-statutory document titled 'Common Core of Skills and Knowledge for the Children's Workforce' in which good communication was identified as central to working successfully with children, young people, families and carers. And the importance – the centrality – of good communication in education, healthcare and parenting is also widely acknowledged, with myriad organizations offering specialized training and an increasing number of books, magazines and journals devoted to the topics.

So, to summarize:

- The vast majority of us recognize the value of communication in all aspects of our lives.
- Most of us are confident in our ability as communicators.

Why, then, are we writing this book? If all is well in the 'communication world' why are we arguing for an essential paradigm shift in our understanding of, and approach to, effective communications? Why are we committed to the notion that we all need to learn how to campaign effectively?

Simply because all is not well. And the evidence is all around us. Most of us clearly believe that we are at least good communicators and yet as the following examples reveal our communications often fail to lead to our desired outcomes. Miscommunication creates misunderstanding and the prices we pay for misunderstandings

---

[2] And despite the implication above it is even true for accountants if Dr John Ball, writing in the *ACCA Accountant*, is to be believed when he described communication as the 'core activity of the accounting profession'.

in the workplace, in healthcare, education, political relations, conflict resolution, policing and in our personal lives are mounting up.

A white paper published in 2008[3] revealed that the overall cost of employee misunderstanding in the UK and the USA totalled a quite incredible £31 million ($62 million) per year. If you are wondering, 'How can such misunderstandings occur given that business folk like our 1,500 MBA graduates value communication skills so highly?', then the answer is that the graduates also reported that only approximately 6 per cent of business schools did a 'moderately effective' job in helping them develop these skills. And if you want to know how simple misunderstandings can be so costly, according to the 400 companies surveyed, unplanned downtime, poor procurement practice and industrial tribunal settlements had a large part to play. However, all the companies also reported that employee misunderstanding had additional negative impacts on brand, reputation, loss of sales and customer service, and led to increased health and safety risks.

In the UK, medication errors caused by poor communication, failure to read notes and miscalculation of doses result in the deaths of two patients every month and a loss of £775 million every year. A study carried out by the National Patient Safety Agency found that 60,000 'medication incidents' resulting in 18 deaths and 54 people dangerously harmed were reported by GPs, community health centres, pharmacists and hospitals in the 18 months leading up to June 2006. As some experts argue that fewer than 1 in 10 of all incidents are reported, the actual death toll could be much higher.

Worryingly, three years earlier, the Parliamentary and Health Service Ombudsman, Ann Abraham, had concluded that poor communication was often to blame for substandard NHS care. She said, 'If only all Health Service staff made sure that they listened to patients and their carers, communicated clearly with them and with each other, then made a note of what had been said, the scope for later misunderstanding and dispute would be reduced enormously.'

Poor communication is one of the most common reasons for patient complaints and is a significant factor in litigation. Research[4] carried out in the USA revealed that primary care physicians with good communication skills were far less likely to be the victims of malpractice claims than those with poor communication skills. In this context, the good communicators educated their patients about what to expect and what course their treatment or visit would follow; they used humour whenever appropriate; they encouraged their patients to ask questions, to share their opinions and feelings; and they demonstrated their understanding of the patient perspective. The research concluded that there were specific and teachable communication behaviours that primary care physicians could develop and apply which would reduce the risk of malpractice claims.

Yet it is also acknowledged that when doctors communicate effectively the overall quality of patient care improves. Patients understand their problems more fully and

---

[3] IDC white paper commissioned by Cognisco.

[4] Levinson, W. *et al* (1997) 'Physician-Patient Communication: The Relationship with Malpractice Claims Among Primary Care physicians', *The Journal of the American Medical Association*, 277(7): 553–9.

are more likely to follow medical and lifestyle advice, Even the doctor's own well-being improves!

If our miscommunications can result in such damaging outcomes within the relative security of repetitive organizational procedures and systems, what are the consequences during the organized chaos of war? Sadly and simply this: unplanned and unnecessary fatalities. One of the most obvious examples, allied to one of the most chillingly inappropriate descriptors, is 'friendly fire'. This is the term originally used by the US military to refer to fire from either one's own side or from allied forces. Friendly fire, or non-hostile fire, has claimed lives for as long as man has been going to war. The notion of 'the fog of war' is often used to describe the complexities and confusion of military engagements and is cited by many as the primary cause of friendly fire. The use of this term stems from a battle in 1471 during the Wars of the Roses when, whilst fighting in heavy fog, a Lancastrian division led by the Earl of Warwick fired and inflicted heavy casualties upon a division of their allies led by the Earl of Somerset.

Whilst to some 'the fog of war' can be used as an excuse for inadequate planning or incompetent leadership, fog of war errors clearly exist and seem to fall into two categories: those relating to errors of position and those relating to errors of identification. Both are the result of miscommunication and misunderstanding. And the cost? A US military study focusing on wars from World War I to the first Gulf War found that 15 per cent of all US, British and German casualties came from friendly fire. Given that, in World War II alone, it is estimated that over 380,000 British military personnel died, it means that over 55,000 of those servicemen were killed due to communication errors.

Not surprisingly, much is being done now to increase clarity within the fog of war. However, friendly fire continues to claim lives and create personal tragedies for all involved.

Miscommunication within the family is, sadly, increasing with about 40 per cent of British marriages ending in break-up. Paul de Graaf, Associate Professor of Sociology at Radboud University in Holland, along with Matthijs Kalmijn, Professor of Sociology at Tilburg University, interviewed over 1,700 divorcees dividing them into three groups: those who had split up from 1949–72, 1973–84 and 1985–96. They found that, amongst couples who had divorced most recently, the motives given by women have changed dramatically, with emotional factors, such as lack of attention and communication, having grown in importance.[5] In support of this, the social and economic research consultants Kieran McKeowan Ltd, also identified lack of communication as a major factor in the cause of marital difficulties.[6]

Given all the above, why are so many of us so confident in our abilities? Perhaps it is because we have experienced success in our personal or professional life and have taken that as an indication of our high-level communication skills? Or perhaps

---

[5] 'Change and Stability in the Social Determinants of Divorce: A Comparison of Marriage Cohorts in the Netherlands' *European Sociological Review*, 2006, 22(5): 561–72.

[6] 'Unhappy Marriages: Does Counselling Help?' (Final Report to ACCORD) by Kieran McKeown, Pauline Lehane, Rosemary Rock, Trutz Haase and Jonathan Pratschke.

because we communicate in so many ways on a daily basis it is too easy for us to assume a level of expertise that we do not possess? Maybe we have made the mistake of confusing a much-repeated habit with a deliberately developed skill set? It might also be that we rarely consider how best to sequence a number of communications, choosing instead to measure our communication skills based on the short-term, often immediate, responses they appear to get?

Whatever the reason, most, if not all, of us can think of times we have miscommunicated and failed to achieve the responses and outcomes we were aiming for. It is all too easy to think of times when we might have succeeded had we communicated more effectively, of occasions when we were completely misunderstood even by people who know us well. Indeed, sometimes it seems easier to miscommunicate with someone we know well than with a complete stranger!

Not surprisingly, the evidence suggests that when we improve our ability to communicate and influence effectively, we improve the quality of our life and the lives of others. The success of our communication and the nature of that influence is not, it seems, determined solely by what we exchange but also by the quality of the exchange process itself.

LEARNING POINTS

- Communication is our primary method of exchange.
- Most of us acknowledge the importance of communication in our lives.
- The costs of miscommunications are significant – and we are all paying them.

The inevitability of influence

Influence is simply an effect that one person has on another. This can be an effect on a person's character, their behaviour, their knowledge or understanding. Just as we can communicate in many ways, so we can influence in many ways. For example, we can motivate, delegate, teach, appraise and criticize. We can make others laugh. We can make them feel afraid, ashamed or just undervalued. We can lighten their days or darken their thoughts. We can create hope, inspiration, aspiration and a sense of self-worth. We can push friends, families and communities apart, or we can bring them together just by how we communicate. That is the power of influence.

Whenever we interact with others we create influence to some degree. The aim of a campaigner is to create only intentional, positive influence.

As we mentioned earlier campaigning is based on three things:

1 an attitude;
2 a skill set;
3 a process and associated principles.

The curious, courageous, caring attitude of a campaigner is based on an acceptance of the inevitability of outcomes and the need to ensure that, no matter how challenging they might be, they are both positive and appropriate within the given context.

> *Influence is inevitable; we always create an effect on others.*

The Latin root of the word 'influence' is 'influere'. It means to 'flow into'. It is through our communication that we flow into the lives and experiences of others and so create influence. It is both a responsibility and an opportunity. That is why we need to know how to apply the key principles of influence. According to Dr Robert Cialdini, formerly Regents' Professor of Psychology and W.P. Carey Distinguished Professor of Marketing at Arizona State University, there are six 'weapons of influence'. They are:

1 **Reciprocity.** Research shows that if you do someone a favour they will, in all probability, return it. They might even return it with interest! So, if you want someone to do something for you, ensure that you have done something for them first. Given this, campaigners need to make clear precisely what they have already done that adds value to the lives of their audiences, and what future benefits the campaign will bring.

2 **Commitment and consistency.** Simply put, people are more likely to act in a consistent manner once they have made a commitment to do so. Interestingly, this is even the case if the original incentive for doing so has been removed. As campaigners we need to realize and employ the power of commitment amongst both our audiences and our campaign team and supporters, considering how we can increase levels of commitment throughout the campaigning process.

3 **Social proof.** This is the accepted truth; the beliefs, attitudes or behaviours that at least the majority of a society subscribe to. Social proof is an extremely powerful influencer. It can install beliefs, shape attitudes and improve, limit or prevent certain behaviours. Campaigns often seek to change some aspect of social proof. If these campaigns are powerful and persuasive, people who had originally held on to the social proof being changed will often experience a sense of cognitive dissonance as they find themselves trying to juggle the old with the new.

4 **Authority.** If we accept a person as a figure of authority, we tend to do what they ask us. An individual can claim such power in a variety of ways including their personal charisma, their acknowledged expertise in a given arena, or their professional role. Campaigns need to be authoritative on many levels. For example, public figures who are supporting a campaign, sharing its messages and arguing on its behalf, need to be viewed by the audiences as appropriate authority figures – whether that is because of their expertise, their celebrity and charisma, or simply their status. Similarly, the authority of campaign leaders needs to be acknowledged and accepted by the campaign team.

5　**Liking.** The more we like someone else, the more easily we are influenced by them. Whilst the research assures us that we are, inevitably, attracted to attractive people, there are myriad ways we can like and be liked by others. For example, we tend to like those with whom we share common interests, backgrounds, experiences or values. It is also easy to be drawn to people who communicate in the same ways that we do; those we feel we can make sense of easily and so create a state of rapport with. Perhaps not surprisingly, we tend to particularly like people who show an unselfish interest in us and, whilst doing so, demonstrate that they really do understand us. Campaigners and their campaigns need, then, to communicate directly and indirectly in ways that both demonstrate their understanding of their audiences and increase their likeability with them.

6　**Scarcity.** One way to create the public perception of value is to limit the availability of a particular product or service. If the restaurant we phone is fully booked for the next two months, we presume that it must be excellent. And, often as not, we make a reservation. If we are told that the antique we have discovered is the last of its kind, we assume immediately that it will be worth a great deal of money. We can, therefore, add value to our campaign if we communicate the unique nature of our proposal, whilst also convincing our audiences that what we are promoting is the *'genuine article'*.

These six weapons can all be applied within a campaign of communications and can overlap.

One of the things we have both learnt from our different arenas is that people are primarily influenced by people. Hence the need for the campaign story to create an emotional response. It is important to remember that, whilst it is necessary to share relevant information, facts and figures alone to do not persuade people to change, as the following story from CP demonstrates:[7]

_____

'These suits sell themselves, sir'

There is a gentleman's outfitter in my home town of Nottingham that I used to shop in. (Notice the use of the past tense.) Once, during what happened to be my last visit, one of the elder salesmen complained to me that business had taken a very serious turn for the worse. 'I don't know why,' he complained. 'After all the quality of our clothes is exceptional.' For the next five minutes he explained to me in great detail precisely why the materials they used and the garments they sold were so good.

_____

[7]　If facts and figures alone were truly influential, scientists would have persuaded us all to eat more healthily, drink less alcohol, to stop smoking and doing the range of other things that we know are bad for us.

He went into detail that, whilst no doubt fascinating and important to a person in his profession, was of no interest or relevance to me. He spoke in the language of the expert and with the dispassionate and clinical style of a surgeon. He had interrupted my search for a new suit and he had failed to engage or motivate me. He concluded with the words, 'The manager is afraid that we might have to close. I don't believe it. I'm confident that people will start purchasing from us again. After all, these suits sell themselves, sir.'

Unfortunately, he was wrong on both counts. The shop closed precisely because suits don't sell themselves. Of course, the perceived quality of any purchase is important, but ultimately people buy from people. It is through our communication that we influence the perceptions of others and enable them to recognize the quality of what we have to share. We influence others emotionally rather than just rationally. My friends in the outfitters hadn't appreciated that times had changed and that to survive they needed to campaign the quality of both their products and their service in ways that excited customers and motivated them to buy their clothes. It proved to be a fatal error.

In summary, communication has two purposes. We use communication to influence ourself and others and also to cope with the demands of our world and develop a sense of place, purpose and power. We exchange with others because we are social animals and because we are hard-wired to give meanings to our experiences.

The more we believe that we understand things, and the more we believe those things fit the meanings we have already accepted, the more sensible we feel. Those things we cannot fit our meanings on to, that contradict our current understanding, are all too easy to dismiss as *non-sense*. When someone proposes an alternative viewpoint or approach, one that contradicts and challenges our own, we tend to feel a discomfort that can lead to resistance.

LEARNING POINTS

- Influence is, quite literally, the effect that we have on others.
- Influence is inevitable.
- Six key weapons of influence are: reciprocity; commitment and consistency; social proof; authority; liking; and scarcity.
- These can all overlap and be applied within a campaign.
- Suits don't sell themselves.

ACTIVITIES!

1   Identify some examples of reciprocity that you have experienced with any of the following: family members; work colleagues; sales staff.

2   Think of one commitment you have made. How has that made you behave (and think) in a consistent manner?

3   Consider the ways an organization or group that you know well creates its own social proof. This might be through the beliefs, values and associated behaviours that are favoured, or through the structures and systems that have been put in place, or even the ways other organizations or groups are referred to. What are the essential elements of the current social proof? How does it both help and hinder this body?

4   Think of two people you know who both exercise authority. What is the source of their authority? Compare and contrast the ways they demonstrate their authority.

5   The next time you are in a public meeting place, for example a bar, a restaurant, a hotel lobby, spend a few moments just watching people in conversation. Identify a couple who really like each other. What do you see or hear that tells you they are in rapport?

6   Notice the different ways marketeers and sales people use the concept of scarcity to promote products and services.

The likelihood of resistance

Every campaign seeks to create a change or maintain the status quo and provides opportunities for other people to join in. Change, however, is not always welcomed or valued. When the proposed change is not supported universally (and few are) the campaign will face varying degrees of resistance. As campaigners we have to be willing to accept and manage resistance.

Cognitive dissonance is the name given to the sense of discomfort people experience whenever they recognize a discrepancy between what they already know or believe and new information or a new interpretation.

When people are communicating with the intention of creating change, those they are communicating to are likely to experience some degree of cognitive dissonance.[8] Indeed, it may be necessary for them to go through this state in order to become open to new possibilities. Whilst a high sense of cognitive dissonance can increase resistance to change it can, perhaps counter-intuitively, also help create the belief that 'the new learning must be good because it was so challenging'.

---

[8]   Actually, we can create this state in others in one-off communications too, and, sometimes, we can even create cognitive dissonance without meaning to!

So if we are campaigning to create meaningful change we do need to know how to recognize, manage and limit cognitive dissonance in those we are influencing. This is one of the reasons why we need to:

- Understand our audience's starting point.
- Analyse our audience and gain feedback from them throughout the duration of the campaign.
- Highlight repeatedly the benefits our cause offers.
- Ensure that we are heard by using the audience's preferred communication channels.
- Ensure that we are easily understood by using the communication style and preferences of the audience.
- Be clear about where we need our audience to be by the end of the campaign.

Throughout the *Campaign It!* approach we use two specific forms of communication. We call them macro-communications and micro-communications. We will explain the relationship between the two in moment. First, though, we will introduce each in turn.

Macro-communications

These are the 'big-picture' skills, attitudes and processes we use to:

- Identify and analyse our audiences.
- Determine our desired outcomes.
- Plan our campaign.
- Create and manage timelines efficiently.
- Determine, develop and manage our narrative.
- Create and execute the activities that constitute the campaign.

When we are operating on the macro-level we are focusing on how best to influence larger audiences including entire organizations, communities, even societies. The ability to create and implement a plan of action is underpinned by excellent, on-going research and the application of analytical, evaluative and systemic thinking. At this level, it is important to be able to recognize the relationships that exist between different factors, identifying accurately and with clarity both causes and effects.

Micro-communications

These are the skills we use to create, recognize and manage the specific details of an interaction so that we can:

- Understand precisely the messages other people are sharing with us.
- Influence through all manner of one-to-one interactions.

- Use the written word to engage and influence others.
- Create and deliver influential presentations.
- Manage meetings successfully.
- Motivate, delegate, and provide inspirational leadership to members of our campaign team.
- Create and execute the activities that constitute the campaign.

When we are operating on the micro-level we are focusing on creating influence by managing specific details. We need to ensure that we recognize accurately the messages others are sharing with us. Micro-communication skills enable us to manage the dynamics of the interaction we are engaged in *now*, whether that is with an individual, a team, or a gathered audience. Such interactions can be planned, however there is an immediacy and, in some respects, an intimacy in these situations which is not necessarily present in 'big-picture' communications.

There is, though, an inextricable link between macro- and micro-communications. The strategies and principles that underpin and run through macro-communications and extended campaigns also apply to all forms of micro-communications. A conversation, for example, can be viewed as a form of mini-campaign especially if one person at least has a desired end outcome and a timeframe within which to achieve it. As we will discuss in Chapter 5, influential conversations are most likely to be successful if based on an understanding of the other person, if the communication is sequenced appropriately, and incorporates persuasive messages supported by helpful facts and figures.

The elements of the *Campaign It!* model apply to a single lesson, lecture or presentation as well as they do to a campaign designed to create social change. Indeed, an extended campaign comprises a range of activities all of which need to incorporate these same elements. Planning a campaign requires the application of a number of macro-skills, yet sharing the details of that plan persuasively requires the application of a number of micro-skills. Likewise, aspects of audience analysis, such as face-to-face research, are dependent upon the use of micro-skills. And, although the ability to determine and create the narrative requires macro-skills, delivering the narrative in an appropriate and influential manner requires a variety of micro- and macro-skills to be employed.

As we progress we will identify the essential macro- and micro-communication skills needed to run an influential campaign, and provide opportunities to practice a range of these. We will also demonstrate how the ability to use these skills effectively is dependent upon the ability to gather and respond appropriately to feedback. It is an ability that also needs to be maintained within a moral framework.

> Macro- and micro-communication skills are the links that make up the campaign chain; avoid having a weak link.

The need for an ethical approach

We are all powerful communicators and influencers, whether we choose to create influence by design or by accident. We believe that every individual has an obligation to themselves and to others to communicate deliberately, respectfully and skilfully – hence our development of the *Campaign It!* model.

The ability to influence others by campaigning communications effectively is a powerful one that, like all other forms of power, brings with it a need for control, tolerance and care. As Rollo May wrote, effective communication:

'leads to community; that is, to understanding, intimacy and mutual valuing.'

We would argue that careless or selfish communication lead to the opposite, to unintended outcomes, confusion and misunderstanding, a breakdown in community and/or the manipulation of others.

An ethical approach to campaigning is based on a determination to understand the attitudes and perspectives of the target audience and is demonstrated in three essential ways. These are in the:

1 value and appropriateness of the desired outcome(s);

2 accuracy and quality of the narrative, the story that is being told;

3 manner in which resistance is addressed and managed.

It is when faced with the pressure of resistance or the frustration of apathy, when experiencing difficulties, doubt or rejection that personal beliefs and values are most likely to be tested. Unfortunately, or fortunately depending on your perspective, these are all likely experiences along the campaigning path. An ethical approach reflects the campaigner's sense of personal identity and becomes part of the identity of the campaign itself in the eyes of the audience. It helps to shape the behaviours, messages and operational processes of the campaign and acts as a form of security and protection, providing something to hold on to in stormy times.

LEARNING POINTS

- Campaigns often create a sense of cognitive dissonance amongst at least parts of the audience; campaigners need to be able to recognize and manage this.
- Campaigners need to be skilled at both macro- and micro-communications, and understand the relationship between the two.
- Communications, when campaigned appropriately, are inevitably powerful and therefore need to be managed within an ethical framework.

The seven principles of campaigning

1. The purpose of any campaign is either to make change happen or to reinforce some aspect of the status quo

Campaigns are fuelled by a cause. This can be anything from persuading an individual to change a specific behaviour to influencing a society to change a government. It can be a change within a family or a change within a multi-national organization. The cause, whatever it maybe, is the emotional compulsion for the desired outcome you are aiming to achieve. It provides both the motivation and, when necessary, the courage to campaign. The cause becomes the story you just have to tell.

2. To make change happen you have to get permission from others

Every change we seek to create will influence someone else. We need, therefore, to identify and understand the people we have to influence, those we need to be on our side. If we fail to get permission from these significant others, the chances are we will fail to achieve our desired outcome. Understanding and influencing your audience(s) appropriately is at the heart of campaigning.

3. To get permission from others you have to tell them a compelling story

People are influenced by stories. The campaign story is referred to as the narrative. It grows out of our understanding of the value of our cause and the benefits it offers, and our understanding of the current knowledge, attitudes and agendas of our audience. We share the campaign narrative through a series of integrated activities. It is through the sharing of this compelling narrative that we gain permission.

4. A compelling story needs to be structured, sequenced and planned and create an emotional response

For any story to be engaging and compelling, it has to be structured and sequenced appropriately and it has to be delivered through the most appropriate channels at the most appropriate times. Novelists, screenwriters and playwrights are all acutely aware of the importance of layering their story to ensure that the storyline is developed at the right pace in the right way. Great storytelling is as much about careful planning as it is creative flair. Both combine to ensure the desired emotional response from the audience. Ultimately, in a fictional story as in a campaign narrative, the order in which you deliver the information to your audience determines the response you get.

5. The plan can change in response to feedback

Whilst it is essential to plan your campaign in detail, it is equally important to be willing to change the plan if necessary. Other things are going on in the world that impact on our abilities to communicate. And some of these may be deliberately organized against our campaign. As campaigners we create and control the plan; a willingness to be flexible and adaptive is one of the core traits of a successful campaigner.

6. Feedback is the lifeblood of a campaign

Seek feedback throughout the duration of the campaign. Because all campaigns operate within a range of contexts all influenced by other peoples' agendas, it is essential that these are monitored continually. Keep asking the right questions of the right people, respond to this feedback as required and be ready and willing to manage resistance if and when it appears.

7. Campaigns all begin and end with a clean whiteboard

The *Campaign It!* model provides a comprehensive approach to creating and delivering influential communications in any context. However, no two campaigns are ever the same. When beginning a new campaign it is necessary to forget, temporarily at least, how previous campaigns have been constructed and to be genuinely and overwhelmingly curious about the new context we are operating within. Only then can our thinking be informed by previous experiences and skills.

AB likes to use a whiteboard when designing and developing campaigns. A clean whiteboard means that the previous campaign is over and that in the next campaign all things are possible. The slate has quite literally been wiped clean and he is ready to make a fresh start.

LEARNING POINTS

- Campaigns create change through the telling of a compelling story that engages the audience emotionally as well as rationally.
- Feedback is the lifeblood of every campaign.
- Campaigns all begin and end with a clean whiteboard.

The *Campaign It!* model

Look at the next page. This is what the *Campaign It!* model looks like.

CAMPAIGN IT!

Cause	Audience	Map campaign	Prepare narrative	Activities	Integrate	Grid	Narrative	Influence conversations	Test	Remember
Your cause provides the emotional compulsion.	Who gives you permission to succeed?	Create a rough overview of your campaign.	The narrative is the heart of your campaign – get it right!	Bring your cause to life.	Create as many touchpoints and interactions as necessary.	Coordinate your activities.	Use the narrative to guide your campaign.	The most powerful messaging is word of mouth.	Gather feedback and test your plan.	Emotional commitment fuels momentum.
The cause becomes the story you have to tell. It gives purpose and a vision. It gives the desired outcomes. It gives power and a sense of identity. There are gradations of cause. And causes can be nested, overlapping, simultaneous or side-by-side. Go first!	Analyse the audience(s). Be curious. How are they defined? Who are the intermediate audiences? What do you know and need to know about them? What are their ambitions in respect of our cause? What other ambitions do they have? Who and what influences the audiences? What knowledge or beliefs do you need to impart?	Plan from the end goals and work backwards - use reverse planning. Know what success will be. Be creative - use imagineering. Work out sequence of story and types of possible activity. Create timelines and targets with milestones along the way. Assess resources and skills required. Create a great team culture.	The narrative is the understanding you need the target audiences to have so they give you permission to succeed. Be true to the vision and purpose. Create and develop: • Key Themes • Flagship Policies • Messages • Lines to Take • A Slogan. Assemble the supporting info, facts and figures. It will pay off to spend early time getting this right.	Explain your cause for your audience. Prove it using as many campaign activities and communications as required, always thinking "and then what?". Create events and activities. Each activity should set up the next. Deliver using all appropriate channels. Have story plans to develop content and collateral, and to integrate across channels.	Integrate message into all appropriate consumer and audience touchpoints & interactions. Use the narrative as a guide to content. Overlap stories. Repeat and reinforce. Repeat and reinforce. Grow and build. Take advantage of opportunities that arise or that you can create.	Have a plan to set out the narrative development over time. Timetable events, communications and other audience interactions to build the understanding of the narrative. Use a message Grid to coordinate activities. Monitor the plan. There's no hiding place from the Grid. Be flexible; update the plan and Grid in light of feedback and opportunities. Build momentum.	After cause, the narrative is the most important element of any campaign. Every communication must tell at least one part of the overall narrative. The whole narrative must be repeated at least once before the end of the campaign.	The aim is to get your campaign talked about in the right ways by the right people so that you succeed. Sequence the narrative. Build and layer the story. Ensure great timing. Do so deliberately and consistently. Develop your micro-communication skills.	Feedback is the lifeblood of the campaign. Act, learn, adjust, act. Ask the right questions of the right people. Look, listen and learn. Be adaptive and flexible. Manage resistance.	Create e-motion. Provide direction and opportunity. Be determined. Be flexible. Be-cause.

Whilst the model identifies all of the essential elements of a campaign, there are 12 important points to note:

1 Campaigns combine macro- and micro-communication skills. The two are linked throughout.

2 There is no need to campaign communications unless there is a desired outcome to achieve.

3 This desired outcome grows out of and reflects a cause.

4 The cause has at least some degree of emotional significance for the campaigners and the audience. The greater the emotion the stronger the cause.

5 The campaign plan is created by reverse planning, working backwards from the end date by which the outcome must be realized.

6 The story, or narrative, is at the heart of the campaign.

7 Messages and themes of the story need to be integrated into all activities.

8 A compelling campaign story influences emotionally as well as rationally.

9 Campaigns are cyclical rather than linear in nature; think only of an ongoing feedback loop.

10 Feedback is gathered through continual audience analysis and scanning of the environments within which the campaign is operating.

11 The plan can change in response to feedback.

12 Campaigning is an attitude, a state of mind, which is supported by a skill set and a process.

The story that follows, told by AB, is an example of a highly successful campaign that combined all of the above.

A new future for Wales

When a Labour government was elected in 1997, one of its pledges was to hold referenda in Scotland and Wales about devolved government. It was widely expected that a vote for a Scottish Parliament was a foregone conclusion. It had been a powerful cause for many for a long time and there was a large coalition of support for it. The public wanted it.

Wales was different. There were certainly some for whom it was a strong cause. There was a coalition of institutional support, but by no means as strong as in Scotland. And there was ambivalence about it amongst the voters – at best they weren't dead-set against it. The fact that Wales was being offered an Assembly without tax-varying and law-making powers was telling in itself.

I was asked by Tony Blair to go and take charge of Labour's campaign to win a 'Yes' vote.

It was going to be a tough challenge in Wales. Coming straight after the General Election wouldn't make it any easier. And it was always tough going from head office to manage campaigns hands-on in other parts of Britain. Local volunteers and staff would mostly resent an outsider coming in to take charge. Usually I would be going to run a parliamentary by-election in a single constituency. By comparison the constituency this time were slightly larger and more complex as it was the equivalent of 40 individual constituencies, with so many more agendas at play, much more politics and plenty more opportunities for people to be resentful that they are 'being told what to do' by someone from head office. And I was English! (Still am, actually.)

After the General Election the coffers were bare and the budget was small. My job was to manage it well, and protect it from being frittered away on ineffective activities, which is always possible given the participation of politicians in campaign management – and this was a campaign with very senior politicians all over it.

The first thing was to work out my end point. Then I could work backwards and think about what I needed to do to get there. In this case – a straight two-horse race between 'Yes' and 'No' – my end point was quite simply to secure more votes than the opposition. So I looked at the numbers. I needed to know how many voters there were, and estimate the likely turn-out for the referendum. I needed to get at least half of them to vote Yes. From previous election results in Wales I was able to calculate how many votes we'd need to win.

From the spread of political support throughout the country I could work out where those votes might best be found by a Labour campaign. There was also an official 'Yes' campaign as well as an official 'No' campaign. The nationalists and the Liberal Democrats were campaigning under the umbrella of the Yes campaign. Labour was mounting its own campaign. Loyalty to the Labour cause was judged to be stronger than loyalty to the cause of devolution.

I looked for Labour strongholds because I wanted to target the budget and activities well. I knew from all my political campaigning roughly where they were – the south Wales valleys and north-east Wales. I wanted to avoid spending it in areas with strong Tory support as my research indicated I wouldn't get enough return from it in terms of votes at the ballot box. The Tories were campaigning for a No vote in the referendum. And there were areas where I expected the nationalists to deliver votes so I could save my money in those. I didn't expect too much campaigning from the Welsh Lib Dems. I had to deliver the bulk of the votes in favour of a Welsh Assembly.

Back in 1997 Wales was a Labour stronghold, and this was Labour Government policy. Although Labour won many seats in Wales easily, the strength of support in those seats was so great that many didn't bother to vote. They knew their man – and it was almost always a man – was guaranteed to remain their MP. People had got out of the habit of voting and our local parties had got out of the habit of campaigning. So as well as selling a future Welsh Assembly to an ambivalent nation, there was a mobilization problem.

For me, every campaign starts with a clean whiteboard. Every campaign is different, albeit drawing on my skills and experiences learnt in previous campaigns. And campaigns have to be flexible. Immediately this proved to be the case. Labour had just been through a long General Election campaign and had been both relentless and ruthless in deploying their activities in the most marginal seats. Labour ignored those seats where it was certain of winning. My strategy would have to challenge this and the mindset of seasoned campaigners.

My immediate task was to convey the mathematics of the referendum campaign to my team – over 2 million voters across one country rather than 40 constituencies of 60,000 or so voters each. In Wales many assumed that the high-intensity campaigning in the key seats would continue and they had been preparing accordingly. Instead, I told them that we had to mobilize our core support in our Labour strongholds.

Time is always a factor in campaigns and this one was no different. We simply didn't have enough time to find the 'No' voters so we had to operate in areas where, if everyone turned out, we would get overwhelming support. This was more a campaign to mobilize voters, not so much a campaign to win hearts and minds. I wasn't expecting my volunteers to go door-to-door talking to voters and recording information – we had to create some noise and get people talking to each other about the campaign and were never going to have the time or resources to compile a database of voting intentions to enable me to segment the electorate let alone make use of it.

I set targets for the number of votes required by every constituency, with it being weighted disproportionately to traditional Labour heartlands. I had to equip the Labour stronghold seats to mount a vigorous campaign for the first time in many years. And I had to decide upon the narrative and messaging for the campaign.

Labour assumed that although there wasn't the clamour for their own parliament as in Scotland, Labour voters in Wales would support it out of loyalty to the party. However, I needed to test this hypothesis in research. Tony Blair proved to be a powerful motivator – Labour voters in Wales loved him and trusted him. They would do what he asked. I decided to make him the campaign message carrier.

I found there was an uncertain sense of Welsh identity. In south-east Wales they looked towards Bristol, the M4 corridor and London, whilst in Wrexham and north-east Wales they were pulled towards Manchester and Liverpool. In the Welsh valleys there was a strong sense of community from the mines, but most people recognized themselves as being first and foremost part of the United Kingdom. There wasn't yet a burning desire to express themselves as Welsh other than for sport.

I decided that we would work the south Wales valley seats very hard. I wasn't too fussed about Newport and south-east Wales. After analysing our research I didn't think we'd get much return on our investment. I wanted to put some effort into Wrexham, though. There were a lot of Labour voters there but they thought Cardiff was remote and not interested in them. However, I had an instinct that they could be enticed with our messaging, unlike Newport.

Our campaign had to build a sense of pride and of possibilities for the future. It had to have a vibrancy, energy and hope. We were hampered because the Welsh Assembly wouldn't have the same powers as the Scottish Parliament, and the Westminster Parliament would still dominate. Timetabling the Scottish referendum was part of the strategy that would enable me to generate momentum in the last week – Welsh voters could get a sense of a possible future by watching Scotland vote for their new future a week before.

We created our themes around the notion that 'Wales deserves a voice', bringing jobs, improving health and education through local control whilst still retaining the security of being a strong voice in Britain. We devised our story, message and activity grid to bring it to life. I was determined that Labour should be high profile in their heartlands, concentrating on providing a visible presence, giving confidence and the simple message that Tony Blair and Labour wanted them to vote 'Yes' because it opened up a new future of possibilities for Wales.

I allocated the bulk of the budget to setting up high-profile visits, stunts, creating media coverage, street activity and imaginative leaflets and advertising. Balloons and street stalls were a staple of the campaign, not forgetting good old-fashioned meetings in public halls and people's homes. I knew that we should be in amongst the community, so I took out adverts on buses and used scratch cards that volunteers took around the pubs, clubs and Miners' Welfares to convey a political message. Everything was on message. I made sure of it.

I needed feedback during the campaign so I made use of the campaign phone bank to provide real time feedback on voting opinion. I knew it wasn't as robust as paying for quantitative polling but my budget was limited and I needed information otherwise I was flying blind. I had a budget for qualitative polling (focus groups to assess attitudes) to help refine our messaging throughout the campaign, but not for quantitative analysis.

We built campaigns in our heartlands, and we grew the momentum, using our resources wisely knowing that the nationalists would deliver 'Yes' votes in south-west and north-west Wales. Our final week of messaging was based on the hope that would be created both by a 'Yes' vote in Scotland and a direct appeal by Tony Blair.

The first result in was Wrexham and although 'No' won we got a far bigger vote than had been anticipated at the start. We did badly in Newport and Monmouthshire just as we expected. Turnout was decent in the south Wales Valleys seats, as we planned. It went right down to the last of the 22 local authority areas to report before the winner was known. The final result was that 'Yes' won by 50.3 per cent to 49.7 per cent on a 50.1 per cent turnout. More than 1.1 million people had voted and we had a majority of 6,721.

It was close but the campaign had delivered enough votes. A win's a win, but I also knew that people are motivated to vote against something far more easily than they are motivated to vote for it. The 'No' campaign would have maximized their opposition to the Assembly. Those who didn't vote weren't against it, else they most certainly would have voted to stop it. They were either willing to go with the consensus, were prepared to see how it went once it was up and running or simply didn't care.

It was a just result. Wales got what it wanted, and history can already judge that in Wales there is a new sense of pride in the Welsh identity and confidence in their country as a result.

ACTIVITY!

Read Alan's story again and identify how all the elements of the *Campaign It!* model were applied.

Final thoughts

'It takes tremendous discipline to control the influence, the power you have over other people's lives.'

Clint Eastwood

We don't need to be a leading media star, a famous actor or film director, to influence others. And until we accept the inevitability of the influences we create we have no real reason either to exercise discipline over them or to develop the power to manage and direct them appropriately. The *Campaign It!* model is one way of developing a deliberate, disciplined capability that grows out of our care and respect for ourselves and others. After all, inadequate communication costs everyone dearly and, as Aristotle wrote: 'We are what we repeatedly do.'

If we want to become excellent communicators and therefore great partners, parents and professionals, as well as influential members of our communities, we need to work repeatedly to develop the required attitudes, strategies and skills.

No matter where we work, or what the context, our communications need to be planned, ongoing, timely and targeted. They need to be integrated and sequenced appropriately. They need to be accurate and adaptive and perceived as relevant. They need to create emotional as well as intellectual responses in our audience. Most importantly, they need to have a purpose, a value, a cause.

As campaigners we know that our communications can themselves be influenced by other, sometimes seemingly unconnected, events. For that reason we have to scan and analyse constantly the environment within which we are operating, being willing and able to adapt our communications in response to any unexpected influencers.

In our rapidly changing, high-tech, media-rich world our communications need to be deliberate, elegant and powerful. Most important of all, they need to be part of an irresistible campaign, fuelled by a powerful cause. That is what we are going to explore next.

02 Cause

> *Unless you give yourself to some great cause*
> *you haven't even begun to live.* **WILLIAM P. MERRILL**

> *I can't imagine not having a cause.* **MARGARET MCDONAGH**

The purpose of this chapter is to:

1 Define and discuss the nature of cause.
2 Explain how campaigns and key elements of campaign management grow out of having a cause.
3 Identify the personal challenges we face when campaigning a cause and discuss how to manage these.

In this chapter we:

- Define the nature of cause and explain how it is of meaning and relevance to all aspects of our professional and personal lives.
- Introduce and discuss the notion of gradations of cause.
- Discuss the inevitability of simultaneous causes.
- Discuss the power that comes from having a cause, explaining how it creates a purpose, vision and a sense of identity.
- Explain the difference and relationship between objectives and cause.
- Discuss and demonstrate how campaigns begin with a cause.
- Explain that success comes from sharing your cause.
- Discuss the relationship between personal values, ethics and campaigning for a cause.
- Justify the need for campaigners to have high levels of emotional intelligence.
- Explain why if you truly believe in your cause you need to *Campaign It!*

Introduction: from law-suits to the pursuit of principle and a click-whirr

Our modern word *cause* comes from the Latin *causa*, meaning *reason*, *motive* or *law suit*. It became part of the English language via the Old French word *cause*, which meant either *a cause* or *a thing*. The French phrase *cause-celebre* was (and is) used to describe a much-talked about legal case and the word *cause* remains a part of English legal language,[1] even though it has taken on additional usage and meaning. Today most of us use the word as a noun that identifies either:

- the source or reason of an event or action; or
- a principle or aim that exceeds selfish desires and is worth striving for.

Both of these usages are essential in our approach to campaigning. For us, cause is the pursuit of an outcome, a principle or an aim that will improve at least some aspect of a current situation. Moreover, it is the emotional compulsion to achieve this desired outcome. It provides both the motivation and, when necessary, the courage to campaign. The cause becomes the story you just have to tell. It is something that we feel is worth committing to and working towards and so it becomes the source, or reason, for the creation of a campaign.

Having said that, we need to make an important point:

'Causes range in size and scope. They can be simple, complex, personal, shared. Some causes can be achieved literally in minutes through a campaign delivered in a single communication, some require a handful of communications, whilst others might need complex sequencing and layering of communications and take several years to achieve.'

The media tends to report mostly about causes that influence communities, societies or nations, and about campaigns that are significant on a national or international level. This has encouraged the perception that campaigns only occur on a grand scale and that they are only about issues that affect many, if not all, of us. Our new paradigm, however, encourages a different view. It is based on the belief that if we care enough about achieving any particular outcome irrespective of size – in other words, if we have a cause – the best way to gain the permission needed to make it a reality is to campaign our communications. The cause can be something as personal as getting a promotion or a new job, or it can be as all-encompassing as reducing global carbon emissions. It can be anything in-between.

In the final analysis we decide what is or isn't a cause in our lives. We decide because a cause is identified and defined by our level of care, by how important we believe something is for ourselves, our families, our organizations, communities or world. In the first instance we don't need anyone else to agree with us about the value and importance of a topic. Obviously, it is nice and it makes life easier if we do have a lot of immediate agreement or support, however a cause begins as a personal commitment and develops into a shared purpose through a successful campaign. In an interview with AB screenwriter, director and founder of Comic Relief and

---

[1] For example, within the term *cause-list* which refers to a list of cases needing to be tried.

Make Poverty History, Richard Curtis OBE, and his partner, presenter and script editor Emma Freud, Spoke of the importance of emotional commitment in campaigning. They emphasized:

> 'What is crucial is, at the core of it, not to separate yourself from the cause and to be very passionate about it.'

Sometimes the audience we need to influence and gain permission from is limited in scope if not in importance. It might be our life partner, or other individuals in our family, or our neighbours, or our boss at work. Sometimes it will be sufficient numbers within a community or a country. A cause is whatever motivates us enough to take persuasive action by campaigning our communications thoroughly.

The value of the *Campaign It!* model is that it can be applied to the most simple cause as well as it can to the most grand. We will return to this topic later in this chapter when we discuss gradations of cause.

It is important here to spend a moment or two explaining the relationship and the differences between the desired end outcome and the cause itself. Essentially, there are two ways a campaign can begin:

1 It can start with a cause to which an individual or a group has made an emotional investment, which can only be achieved through the creation and implementation of a desired end outcome.

2 Alternatively, it can start with a desired end outcome (which might or might not be clearly defined) from which the cause and associated emotional commitment have to be drawn and placed centre stage.

Either way, a cause is far more than just a detailed and clear vision of the future. The cause is the *why*, not simply the *what*. It reflects values whilst promising value. It is worth striving for because we *feel* its worth rather than just being able to measure its reward. The cause is the story we have to tell now, not the novel we might get round to writing one day. Our cause, whatever it might be, is brought to life by the implementation of the desired end outcome, however it is born out of our emotional need. It is because of the need for, and power of, cause that we say quite simply:

> 'If you care enough, *Campaign It!*'

ACTIVITY!

Write a list of your personal, social and professional causes.

Wonderfully, at the very heart of campaigning a cause, of making that commitment, is a single word. It is a word that by its very structure emphasizes the importance of campaigners holding dear to a cause, of making it almost a part of themselves. The word is: *because.*

> Causes range in size and scope. They can be simple, complex, personal, shared.

The word *because* grew out of the phrase *by cause* which, in turn, was modelled on the French *par cause*. We use the word *because* whenever we need to add a reason (or two) to the main clause in a sentence. In other words, if we have explained what has happened and feel the need to then explain why it happened, we link the two with the word *because*.

According to Robert Cialdini *because* is a powerful influencer *because* whenever we hear it we are conditioned subconsciously to expect reasons or a justification to follow. Consequently, we are far more likely to agree with someone who uses the word whilst explaining their situation, or behaviour, or request, than someone who does not. If their explanation strikes an emotional chord it becomes even more powerful. *Because* stimulates what Cialdini calls a 'click-whirr' pattern, an automatic response that can happen so quickly it supersedes conscious and rational thought.

In one experiment a Harvard psychologist told a subject to approach a queue at a photocopying machine and ask for permission to print her papers first by saying, 'Excuse me, I've got five pages to do, may I jump in and use the machine?' Using these words, the subject was successful 60 per cent of the time. Significantly, though, when the subject used the word *because* in the midst of the sentence her success rate shot up to over 90 per cent! This remained constant when the reason that followed the word was weak, for example, 'I'm in a rush' and even when there was no reason at all, for example, 'I need to make some copies'!

People are, it seems, keen to justify their behaviour and the behaviour of others and are willing to be persuaded when approached by someone with what appears to be a reasonable request. We know instinctively the role the word *because* plays in connecting behaviour and desire with motive and cause, even though we might never have stopped to consider the intimate relationship that exists between the words *because* and *cause*.

> The first thing to do with any project is identify the cause.

Whether or not a cause ever truly exceeds our own selfish desires, is a question for philosophers to discuss. Can we be genuinely altruistic? This is a debateable point, given that most of us tend to draw pleasure from the very act of helping others and from the feeling of having made a worthwhile difference. Of course, a cause can be to achieve a selfish aim – to succeed in getting the job of your dreams, for example – although most of us would say that such a selfish ambition will also bring benefits elsewhere, especially if you truly believe you are the best candidate for a job. What we can say for certain, though, is that there is a significant difference between running a campaign that is designed to create purely personal gain at the expense of others and one that seeks to establish mutual benefits.

We, of course, are focusing on the latter and as AB explains when working with, or for, others the ability to create a shared cause and the associated level of emotional commitment is a prerequisite for success:

A cause, a cause, my company is for a cause!

I can create many causes. Some are more important to me than others, but they all propel me to act. The more important the cause to me the more powerful and determined is my campaign to achieve it. And I can have nested causes as well.

For example, at work my cause is to build my company up to be the best it can be. And in order to do that I have to deliver campaigns that realize the goals of my clients. I have to find their causes and work out how to use them to bring them success.

Clients come to us with a problem to solve, or an objective to achieve. They know we will run a campaign to help them succeed, but first I have to turn their brief into a cause. I need to find the emotional element that will enable others to give them the support and the necessary permissions to be successful.

Once I have turned their ambition into a cause I assume that it has become my cause. My company has an unwritten slogan: "We only help the good guys". If we can't make their cause our cause then we can't help. I can't make it up. I have to believe. My company has turned clients down because we couldn't support their cause. It's an important element of any initial discussions and interactions with potential clients. We have to be sure we can believe in their cause.

Cause is that important to our work. I'm not saying that the causes we campaign for in the course of our work have to be big and worthy. They just have to fit with the identities of those who run the company and who we ask to work on any particular project to allow us to give our all to the campaign we will create. External observers may say that some of the causes we work on are insignificant compared to others. That doesn't matter, after all there are gradations of cause.

Our task, once we have accepted the commission, is to build the necessary support for the new cause that we now believe in. When I'm with a client my language changes. I become part of them, using "we", "us" and "our", rather than "you" and "your". I share in their desire to succeed because their cause has become my cause. I always take sides.

However, I need to be able to give independent third-party advice. I am always thinking about the cause from the perspective of our target audience(s) and what is in it for them if we succeed. And I keep one step removed from the short-term compulsions, keeping an eye on the bigger picture and longer term strategy. I can't afford to let my emotional commitment blinker my perception and yet unless I believe in my clients' cause I can't help them. And by helping them with their causes I am helping to achieve my cause – that of making my company better and stronger. The campaigns I run for my clients are all part of my own over-arching campaign.

LEARNING POINTS

- Campaigning a cause is the pursuit of a desired end outcome driven by an emotional compulsion.
- Cause is the story you just have to tell.
- Causes range in size and scope.
- A campaign can start with a cause or it can start with the desired end outcome from which the cause can be drawn.

ACTIVITY!

Over the course of one day practise using the word 'because' to help you gain agreements or support in different contexts.

Observe how people react to the word and what you say subsequently.

Through his brief insight AB introduces three key issues relating to creating and managing cause. These are:

1 managing personal emotions;

2 creating a cause;

3 the inevitability of simultaneous causes.

Managing personal emotions

The challenge of managing our own emotions when campaigning a cause grows out of a simple yet powerful double bind, which is this:

'The more we care about the cause, the more powerful our emotional compulsion to campaign it, the greater the risk that our emotions will impair or, in some other way, damage our performance.'

Just consider for a moment an individual you love dearly and then consider to what extent your emotional commitment (and need) has made you struggle on occasion to say or do the right thing. For many of us love can, at times, act to bind and confuse as much as it can to liberate and empower. Managing the most meaningful relationships in our life can often be more challenging than managing those in which we inherently feel a degree of emotional distance. And yet, ultimately, it is these meaningful relationships that make life worth living. So it is with campaigns. We talk later in this chapter about gradations of cause. Inevitably, our level of emotional commitment is a crucial factor and, as campaigners, we have to be able to manage our emotions so that they enhance rather than detract from the pursuit of our cause. The ability to manage our emotional states is known as *emotional intelligence*.

Essentially, the term emotional intelligence refers to those aspects of a person that are not related to the rational, analytical or intellectual domains. According to Daniel Goleman, a leading researcher and writer in the field, an individual with a high level of emotional intelligence demonstrates this by:

- recognizing what emotion, or emotions, they are feeling at any given time and being able to manage these without ever being taken over, or overwhelmed, by them;
- being able to motivate themselves to complete tasks appropriately, to be creative and to perform at their very best when required to do so;
- sensing what those around them are feeling, recognizing the emotional responses of others, and managing relationships effectively.

Developing this further, Malcolm Higgs and Victor Dulewicz list the essential components of emotional intelligence as:

- self-awareness,
- emotional resilience,
- motivation,
- interpersonal sensitivity,
- influence,
- decisiveness,
- conscientiousness and integrity.[2]

A campaigner with high levels of self-awareness will recognize their own emotional responses to situations as they occur. They will be able to relate and manage their personal feelings towards the cause, campaign and the responses it is eliciting at any given time. They will be accurate in an assessment of their own strengths and weaknesses. The emotionally resilient campaigner will couple this awareness with the ability to resist being swamped, or overcome, by their emotional states. They will be able to walk the emotional 'high-wire', managing the difficult balancing act between emotions and results.

The willingness to campaign is fuelled by our motivation to achieve a cause that, in turn, is influenced greatly by our degree of emotional commitment. Motivation is demonstrated through the willingness to take action in pursuit of what might be perceived as a challenging or demanding goal, even in the face of doubt, opposition or rejection. Campaigners not only have to manage their own levels of motivation they need to create and manage it in others, including significant parts of their audience(s) and their campaign team. To do this they need high levels of interpersonal sensitivity

---

[2] Higgs, M., Dulewicz, V. (1999) *Making sense of emotional intelligence.* NFER-NELSON Publishing, Berkshire.

based on a clear understanding of others' needs, expectations, perceptions and desires. This, when combined with great communication skills, increases the likelihood of creating the desired influence and so progressing the campaign.

In the final analysis, the person leading a campaign takes responsibility for making the decisions that move that campaign in a given direction at a given time and in a given way. Inevitably, there will be times when a decision has to be made in the face of ambiguous or incomplete information. Decisiveness is the

> *A campaigner with high levels of self-awareness will recognize their own emotional responses to situations as they occur.*

ability, and willingness, to make these decisions, often by combining both rational thought and emotional 'gut-instinct' and then testing the outcome against the measure of one's personal values and integrity.

In summary then, as the following diagram shows, the emotionally intelligent campaigner has a high level of self-awareness coupled with an equally high level of self-control, which is influenced in part by their beliefs and values. They also have an understanding of, and sensitivity towards, other people that enables them to communicate, motivate and influence powerfully and with integrity.

Given the inevitability of influence and the fact that the *Campaign It!* model is a powerful, influential tool, we believe that campaigning brings with it an inevitable moral requirement. Simply put, if we are capable of influencing others we need to ensure that we do so with care and respect, both core traits of a campaigner. And, whilst we can never run a campaign that will be valued and supported by all, we do need to ensure that, no matter how committed we are to our own cause, we avoid the selfish manipulation of others and the use of unethical tactics.[3]

The emotionally intelligent campaigner

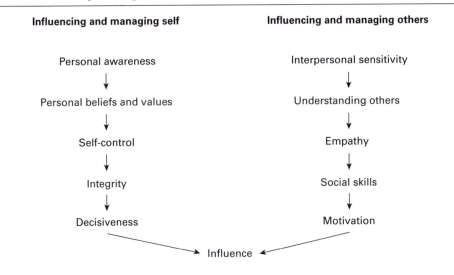

Influencing and managing self	Influencing and managing others
Personal awareness	Interpersonal sensitivity
↓	↓
Personal beliefs and values	Understanding others
↓	↓
Self-control	Empathy
↓	↓
Integrity	Social skills
↓	↓
Decisiveness	Motivation

Influence

---

[3] More about cause, campaigning and ethics later in this chapter.

Creating a cause

As we mentioned earlier in this chapter, sometimes we campaign because there is a cause we hold dear and sometimes because we have committed to achieving a desired end outcome. In the second case, before we can create a campaign we have to unearth the cause within it. Either way, our cause has to be clear and bright and powerful and, most importantly, it has to be shared. And this has two significant implications. These are:

1. Every one of us is allowed to create a cause

Really! You have as much right to create and then campaign a cause as anyone else. Campaigning is not the prerogative of a particular social sector or of particular professions. Our ability as humans to communicate allows each of us to campaign. We all have the opportunity, the potential and, if we exercise it, the power to create a cause. This is the foundation upon which we develop the capability and the courage to shape both our life and, when appropriate, the lives of others.

It is why the ability to create a cause is both a right and a responsibility.

2. Campaign teams need a cause-creator

Whether a team is seeking to create change or maintain the status quo, whether it is operating within their community or organization or beyond it, someone within the team has to be capable of creating the cause around which the campaign will be developed. A cause-creator can identify, clarify and shape the emotional meaning and value that runs through the campaign and which justifies the desired end outcome. They will know how to question others and themselves. They will know how to dig below the surface and find the emotive seam that is essential for both motivating those around them and for persuading those they need to gain permission from.

However, no matter who creates the cause it has to be shared for it to come to life and for its value to be accepted and then experienced. For that to happen, they also have to be able to manage it as well as the other causes in their life that they campaign about.

The inevitability of simultaneous campaigns

AB's story highlights how, for him at least, the causes that he decides to support have to fit comfortably within the range of causes that are already at the heart of his life purpose. Whilst we might not have thought of our lives in this way, we all create and manage a variety of campaigns simultaneously. Arguably we have little or no choice. Our personal beliefs and values lead us to identify or create the various causes we feel compelled to support. And, because we play a variety of roles in a range of personal, social and professional contexts, we can become involved in causes relating to any or all of these various contexts. These can, for example, include causes relating to our family life, our personal and professional development, even our work–life balance. Irrespective of what these causes are (or how well we campaign them), our campaigns tend to fit into one of three types. These are:

1 nested campaigns,
2 overlapping campaigns,
3 side-by-side campaigns.

Nested campaigns are those that run within each other, with each individual campaign an essential part of the over-arching campaign and cause. For example, AB and the team at bbm (bbm consultants) agreed to develop a campaign on behalf of the Law Society. The cause was to save Legal Aid provision from proposed cuts. Within this one campaign, in support of this one cause, the team had to create and manage a series of interlocking campaigns designed to influence a wide variety of different audiences, including specific MPs, the media, third party organizations and Law Society members and staff.

Overlapping campaigns are different campaigns that share a common connection. For example, you might choose to run two campaigns influencing your local authority to: a) make changes to parking zones in your area; and b) repair the broken drains in your street. These separate campaigns clearly overlap and yet they are not dependent upon each other in the ways that nested campaigns are.

Campaigns that exist side-by-side have no connection other than the very important fact that you are involved in them. These might include campaigns to get a job, or to teach your children the importance of citizenship, or to persuade your local authority to sort out those blasted drains!

When talking to AB Richard Curtis discussed the relationship that can exist between different campaigns:

'"Live Aid" and "Band Aid" were absolutely key in making me think I ought to do something. So I think it is an important point that campaigns are based upon campaigns! The things that one person does cause another person to do things. Oddly enough, the major things that you achieve in life may be what is achieved by the next person who does that thing.'

To commit to campaigning a cause is to make a commitment to some degree. If, and when, we feel the pull of a new cause we need to ensure that it belongs within the family of causes we have already accepted and developed. There needs to be congruency between it and those forces that currently shape the structure, manner and demonstration of our life and who we are. There also needs to be an appropriate level of balance. Before committing to campaign a cause, we need to be sure that we have sufficient resources available – these include time, skill, emotional energy – and that by doing so we will not irreparably damage the relationship that exists between those other essential causes in our life.[4]

The ability to create and manage different causes simultaneously is based to a great extent on our level of emotional intelligence coupled with a clear understanding of, and commitment to, those personal and professional goals that reflect both who we are and what we value and believe in. Of course, not every cause creates within us the same degree of emotional commitment, nor requires the same amount of time or energy to campaign successfully. There are, what we refer to as gradations of cause.

---

[4] Unless, of course, it is such a powerful cause it supersedes all others.

Gradations of cause: why size really doesn't matter

Where cause is concerned, size really doesn't matter. Within the *Campaign It!* model we acknowledge gradations of cause simply because there are different types of cause that require different types of campaign.

Campaigns can be simple, complex, personal, shared; they can be nested, overlapping or side-by-side simply because they reflect the nature of the different causes in our life. Some causes are personal. Some are complex. Some necessitate a series of nested campaigns, whilst others can be achieved through a conversation.

To determine the gradation of cause we need to consider the following factors:

- the type of campaign needed to achieve it;
- the number, power and types of audience we need to gain permission from;
- the resources required to do so;
- the timeframe within which we have to operate.

Most importantly, though, gradation of cause is determined by one factor above all others:

How much it matters to us.

And it can matter to us for a variety of reasons. It can be because we care about someone else and wish to help personally. It can be because of a matter of principle. It can be because of a professional or social commitment. Whatever the type of cause, gradation of cause is determined ultimately by our level of emotional commitment. However, different types of cause will inevitably stir different levels (and sometimes different types) of emotion within us. To keep our earlier analogy running just a little further, not every cause will turn into the 'love of our life'. And neither should it.

Just as we all have people in our lives we are closer to than others, so we have differing priorities and different levels of commitment to different aspects of our world. To campaign, we just need to care enough to act and we should perhaps all be willing to act at times on behalf of others who are not emotionally involved in our lives and/or in response to situations that do not affect us directly.

> Ultimately, gradation of cause is determined by how much it matters to us.

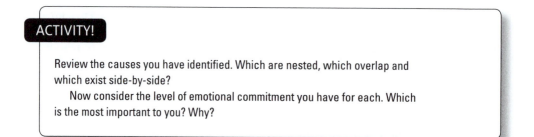

ACTIVITY!

Review the causes you have identified. Which are nested, which overlap and which exist side-by-side?

Now consider the level of emotional commitment you have for each. Which is the most important to you? Why?

What to do with a cause

The most basic requirement of a commitment to a cause is the willingness to 'walk the talk' in pursuit of your desired outcome. Ultimately *campaign* is a verb not a noun. We measure our commitment to a cause by the extent to which we campaign it actively and ethically, rather than by how much we simply make reference to it during idle conversation.

At the heart of ethical campaigning is the answer to the question,

'What are you prepared to do to win?'

As campaigners our personal values act as the boundary within which we are willing to operate. We have already said that, no matter what the context, we are never operating in a vacuum. Consequently, whenever we pursue a cause we can expect a range of responses throughout the campaign. These include:

- apathy,
- support,
- doubt,
- resistance.

Whenever we feel an emotional commitment to a cause it becomes easier for us to forget that some other people don't; that they might be disinterested, confused or just plain antagonistic towards our desired outcome. Whenever we care about a particular topic we often presume that others care too and that they care in the same ways we do. It can be emotionally challenging to discover that this is not the case. The challenge is to respond to apathy, doubt, opposition and even, in some circumstances, support in ways that are in keeping with our value system.

The bottom line is simply this: because we never operate in a vacuum we should expect others to respond in a variety of ways to our campaign. It is their right to be able to do so. Just because we are certain of a particular way forward, it doesn't mean that others have to agree with or, indeed, even be interested in our approach. As Baroness Margaret McDonagh, the former General Secretary of The Labour Party, says:

'People have the right not to agree with you nor even to like you.'

And we have the right to engage with these people, to seek to persuade them, or to just ignore them.

All of which reflect the power we gain from having a cause. The degree of power is determined to an extent by the level of our emotional commitment. The ways in which we exercise our power is determined in part by our level of emotional intelligence. No matter what the context, we need to ensure that we use this power wisely.

LEARNING POINTS

- Campaigners need to develop high levels of emotional intelligence.
- Everyone is allowed to create and campaign a cause.
- We all create and/or manage a variety of campaigns simultaneously.
- There are gradations of cause.
- Campaigning brings with it an ethical responsibility.

ACTIVITY!

What are you *not* prepared to do to win for your most important cause?

The power that comes from having a cause

This is created and reflected in three essential ways:

1 by our purpose;

2 by our vision;

3 by our sense of identity.

Whilst there is an obvious overlap between purpose and vision, the purpose of every campaign incorporates our desired process outcomes as well as our desired end outcome. How we campaign, those things we are both prepared to do and, equally, those things we are unwilling to do, in order to win, reveal our sense of identity. A cause is far more than just an objective or an outcome. A cause is made manifest through the process we call campaigning and our purpose is to create and manage a process that is both ethically acceptable and effective in making our desired vision a valuable, and valued, reality. Given this, our purpose grows out of our sense of cause and the clarity of our vision and it, in turn, influences the processes we use throughout the campaign.

Often, as the following story illustrates, a campaign is fuelled by a powerful vision that is tied to very specific objectives and purpose. What follows is the story of the London 2012 Olympic bid, as told to us by former Secretary of State for Culture, Media, and Sport, Tessa Jowell.

The London 2012 bid: a vision and a legacy

The vision

The London 2012 bid was a vision. It was a vision that was tied to two legacy objectives. The first was to transform a generation of young people through sport and the second was to transform East London through the accelerated regeneration of the Lower Lea valley.

I think vision has both content and process. If I take those two legacy objectives, East London had always been a priority for regeneration as and when investment became available and so there was never really any serious question that if we were going to stage an Olympics we would stage them anywhere other than in East London. What the effect (of the successful bid) has been is to accelerate that regeneration by about 25 years. So in 6 years we have seen 60 years' regeneration. Linked to this, is the importance of the legacy promise being not only focused on the physical infrastructure but also the change in demography, the aspiration of the 5 Olympic boroughs.

On the transformation of a generation of young people through sport, that is really what drove our Labour Government's School-Sport programme. And we started back in 2002, maybe even earlier, to promise that every child in primary or secondary school would have at least two hours a week of high-quality sport or physical education. That increased to three hours and was set to increase to five hours for about 70 per cent of children (and rising) by the time we got to 2012. That was linked to a growth in facilities, a growth in the number of coaches and, critically, a growth in the number of sports that children could choose from.

We then also built a second leg to that through our International Inspiration Programme, because the Singapore Promise had been to the children of the world not just the children of the UK and I think this was incredibly important. So, by the time we get to the summer of 2012 we will have International Inspiration Programmes running in 20 countries around the world. Every programme is taking a different aspect of child development and applying it; every one is using sport as a force for good, for transformation in the lives of children.

The vision, then, was a pretty full-square vision for a Labour Government. What made sense of it all and gave it greater impetus and purpose was the Olympics. Both in terms of school sport and regeneration we went faster than we would otherwise have done because of the Olympics. That is the Olympic effect.

The campaign process

The Olympic campaign process is like none other. It's a bit like three-dimensional draughts, having to take pieces out and create a critical mass and advantage. There are distinct spheres of influence that you have to win over. These include the IOC, the international governing bodies and the athletes themselves. Once I had decided that we should at least throw our hat in the ring to bid, the first sphere of influence that I had to affect was the Cabinet. I had to persuade the Cabinet that this was something we should support. And remember, this came to be a commitment of £9.325 billion of public money.

I had to build sufficient confidence in government that we could win, because Paris was the strong contender. The three key tests were:

1 Could we win it?

2 Could we deliver it?

3 Could we afford it?

Basically, I spent a year demonstrating how we could meet each of those tests. I talked to every member of the Cabinet, finding out their views and also what might be in it for them – and what it might cost their department. If you are the Secretary of State for Culture, Media and Sport, the Olympic bid is precisely what you care about. If you are the Secretary of State for Transport, you don't. The crucial thing was getting the Prime Minister and Deputy Prime Minister to support it, and this meant getting the PM's attention at a time when we were just about to go to war in Iraq. All of this was very difficult, but I was resolute. I never thought of failure. One person can start a campaign.

For example, at an early stage I was handed advice that said we should reconsider bidding for the Games. I handed it back and said, 'Can you bring me advice that says we should consider this and which offers a more balanced view.'

This was one of those things that sometimes you just have to do in government that takes you right outside of your comfort zone. However, if you only live in your comfort zone, nothing changes.

To persuade others in situations like this you need to do two things:

1 You establish who the real leaders of opinion are.

2 You mobilize the people who will automatically support you.

Also, you cannot win a campaign if your message is badly worded. I had a very clear vision and a script that just kept getting better. If your proposition is not worked out clearly and is delivered badly, you are not going to get off the ground. You also need to determine the ecology of the campaign, to understand the impacts it will have and how others regard it and will respond to it. Then you have to want it more than anything else you can imagine – and that is exactly how I became during the campaign. Sometimes you hit things in your life where you have to shut down everything else that's going on in your life and just focus on that. You handle it every minute of the day. You never stop thinking about it. You never stop talking to the people you are working with. You reach a point where you can almost live in each other's minds. That's how it became. I was absolutely fixed and focused as were all the other key people, including the Campaign Chair, Seb Coe.

I remember that Seb and I had a conversation in the run-up to Singapore and we said, 'If we play this safe Paris will win. We have got to take some risks.' So, the risk we took was to take to Singapore not 30 suited sponsors but 30 young people from two of the schools in East London next to the Olympic Park. Thirty children, 22 nationalities, 24 different languages. And what they did in Singapore was to stand up, turn round and wave at the IOC. It was such a picture! It was incredible! When I flew out to Singapore with the lobby I thought that we were going to win by three votes. We won by four.

ACTIVITY!

What was the cause that fuelled the 2012 Olympic bid?
Identify the attributes of a campaigner demonstrated in this story.

Whatever the cause, the vision that derives from it needs to be clear, detailed, appealing and motivational. Inevitably, it will also be to some degree distant and challenging. This is why it will require an emotional commitment and, often, a willingness to make sacrifices. The vision is the shining picture of the cause brought to life. It needs to be shared fully with the most appropriate audiences and its value and benefits accepted if it is to become reality. The creation of our vision is not only the driving purpose, the desired end outcome, of our campaign, it is also a reflection of who we are and what we stand for – our identity. To commit to a cause requires us to take sides.[5] To craft, share and strive to implement a vision that is at once rational and emotional, engaging and frightening, capable of uniting and dividing, is to make clear one's personal beliefs and values. It is a statement, in part at least, of who we are as well as how we think things should be and how we think they should be achieved.

This combination of purpose, vision and identity combine to help develop another essential quality for a campaigner: courage.

Courage

What is courage? In some ways, it is easier to say what it is not. Courage is not:

- the absence of fear;
- the refusal to acknowledge or respond to feedback;
- the desire to take unnecessary risks;
- the willingness to disregard all personal beliefs and values in order to achieve our goal.

According to Winston Churchill:

'Courage is what it takes to stand up and speak; courage is also what it takes to sit down and listen.'

To be courageous in pursuit of our cause is to acknowledge the doubt, indifference and even hostility of others and to make public our commitment despite this. It requires us to acknowledge and manage our own fears so that they never limit our performance or planning nor cause us to over-react. It enables us to seek out and respond to feedback, to be willing to accept errors and change aspects of our plan if necessary. It is at once a source of control, reflected through a strategic and structured urgency and a measured approach to risk taking, and a willingness to break through boundaries, reflected through the confidence to 'go first', to be different and challenge accepted thinking and behaviours. If, as Hemingway wrote, courage is:

'grace under pressure'

it is a grace that is shaped within the context of our beliefs and values, and is demonstrated through a campaign that reflects these throughout.

---

[5] The question 'Whose side are you on?' is a very powerful one that we shall explore later in the book.

Courage is necessary because of the professional and, often, personal challenges that campaigning some causes create. Not all campaigns require us to be courageous, though, and certainly not all require us to be courageous throughout. Often, we simply need the courage to start, the willingness to go first – which, of itself, can be a brave act – followed by the occasional need to summon our courage in the face of challenges along the way.

> Courage is grace that is shaped within the context of our beliefs and values and demonstrated through action or stillness, silence or speech.

Whatever the gradation of cause, our commitment to it reflects a degree of personal care and an acceptance that others have the right to disagree and/or oppose us. We know, as Tessa Jowell discussed, that to make our cause a reality we have to influence a range of people each with their own agendas and persuade them to trust not only in the value and benefits of our vision, but also in our ability to achieve it. To be willing to defend the status quo or to make a significant change we need the courage to commit, to disregard thoughts of failure and to focus only on doing the very best we can. It is the cause that determines and then unlocks our emotional investment, giving us the courage to stand up and speak or to sit down and listen. It is our level of emotional intelligence coupled with our strategic capability and our sense of personal identity that enables us to know when to stand up and speak, when to sit down and listen and how to do both wisely and well.

The following story, told by CP, is just one example of how finding the right cause and tapping into the power of individual identity unlocks a great sense of personal courage and commitment.

'She's behind you!'

I used to teach a self-defence programme for women. It was made up of six two-hour sessions taught over a six-week period. The training was divided into three parts. It began with a focus on awareness, avoidance and image management, in other words how to maintain appropriate states of alertness, recognize and avoid potential threats and present yourself in ways that it made clear you were not an easy target. The second stage was on the development of the all-important mental attitude needed to survive an assault. Only in the third and final part of the course did we identify and practise any actual physical techniques.

Most of the women who attended the programmes found the first part easy to understand and implement and also made fairly rapid progress in learning how to deliver a number of physical techniques. The most difficult aspect by far was in developing the actual desire to hit and hurt another human being if the situation demanded it. To be honest, this was no great surprise. Many people, both men and women (although in my experience women tend to be far more honest about this), find the idea of hurting someone else a deeply distressing and challenging prospect. Inevitably, though, having the right attitude is as important in a self-defence situation as it is in campaigning – as it is, in fact, in all different contexts. There are countless stories of untrained and inexperienced individuals defending themselves successfully simply because of their sense of moral outrage and their refusal to submit. My task, then, was to help each individual find a reason, a *cause*, that would spark a powerful desire to fight back if they ever decided that was the right option in a given situation.

Mary (not her real name) joined the very first women's self-defence programme that I ran. She was a small, delicate, softly spoken young woman who was a counsellor by profession. Whilst she understood, and found it easy to practise, the principles of awareness and avoidance she was less than enthusiastic about learning any actual physical techniques and was adamant that she could never, no matter what the circumstance, deliberately hurt another human being. Mary's certainty, underpinned by her principled resistance to the notion of ever causing physical harm to another, presented a significant challenge to me and threatened to undermine the value and validity of the entire programme. Her argument was receiving growing support from other participants who, like her, were convinced that they would sooner be hurt themselves rather than hurt their attacker.

After several failed attempts to persuade Mary and, with the final session looming, I found myself running out of options. What made it worse was the fact the final class culminated in a pressure test in which several large, and very well padded, men attacked each participant as they walked through a carefully designed dimly lit course. Without a change of heart I knew that Mary and possibly some others would refuse to join in. With time running out I decided that the best way to go forwards was to step back a few paces and find out some more about Mary. As we chatted over an orange juice after the penultimate session, she told me for the first time about her two-year-old daughter, Hettie. It took little persuasion for Mary to show me several photos of her beautiful first born. Hettie was truly adorable and the answer to my prayers. The more Mary talked about her daughter the more her face glowed with pride and affection. There was, it was clear, nothing Mary wouldn't do for her daughter...

Although she wasn't keen to attend, Mary did agree to be there for the final session. As the other women prepared themselves to walk the course, Mary and I stood on the sidelines and talked again about her lack of motivation to join in. 'I do know intellectually that I should want to stop a criminal from hurting me, it's just that I can't find it within myself to hit back,' she said. 'It's almost as if I don't think I'm worth it.'

'How about Hettie?' I asked. 'Is she worth it?'

'Of course!' The reply was instantaneous and strong.

'Tell me about her again,' I said. 'Tell me how she smiles, tell me what she does to make you smile.'

With that the course was temporarily forgotten as Mary drifted off into a world of wonderful memories. When she stopped talking I let the smile disappear from my face and asked her how she would feel if someone took Hettie from her. The sudden shift rocked her back on her heels and, before she could answer, I asked, 'What would you do to stop them?'

'Anything!' She said, glaring at me as if I were the enemy. 'No one is ever getting passed me to my daughter!'

'Then why don't you walk the course and just imagine that she is behind you?' I suggested. 'Just imagine that the men are coming for her, not you.'

And with that Mary's cause was established so completely that I felt a sudden concern that the padding the men were wearing might not be sufficient...

It was, but only just. What Mary couldn't do for herself, she was more than capable of doing for her daughter. Indeed, during the test, she combined a high level of emotional intent with an appropriate level of strategic thinking. When we talked about it later, Mary realized that the source of her motivation in many aspects of her life was the desire to help and protect others. She had found a way, whenever she doubted her own capability or worth in any situation, to create a clear intention and response. She had learnt how having a cause combines purpose, vision and identity to create a powerful and congruent motivating force. Moreover, she realized that she was at her most effective when she combined emotional commitment with strategic and tactical awareness. Emotion alone was not enough to ensure that she achieved her objectives and secured her cause.

Cause, objectives and a washing line

Although a cause is far more than just a rational objective, every cause is realized through the setting and achievement of a range of objectives. According to Margaret McDonagh (General Secretary of the Labour Party 1998 to 2001):

'Cause is the big thing, the Dream. An objective is something you have to achieve to realize the cause. Generally you have a cause to achieve something bigger and this then funnels itself down into specifics.'

Margaret uses the image of a washing line to show the relationship between cause and the objectives and policies of the campaign. In the same way that clothes are hung on a washing line so the specifics of the campaign, the objectives and what Margaret refers to 'symbolic policies', are 'hung' from the line created by the cause and its associated messages.

The washing line of cause: Labour's symbolic policies from the 1997 General Election

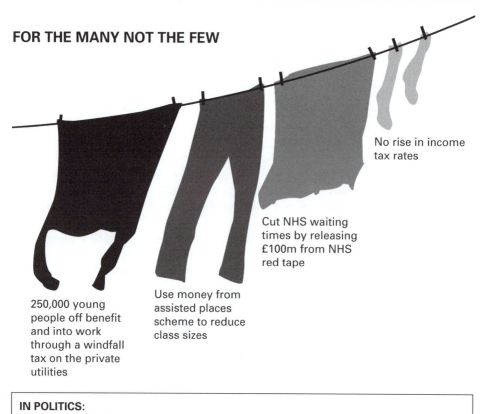

FOR THE MANY NOT THE FEW

No rise in income tax rates

Cut NHS waiting times by releasing £100m from NHS red tape

250,000 young people off benefit and into work through a windfall tax on the private utilities

Use money from assisted places scheme to reduce class sizes

IN POLITICS:
Washing line is the values/position/what you stand for that everything hangs from
Wet clothes are the symbolic policies that explain and bring colour to the washing line

If our cause is the source and the driving force of our desired end outcome, the objectives we set in place are the milestones we need to achieve along the way. They are specific targets in their own right, which also help to create the funnel that leads from the dream to the particular actions we take to realize it[6]. Whilst the cause creates our emotional commitment, objectives reflect and reinforce our strategic and tactical thinking. In her interview with AB, Baroness Tanni Grey-Thompson talked of how she set objectives and planned her training over a four-year cycle. She said:

> 'I'd always be thinking four years ahead in global terms. I'd have a four-year cycle because as soon as one Games finishes it's like a conveyor belt. You've got World, Europeans, national selection and so on. It's all a stepping stone to moving somewhere else.'

Whether or not there is a series of externally organized events to target, objectives need to be:

- specific,
- measurable,
- achievable,
- realistic,
- timeframed.

Objectives, like milestones need to be lined up along the way.

Specific objectives are detailed, well defined and positive. In other words, they specify what is to be achieved and, often, how it is to be achieved, rather than what is to be avoided or stopped. A focus on the questions:

- Who?
- What?
- When?
- Where?
- Why?
- How?

encourages the creation of specific objectives which, in turn, enables the application of appropriate measures. Measurable objectives are essential because they help us to identify the progress (or lack of it!) of our campaign and can help motivate the campaign team. A focus on the questions:

- How will we recognize when an objective has been achieved?
- What are the key measures of success?

helps us not only to measure the results of our actions but also to set objectives that, whilst they may be challenging, are achievable. Of course, because objectives are future targets, people have to believe that they can be reached. Baroness Tanni Grey-Thompson emphasized this point when she said,

> 'If you start out believing that you can do it, that's a good place to start. If you go to the start line believing you can do it, you will find that a lot of the time you can.'

---

[6] More on the activities of a campaign in Chapter 7.

Positive beliefs about the capability of the campaign team and the individuals within it can be created or strengthened by the sharing of a campaign plan that is acknowledged to be appropriate, and by the positive ways the campaign leader, or other members of the team, talk about the objectives. Again, objectives that are believed to be achievable can act as a source of motivation. One of the key skills when setting objectives lies in getting the balance right between making them appropriately challenging and undeniably achievable. A focus on providing answers to such questions as:

- What resources do we need?
- What is the timeframe?
- Why is achieving this objective important to our campaign?
- What are the limitations and constraints we face?
- How do we know that we can be successful?

serves to make objectives appear both achievable and realistic, and as campaigners we need to be certain that the objectives we set are both. Whilst it could be argued that with sufficient resources and determination most objectives can be achieved sooner or later, it does not always follow that it is realistic to do so. Realistic objectives fit appropriately within a given context; their value outweighs the effort needed to achieve them; they play an obvious role in helping to make our cause a reality. A focus on such questions as:

- What is the value in achieving this objective?
- How do we know that we can do this?

helps us to imagine, plan for, and work towards our objectives confident in our ability to realize them within the allotted timeframe. Every objective has what AB refers to as its own '*polling day*',[7] or deadline.

Perhaps even more importantly the entire campaign has a final polling day. It is the time when the audience makes its decision, when permission is, or is not, granted. Sometimes the precise date will be fixed before the campaign begins. Sometimes it will be changeable. Sometimes it won't be known. Either way, it sets the timeframe within which the campaign operates. No matter how long or short the race, polling day is the finishing line. It is what the campaign is ultimately working towards. And, remember, it does that paradoxically by reverse planning.

Setting deadlines throughout the campaign creates a sense of urgency and prompts action. Sometimes a deadline is determined by external factors, sometimes we can set it ourselves. Either way, deadlines play a crucial role in influencing peoples' attitudes, which is why it is essential that the deadline is set accurately, known by all involved, and seen to be achievable. A deadline that is set too early can be as damaging as one that is set too late. The message, therefore, is three-fold:

1 Sequence your objectives appropriately.

2 Set the right deadlines.

3 Meet them!

---

[7] Guess where he got the idea to use that term from! CP.

When talking to AB Tanni Grey-Thompson stressed the importance of creating and then meeting a sequence of objectives. She said:

> 'Winning at the Paralympic means winning gold and it doesn't matter about the time and who I beat because it's gold or nothing. There will be other events that would be about beating people or trying out new tactics. There would be a goal in every race and those types of goal would change. It would only be the end goal that I would publicly articulate because no one is interested in all those other things.'

Campaign objectives are targets that we just have to meet in pursuit of our cause. They enable us to measure our progress, motivate our team, and provide a focus for our actions. By publicly meeting our objectives we can also enhance our credibility with those we are seeking to gain permission from.

Whether or not you imagine your objectives hanging on the washing line of cause, you absolutely have to act upon them. Never just leave them out to dry.

LEARNING POINTS

- People have the right to respond in a variety of ways to your campaign.
- The power that comes from having a cause is created and reflected by our purpose, our vision and our sense of identity.
- Campaigners often need to be courageous as well as ethical.
- Objectives are those things you have to achieve to realize your cause.
- Each objective has its own deadline.
- Polling day is the day the audience makes its decision.

ACTIVITY!

Select one cause, personal or professional, from your list to be the focus for the campaign you are going to develop as you progress through this book.

Write down in detail how you will know when you have achieved it.

Final thoughts

'Show me a candidate with a cause, and I will show you a candidate who is difficult to beat.'

Roger Ailes

There is a wonderful paradox about cause that has run, just below the surface, throughout this chapter. Cause, according to Margaret McDonagh, is 'the big thing, the Dream'. We have talked about the powerful emotional compulsion that having a cause creates. We have argued that without a cause there is nothing to campaign for and that, although there are gradations of cause, ultimately what determines the importance of a cause is how much it matters to you. We have made reference to a world filled with a variety of causes and to different types of cause. We have suggested that it is the pursuit of a cause that creates values and shapes our life and the lives of others. Cause is an emotive, motivational driver of action. It is the story we just have to tell; the *why* not simply the *what*. It is a thing worth striving for. It is at the very heart of the *Campaign It!* model and, therefore, of this book. And yet in one sense cause is as difficult to show as a dream; as difficult to actually hold in your hand as the strongest belief. It is the big thing that needs us to breathe life into it. It is the story you have to create, not the story that is there for you to read.

The relationship between cause and campaigning can be summed up as follows:

- Without the realization of a cause there is no need to campaign.
- The purpose of a campaign is to share our cause with our audience(s) in ways that will gain their understanding, their emotional 'buy-in', and their permission.
- We live in a world of competing causes and, therefore, of competing campaigns.
- Many people run a variety of campaigns simultaneously.
- People have as much right to oppose our campaign as they do to support their own.

However, that isn't the whole picture because cause, like beauty, is a matter of personal judgement. It is in the eye of the beholder. You will certainly know when you recognize a cause and yet not everyone will necessarily share either your perception or your emotion. Indeed, whilst some people will be indifferent to your cause, some might even be antagonistic. Which is why, if you need to convince them of their value of your cause, if you need their permission to progress, you need to know how to campaign.

And that begins with understanding your audience.

Recognizing and understanding your audiences

03

> *Your audience gives you everything you need. They tell you. There is no director who can direct you like an audience.* **FANNY BRICE**

> *Get the habit of analysis – analysis will in time enable synthesis to become your habit of mind.* **FRANK LLOYD WRIGHT**

The purpose of this chapter is to:

1 Discuss the purpose of audience analysis.

2 Identify and explain the key principles and methods of audience analysis.

In this chapter we:

- Explain what we need to know about our audiences and why we need to know this.
- Identify the various ways we can gain this knowledge.
- Highlight and discuss the attitudes and skills that underpin this capability.
- Identify and consider barriers to audience analysis.

We will begin, though, by going on a brief journey together. We are going on holiday with a man called Michael.

Tourism, campaigning and a casual glance

For many of us, one of the great excitements about going on holiday to some-where new is the opportunity it brings to see so many new things and to experience different ways of living. This is certainly true for Michael. He had booked a three-week holiday in Japan and, as the day of his holiday neared, he was feeling that curious mix of excitement and nervousness that he always felt when going somewhere for the first time. He managed this by packing everything he needed (and many things that he didn't) one week before his departure and then unpacking his cases every day to check that he hadn't forgotten anything. Michael told his friends that his greatest joy in life was learning about other countries and cultures. Despite the fact that he had lived all his life in Slough,[1] he was, he said, 'A citizen of the world'. The fact that he always took with him half of his home stuffed into suitcases that invariably exceeded the acceptable weight did not strike him as at all ironic. Michael was, he reminded himself on the morning of his flight, an experienced traveller. As he watched the taxi driver struggling to fit all of his cases into a Ford Mondeo estate, Michael couldn't help but reflect that he was, indeed, a man who had been to more places than most. And soon he would be in another one.

Fifteen hours later he was. Tokyo surrounded him with its neon lights, busy, bustling streets filled with signs that gave absolutely no clue as to what they were about, and endless streams of rather small people going in all directions, all somehow managing to avoid looking anyone else in the eye. Michael was just less than six feet in height. In England he was used to many people being taller than him. Truth be told, he found it quite disconcerting to stand in a Tokyo street and look over the heads of the crowd. He had never been big before. Interesting and sophisticated, certainly. Worldly-wise, he would say if pushed to offer the most appropriate descriptor of himself (not that he ever was), but never big. This new perspective, coupled with the lights and signs and the belief he had brought with him from England that he really wouldn't be able to stomach most of the local food, served to make his nervousness exceed his excitement, and justify the decision that an early night was in order.

In the following weeks Michael experienced many aspects of Japanese life and culture, doing everything he could to integrate himself into local society. Despite his best efforts he was forced to admit upon his return, that his time in Japan had been confusing and, often, downright unpleasant. Michael had been amazed by the way so many people could live together in small, densely populated areas without obvious signs of tension or disruption. He put that down to the fact that, as a race, the Japanese clearly lacked the range of emotions that healthy English people felt. He had found it frustrating and somewhat rude and it had made him frown with irritation and confusion when Japanese people agreed to do something for him or to meet him somewhere and then didn't keep to their word. He had decided that the Japanese didn't like the English very much because no one seemed keen to greet him whenever he approached and introduced himself. He thought that, for people who clearly placed such an importance on etiquette, the way they slurped their noodles and soup at the dinner table was most inappropriate. He was offended when he bought one of his Japanese hosts a thank-you present and the man couldn't even be bothered to open it. He had found it patronizing that, whenever he dined out with a group of locals they took it upon themselves to decide when he needed his next drink pouring.

---

[1] A town 40 kilometres west of London immortalized (perhaps unfairly) by the Poet Laureate, Sir John Betjeman.

In the final analysis, he explained to both his friends during the 'Michael-is-back-from-Japan!' dinner party that he had organized himself, the Japanese were incapable of expressing themselves and building relationships. Japan was a land worth travelling through, but the people lacked the social skills and attitudes necessary if they really wanted to establish themselves as a leading holiday destination.

Michael, like the rest of us, has the right to his own perceptions and opinions. In this case, though, they are limited, inaccurate and lacking insight because they are the result of what we can think of as the tourists' casual glance rather than rigorous analysis. As a tourist, Michael experienced things on a surface level. He didn't do the research, ask the questions, or have the curiosity that underpins a real understanding of others. Consequently, he didn't know that, because of the geography of the Japanese islands and the often cramped living conditions this creates, the Japanese people value *wa*, or harmony, most highly. This expresses itself in the overwhelming desire to respect another's privacy and space, to avoid causing embarrassment or creating conflict, and in the creation of a hierarchical, ritualistic society in which uncertainty is avoided if at all possible. This is why Michael noticed that the people on the Tokyo streets avoided eye contact and why there was so little obvious tension or disruption. It is also why individuals appeared to agree with him and then didn't act upon their apparent agreement. Had Michael given his hosts more than a casual glance he would have learnt that the Japanese word '*hai*', which we translate as 'yes', means 'Yes, I am listening to you' more than it does, 'Yes, I will do as you ask'. By saying '*hai*', a Japanese person can at once avoid disagreement or conflict and help the person they are with to save face. Michael might also have known that, in Japanese culture, frowning is interpreted only as a sign of disagreement and that it is seen as impolite to introduce yourself to others. He might have learnt that gift-giving is highly ritualistic, that the way the present is wrapped is as significant as the actual present itself, and that gifts are never opened immediately. He would have also realized that, given the hierarchical nature of a society in which age and status are valued highly, his hosts were treating him with respect whenever they poured his drink for him.

Had Michael undertaken some thorough research before he went to Japan his time there would have been more enjoyable, productive and, certainly, less awkward for both himself and his hosts.

The point of the story is simply this:

'We cannot understand others if all we give them is a casual glance.'

There is a world of difference between a penetrating, informative study and a casual glance. The former reflects, interest, enthusiasm, focus and a willingness to learn and change. It is undertaken by someone who needs to develop a thorough understanding, who acknowledges that their current level of understanding is limited both by their experience and their personal perception filters. The latter reflects a lack of interest and a distracted state of mind. It is appropriate when there is no real need to create influence or to adapt, when one is just 'passing by'. A casual glance is the prerogative of the tourist. A penetrating and insightful audience analysis is a prerequisite for a successful campaign.

> *To understand others you have to give them more than just a casual glance.*

The analysis we undertake of our audiences needs to:

- be driven by a clear sense of purpose;
- have specific objectives;
- be thorough, incorporating all appropriate methods and using all appropriate feedback channels;
- continue throughout the campaign.

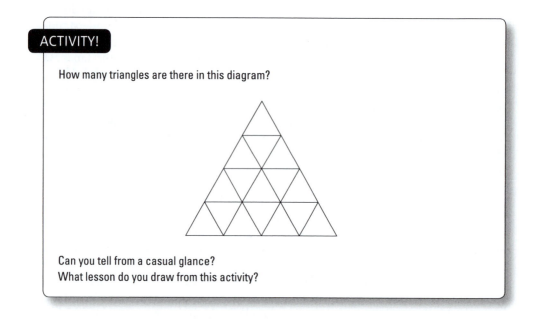
Thinking of an audience

Before we can begin our audience analysis we have to answer an initial, and vitally important, question:

'From whom do we need permission to succeed?'

Depending on the nature and purpose of our campaign there might be a number of audiences we need to influence, each with their own degree of power, each influenced by significant others. The task, then, is to:

- Identify the global audience.
- Segment this global audience into a hierarchy of sub-audiences.
- Identify the audiences and/or individuals that influence these audience segments.
- Decide what we need each segment to do.
- Learn about each segment (including their beliefs, values, behaviours, knowledge, agenda, desires).
- Identify possible communication channels to reach each segment.

Only when this is done, and we have a clear understanding of those we need to gain permission from, can we begin to work out the content and nature of the message(s) we need to share with each audience segment and the best ways to deliver these.

As campaigners, we think of those we seek to influence as an audience quite simply because we have a story to tell. The Latin root of our word 'audience' is '*audire*', which means 'to hear'. However, an audience does far more than receive, and listen passively to, a story. Audiences influence throughout the storytelling process and for us, as campaigners, they make the final decision about the quality, value and relevance – the *meaning* – of the stories we tell.

As we mentioned previously, the narrative is at the heart of a campaign and every storyteller, every narrator, is influenced by their audience in the following ways and for the following reasons:

- In the first instance, there is no need for a narrative, or story, if there is no audience to share it with.

- The structure, sequencing, content and delivery of the story is based to a great extent on the narrator's understanding of their audience, of their expectations, their needs, their knowledge and their desires.

- The audience has to be drawn to the story and then persuaded to engage with it, building their involvement, commitment and enthusiasm throughout; for this to happen the story has to be relevant to them.

- The very presence of the audience ensures feedback which, in turn, can influence both the content and the delivery of the story.

- Audiences respond emotionally and these emotional responses need to be created and managed through the content and delivery of the story.

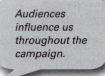
Audiences influence us throughout the campaign.

- Audiences can choose to ignore or dismiss any given story (or part of it) at any time and turn their attention elsewhere.

In short, there is an ongoing dynamic between the storyteller and their audience. An audience needs to be engaged and inspired. It needs to be able to make sense of the story, enabled to make decisions about the information, the dilemmas and the characters it contains, and encouraged to respond emotionally to the drama, the need for change, that is presented to them. To think of those we seek to influence as our audience reminds us of all these things and, in doing so, it reminds us also of the interactive nature of communication and of the need to make our story more engaging than either the stories of those who call our audience to focus in a different direction or the normal daily routines and experiences that demand their attention. As Ada Teixiera observed:

'The sun puts on a wonderful show at daybreak, yet most of the people in the audience go on sleeping.'

We have to present a story that wakes our audience up to the issues, and solutions, it contains. And we do have to present it. Which means it must be delivered, performed, in a way that is truthful, congruent and emotionally engaging.

Of course, when we first began working together we had very different ideas of what constituted an audience. For CP an audience was anything from a single individual to a theatre full of people. For AB it ranged from a community to a nation. In subsequent years we have come to realize that, for the reasons given above, all of these interpretations are valid. The challenge lies in delivering the right story to the right audience in the right way. To do that we first of all have to identify and then understand the audiences we need to influence and we need to be clear about our purpose.

LEARNING POINTS

- A penetrating and insightful audience analysis is a prerequisite for a successful campaign.
- To create influence we need to share emotive, relevant, engaging and congruent stories. Which is why we think of those we seek to influence as an audience.

ACTIVITY!

Identify the audience(s) from whom you need to gain permission to achieve your cause.

The purpose of audience analysis

In the simplest of terms, the purpose of audience analysis is to:

Inform action throughout the campaign!

For campaigners, analysis is never an end in itself. It helps provide the knowledge, understanding and awareness necessary to craft a relevant and compelling narrative and then inform the activities of the campaign.

The essential questions to ask before beginning a campaign of communications are:

- Whose permission do we need in order to achieve our desired outcome?

- What actions do we need them to take?
- What will these people do – for example, where will their perspectives, behaviours, attitudes, lifestyle be – if we do not influence them successfully?
- What do we need to know about them to be able to influence them sufficiently?
- What and who are the influencers on our audiences?
- Who, and what, motivates them indirectly and directly?
- What's their agenda, what's in it for them?

Those people, whether it is one individual or an entire community of people, are our audience. They are the people without whom we cannot either make change happen or reinforce the value of the status quo. Our purpose is to get to know them so well that we can create and share a story that:

- attracts, maintains and develops their interest and attention;
- acknowledges and satisfies their agendas;
- reflects their beliefs and values;
- creates within them positive feelings towards both our cause and the characters central to it;
- encourages and enables them to support or make all necessary decisions and/or changes;
- reinforces that it is a good thing to support our cause or give us the permission we require for success.

Through our analysis we aim to understand the opinions, beliefs and behaviours of our audience and, importantly, to identify those individuals, groups or organizations they trust and are influenced by. We seek also to understand and to identify the channels through which we can most appropriately communicate with them.

We also use audience analysis throughout the campaign to measure the effects our narrative is having on peoples' attitudes and behaviours. It would be a serious error to base a campaign on some initial audience analysis and then wait until 'polling day' to determine how our audience has been responding. Rather, we ensure that audience analysis is an ongoing, iterative process with research being undertaken at certain key points, or staging posts, along the way, to determine the degrees of change we are creating. Used in this way, research enables us to track the progress of our campaign and informs our decision-making, providing the feedback we need to make adjustments if necessary, whilst also limiting the likelihood of unexpected and unpleasant surprises.

In the first instance, though, we use our research to understand the current state of our audience, including their relevant experiences (past and present), their values, fears and concerns. The primary purpose of this audience analysis is to enable us to begin our campaign in ways that are immediately relevant to those we need to influence, to ensure that we meet them in their world rather than shouting at them from ours. We think of this as:

The starting point

This is made up of a combination of three things:

1 The audience's current knowledge of, and attitudes towards, our cause.
2 Their personal and/or shared agendas in this regard.
3 The current sources of influence they trust.

When creating influence, whether on a macro or a micro-level, it is necessary to start where your audience is and, once their attention, trust and respect have been gained, to begin the process of moving them towards the desired state. Analysis enables us to determine our audience's current state and their understanding of the situation and so begin our story at a place that makes sense to them, in a language and style that most appeals to them. By doing this we begin to share the message that:

'We understand and respect you.'

In an interview with CP, Charles Dunstone, the CEO and co-founder of the Carphone Warehouse, talked about the importance he places on understanding the customer perspective. He explained that his staff are encouraged to view their store by looking in to it from the pavement just as all customers do. According to Charles it is essential for any organization to find ways to perceive and experience the business from the customer's viewpoint. For him, this means reminding his employees that the customer's first impression of each store begins on the street outside. It is a wonderful example of how to appreciate the perspective of others by breaking the inside-out perspective that working in any organization creates.

For campaigners, the aim is to enter into the world of the audience and to match their preferred communication styles and patterns, and demonstrate an understanding of the most common beliefs and values and of their shared experiences and aspirations. Thus we can identify the audience's attitudes towards our cause and improve the likelihood of creating and managing a campaign that is received and understood as intended by the majority of people. We also increase the chances that our story, the central messages it contains, and the people who deliver them will be liked by the audience or be like the audience in some essential ways.

As we noted in Chapter 1, likeness is one of the six key principles of influence. We are far more likely to be influenced by people we like, those who demonstrate that they like us, or those who are, indeed, like us. We are also likely to be influenced positively by people who quite clearly give us their undivided attention with the aim of helping us create a desired outcome. Psychiatrists refer to this as the 'therapeutic alliance' and its value in empowering change is accepted widely in the world of personal development and micro-communications. Analysis of a much larger audience enables us to create an equally important and powerful alliance. It is one in which all involved acknowledge their shared interest and, ideally, their emotional commitment. It is one that unites and empowers through that unity. It is an alliance that is essential if the campaign is genuinely to develop the momentum it seeks as it closes in on polling day. We think of it as:

'an alliance of action'

through which shared ideas, beliefs and desires are transformed into a common response intended to achieve the desired outcome.

ACTIVITY!

Just take a moment to consider how often a person has given you their
undivided attention.

When was the last time someone put their own biases and perception filters
to one side and just sought to understand you better, to get to know you so well
that they could then communicate with you in your way about things that really
mattered to you?

If you have had this experience, how did it make you feel about the other
person? (If you have never had this happen, just imagine how you would feel if
it did.)

It is naive to assume that we can gain the support of others without providing
obvious benefits to them in return. Whether a campaign seeks to create change or
reinforce the status quo, its chances of success are
determined to a great extent by the ways in which it
is shown to further the primary agendas of the audience whilst also reflecting the values that underpin
them. People who like us, with whom we have important things in common, might well grant us permission
just because of the emotional or social closeness they
feel. If they also recognize that they will gain specific
benefits for themselves by doing so, they are even more
likely to support our cause.

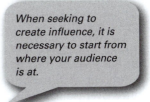

*When seeking to
create influence, it is
necessary to start from
where your audience
is at.*

Understanding the starting point for our audience also means answering the
following questions accurately:

- Who will instinctively and inevitably support our cause regardless of anything
  we do?
- Who will instinctively and inevitably oppose our cause regardless of anything
  we do?
- Who will instinctively want to support our cause but might choose not to
  engage?
- Who will instinctively oppose our cause but might choose not to engage?
- Who can be influenced one way or the other?

Strategic awareness and, arguably, a good degree of courage, are needed when responding to the answers to these questions. It is a strategic error, for example, to

spend a great deal of time and other resources targeting those groups who will support you regardless. No matter how great the temptation to do more, simply acknowledging their support, being grateful for it and making clear your reasons for focusing elsewhere, might well be sufficient. After all, people who already share your cause are relying on you to turn it into a reality and to do that and meet their needs and desires you might well need to gain the support of other parts of your audience. However, it remains important to guide their contribution to the campaign – getting them on-message and taking the correct supporting actions.

Likewise, it is equally flawed to focus time and energy on those who can never be persuaded to agree with you. For whatever reason, be it personal agendas, family beliefs and practice, peer pressure, or even regional or national culture, there will always be those who disagree fundamentally and irrevocably with your cause and the implications associated with it. The only appropriate response to such individuals or groups is to ignore them and channel your activities more profitably elsewhere. The phrase:

'You can lead a horse to water, but you can't make it drink'

is only half right. Some horses simply can't be led to water, at least not to our water and not by us.

Moving on then, those people who instinctively support our cause but might not choose to actively engage and support it are clearly an important part of our audience. We need to understand what might prevent them from expressing themselves and then determine what will motivate them to join in.

There is ample evidence to support the argument that people do not always act in ways that accurately reflect their purported beliefs and values.

In other words, just because we say that we think something is important and that it must be supported or protected it does not automatically mean that we will act on this view at the appropriate time. Just as a campaign never takes place within a vacuum, neither do our individual decisions and actions. Context is a powerful, often over-riding, influence, which is why campaigns have to define and determine the context through the telling of a compelling story if they are to be influential.

It is also true to say that many of us can appreciate different points of view at the same time and, if asked to choose which is the most valid, can find it difficult to be decisive. If we are to create and share a narrative that demands attention and support, we must first understand the beliefs, the fears, the agendas, and the emotional connections that exist in the minds of our audience. This is especially true for those parts of our audience who might choose to support us and those who are, as yet, undecided which way to turn.

The types of people that AB in his political life would have referred to as 'floating, or swing, voters', who can be persuaded to give their support to either side of the argument, are always there to be influenced and are usually the most important group in determining the outcome of a close-fought campaign. It is this group that must be identified accurately and addressed most completely, because it is this group that is the most unpredictable and whose permission we must work hardest to achieve. The notion of 'floating voters' is appropriate in any circumstance in which we need to persuade those who do not have a dominant, all-pervading bias.

The gap between how these people will think and behave if we, as campaigners, do nothing and if we choose instead to instigate a relevant and emotive campaign, is reflected in the following diagram that AB has used from the beginning of his time as a campaigner:

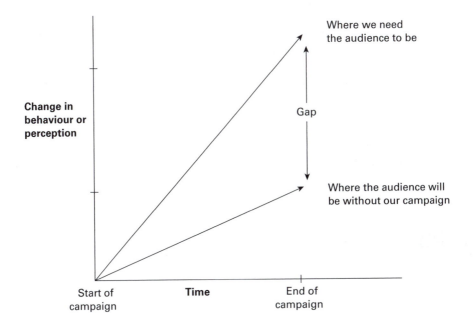

The final degree of separation between the two lines is determined by the nature and quality of the influences upon the audience and the context within which the campaign is operating. The aim, of course, is to create the degree of change that ensures the achievement of the desired outcome. To help us to do this our analysis must provide insights into how our audience is motivated to make decisions.

In one sense, the purpose of every campaign is to close the gap between the current situation and the desired outcome. Every aspect of our communications, every one of our activities, should play a specific role in closing that gap by creating the required audience understanding and behaviours.

LEARNING POINTS

- The purpose of audience analysis is to inform action throughout the campaign.
- To create a meaningful and engaging narrative we need to understand the starting point of the audience.
- Audience analysis is an ongoing, iterative process.
- We need to identify and target 'floating voters'.

The next question, then, is:

'How do we best analyse our audience?'

First and foremost, the desire to understand others has to grow out of an overwhelming sense of curiosity. Before you even consider the range of research methods available to you and develop the skills needed to apply them well, you have got to be just plain curious about what other people are doing, thinking, feeling, aiming for and who they take notice of. You have got to want to walk a mile or two in someone else's shoes even if they don't fit comfortably. Curiosity is the attitude that underpins all research. It is a curiosity that demands to be answered, that cannot be ignored, that wakes you up in the middle of the night because the answers are out there and you need them if you are going to build and run a successful campaign. It is a curiosity that lasts for the duration of the campaign because we are constantly analysing our audiences' responses. Curiosity is at once a sign of our interest in, and respect for, others and the fuel that fires our desire to ask great questions.

ACTIVITY!

Now that you have identified your audience(s) consider:

- their current knowledge of, and attitudes towards, your cause;

- their personal and/or shared agendas in this regard;

- the current sources of influence they trust.

What are your instinctive answers to the above?
How, precisely, can you find out more?

Principles and methods of audience analysis

At the heart of audience analysis is the ability to ask the right people the right questions in the right ways at the right times. The right people tend to be either representative sub-sets and/or key individual decision-makers. For some campaigns, however, it might be necessary to develop an understanding of a specific organization or a corporate community, or just specific aspects of such communities.

Whatever the methods being used it is essential that the nature, content and timing of our research grows out of our clear focus on the desired end outcome. We will outline different methods of research shortly. First, though, we will ask the most important question. The question is:

How do we ask great questions?

As with all aspects of campaigning, this requires an attitude, a process and an accompanying skill set. The attitude, as we have already stated, is based on curiosity and respect. Too often, people who need to influence others positively, for example, experts in education, healthcare, science or law, fail to use the language of their audience and/or to share their knowledge in ways that show either an understanding or a respect for their life experience. One of the reasons why suits don't sell themselves is because no matter how good the material, it always has to be crafted to fit the shape, the expectations and the needs of the buyer. The same is true of all material in all contexts. The ability and willingness to question well, respectfully and repeatedly is essential if we are going to cut our campaign cloth into a comfortable fit for others to wear.

The first question to ask when undertaking any form of research is, 'Do I need to ask a question right now?' The answer will often be 'Yes'. However, there are times during the process when it is best to exercise restraint and to wait for a more appropriate time and place. This might be because we do not have enough knowledge to enable us to form the most useful question yet and so need to do more background research, or because the context is prohibitive, or because we do not yet have the relationship with those we seek to question to begin, or continue, the process.

When we are ready to begin questioning, we need then to be clear about the value and purpose of the questions we are going to ask. We need to determine why we are asking every question we do. Questioning is a crucial part of the educational process. Sometimes we ask questions to encourage development and growth in others; by addressing certain questions and considering their response people can progress their understanding or be encouraged to learn more. Sometimes, though, we ask questions because we need to learn more. In these situations our questions are, initially at least, of value to us rather than others. Either way, we need to preface all the research we do by answering the question: '*Whom are we asking this question for?*'

Whatever the purpose, questions are most valuable when formed in the language patterns of those being questioned. For responses to be informative and reliable questions have to be understood as intended. To create the best possible chance of this happening they need to be asked using the other person's preferred language patterns and style and be framed within their life experience, not that of the questioner.

Nine useful questions to ask yourself before you question another are:

1 Do I need to ask a question *now*?
2 What am I currently unaware of in this situation?
3 What assumptions are driving my behaviour?
4 What is the most useful question I can ask now?
5 What is the best way to frame and ask the question?
6 What size of information do I need to gather?
7 What kind of information do I need to gather?

8 What kind of state do I wish the other person to induce in him/herself by answering my question?

9 How does this question help move us closer to the desired end outcome?

Often, of course, we will need to ask a series of questions. The order in which our questions are sequenced plays an important role in determining the level of focus and engagement of those being questioned and, consequently, the value of their responses. Appropriate sequencing gives the interviewees time to warm up to both the task and the topic and helps create within them the most useful emotional state. Throughout the discussion it is essential that we develop and pursue only the most fruitful lines of enquiry, whilst recognizing, questioning and thus clarifying any ambiguities in the interviewee's responses. Two other factors that influence their willingness to respond and their ability to do so effectively are timing and place.

All involved must feel comfortable that there is enough time available and that it fits well into the interviewees' schedule. No matter how well prepared the interviewer is, responses might be suspect if the interviewee is feeling hurried, or constantly distracted by, for example, thoughts of the important meeting they have to go to immediately afterwards or the challenging encounter they experienced just before. Obviously, we cannot control all external factors, however we do need to manage them as well as we can, and that includes ensuring that the place helps create the atmosphere you want and is conducive to a thoughtful and useful interaction.

It is appropriate to think of this process, as with so many others throughout the overall campaign, as a form of mini-campaign in its own right. When preparing questions know precisely how they will help you move towards your desired outcome and use sequencing, timing and place to create empowering states within the interviewees. Be ready then to manage the feedback.

Managing feedback

We need to ask great questions to get great feedback and we then need to ask great questions about that feedback! Timing is a crucial factor in this part of the process also. The natural desire to search for and identify meanings, to create associations and so gain a sense of understanding, has to be controlled within the campaign team, to ensure that they do not begin to generalize about incoming research results too quickly. Campaigners need a good degree of emotional intelligence and self-control to ensure they avoid analysing feedback before they have collected sufficient data, and also to manage their own perception filters, their personal and collective bias and preconceptions, when interpreting results.

In an interview with CP, Dr Stan Greenberg, former polling advisor to, amongst others, Presidents Bill Clinton and Nelson Mandela, and Prime Ministers Tony Blair and Ehud Barak, said it is important that campaigners:

'Don't talk about early findings. If you do you start creating meanings or possibilities and then you might go looking to prove them or find them.'

The other imperative when analysing feedback is to distinguish between those results that are most significant and useful and those that are less so. Again, a clear focus on the desired outcome helps direct our attention, encouraging us to seek out and focus on the most pertinent cues.

This recognition is crucial if we are to understand accurately our audience and the context within which we are operating. We need to have effective and efficient feedback mechanisms in place to ensure that we receive all feedback in timely and appropriate fashion. And then we need to be able to distinguish between different types of feedback, determining relative values, with the intention of identifying and acting upon only the most significant.

Our research can serve a variety of purposes and focus on different types of data. Invariably, though, it is driven by the need to hunt down the answers to those key questions that will enable us to understand and influence our audiences most effectively and efficiently.

> *The natural desire to gain a sense of understanding has to be controlled.*

Research

Essentially our research can be:

- **Exploratory**: undertaken when we have little or no prior knowledge of our audience; providing the foundation upon which more specific research can take place.
- **Descriptive**: enabling us to describe what is happening within, or to, our audience rather than uncovering why it is happening.
- **Explanatory**: identifying causal relationships between variables; enabling us to answer the question 'Why?' rather than just the questions 'What?' or 'Who?'
- **Predictive**: interpreting the findings of our explanatory research in order to predict likely future behaviours.

The research we undertake can also be defined by the characteristics of the data we are seeking to acquire. This can be quantitative or qualitative in nature.

Qualitative research

This is research that asks 'Why?' and 'How?' rather than 'How many?' The purpose is to gain insights into attitudes, motivation, values, concerns and lifestyles and to develop an understanding of why people behave as they do. It is based, in part, on the belief that the importance and value of experiences and behaviours cannot necessarily be measured by the number of times they occur, and that infrequent occurrences can also be enlightening for the researcher.

Qualitative research tends to focus on the use of focus groups, in-depth interviews, observation and content analysis and, unlike quantitative research, the design tends to emerge as the research develops. The data takes the form of words, pictures and/or objects.

Again, the ability to ask good questions is at the heart of gaining great insights. Use open-ended, discursive questions to explore ambiguities and cause and effect. Look for emotional responses and follow cause and effect arguments. Have a discussion guide mapped out but take the lead from the respondents, taking care to avoid those rabbit holes that divert from the discussions you need to have.

This type of research is often used during the earlier stages of a research project and is based on the presumption that all research is grounded in a qualitative approach and that researchers have to interpret the events, behaviours and responses they experience through their study. This study can be formal and/or informal in nature.

Where budget allows, qualitative research is often followed by quantitative research to check that the insights learnt are not just the preserve of those you have happened to talk with and listen to, and to find out just how widespread the views are. Qualitative research is a powerful way to inform the questions to be asked in quantitative research.

Quantitative research

This is research that is designed to measure what percentage of people in any given population act, think or feel in a certain way. It is research that identifies and draws meanings from measurable quantities. It is based on the premise that human behaviours can be observed and measured, objectively and numerically, and analysed. The purpose of quantitative research is to enable researchers to draw generalizations, create predictions and offer causal explanations. Quantitative research, therefore, tends to focus on large samples using such methods as surveys and questionnaires with the aim of creating precise measurements, classifying features and constructing statistical models that enable analysis of specific concepts. The data takes the form of numbers and statistics. This type of research is often used during the later stages of a research project.

It is worth emphasizing here that, no matter how detailed or thorough your data is, it is worthless until, and unless, you analyse it. Numbers and measurements do not provide a deep understanding of an audience. We have to organize and interpret our data and it is through our analysis that we determine the lessons it provides for how best to influence our audience.

As ever with audience analysis, questions are paramount. Quantitative research is wasted if there is any ambiguity in the questions asked. It is also wasted if you are asking the wrong questions about the wrong concepts, which is why qualitative research should normally come before quantitative.

Responses to questions have to be able to be interpreted absolutely so that valid comparisons can be made. Broadly speaking, there are two forms of statistical analysis. Descriptive statistics help us to organize our data numerically, to calculate, for example, the average number of people in the population who will respond positively or negatively to any given stimulus. Inferential statistics help us to infer relationships between different variables, helping us to identify, for example, the key sources or types of influence most likely to create a specific response from our audience, or parts of it.

Choosing and/or mixing quantitative and qualitative research

It is important to stress that one approach is not better than the other. Each has its place in campaign learning, with their value being determined by the nature of your over-arching research question and the accompanying objectives. If you need to measure a particular phenomenon, or you want to measure progress and change, or you need a benchmark against which to measure that progress, you will use quantitative methods. If you need to identify thoughts, feelings or beliefs you will use qualitative.

However, as a general rule of thumb, AB would spend money on qualitative rather than quantitative research if it came to a choice, because money goes further if you know what you are asking about and is wasted if you don't. Qualitative research also provides the insights and understanding through which the campaign narrative can be developed or strengthened. The approach we recommend for audience analysis, therefore, is to begin with qualitative research to gain insights followed by quantitative research to explore whether these preliminary findings are reflected sufficiently throughout the larger population.

Formal and informal analysis

We can develop an understanding of our audience through very obvious methods including, for example, questionnaires and focus groups, and through informal methods, examples of which include a conversation in a corridor and a chat over coffee. Remember though, that straw polls are at best indicative, never representative.

There are countless text books filled with information about how to research. This is not such a book. Our purpose here is to introduce the purpose and types of research and the data that can be sought and, more importantly, to stress the need for campaigners to develop the attitudes of a researcher – to have the emotional intelligence necessary to recognize and control their own bias and to have a genuine curiosity to understand others more fully. For us, research and the subsequent audience analysis is an iterative process that continues throughout the life of the campaign. Our initial findings provide the basis for the development of our narrative and the beginnings of our momentum. As we share our story through the most appropriate media, delivering the predetermined messages and seeking to achieve our agreed milestones along the way, we constantly research audience responses. Stan Greenberg refers to the floating voters as the 'winnables'. He says,

> 'During the campaign you must go back and check if the "winnables" are shifting in response to you and in the numbers you expected.'

However we choose to use, or how we choose to combine, different formal or informal methods of research either quantitative or qualitative, we must remain clearly focused on our over-arching research question (which is determined by our desired end-outcome) and our understanding of what precisely we are going to do with the knowledge we acquire about our audience. After all, no matter how cute our research, it is ultimately pointless if it doesn't help us to win over the 'winnables'.

> *Your data is worthless until, and unless, you analyse it.*

Using our knowledge

'I try to bring the audience's own drama – tears and laughter they know about – to them.'
Judy Garland

Quite simply, we use our knowledge to influence others elegantly, powerfully and purposefully. Research enables us to understand the starting point of our audience and create a narrative that reflects this. It enables us to monitor audience responses and to demonstrate our understanding, respect and care. It also teaches us how best to reach our audience, which channels to use and when. Ultimately, it is the process that is essential if we are to genuinely connect with others.

As we have already mentioned, we have both been surprised by the many common principles that underpin both macro- and micro-communication processes. Developing a detailed and accurate understanding of those you seek to influence, whether that is an individual, a group, an audience in a room or a social community, is one of the most important of these shared principles. It is easier, of course, to use informal methods when you are working with individuals or small groups. The bottom line, though, is that, as a campaigner, you have to understand others before you can influence them both ethically and effectively. And, the more you understand others, the more capable you are of creating a story and a campaign that reflects the drama of their lives. Inevitably, there are barriers to achieving this.

Barriers to audience analysis

Unless you are engaging in face-to-face communication, one of the most obvious barriers is that you never know for sure that your audience is receiving anything.

This problem is compounded by the fact that there are always competing influences vying for your audience's attention and commitment.

Other barriers are associated with the issue of resource availability and resource management. Three of the most important are:

1 time;
2 access to communication channels and/or to key audience influencers;
3 people.

Every campaign leads to the inevitability of polling day, the time when the audience gives its verdict. Often polling day is determined by significant others and we find ourselves working within their timeframe. If we have the power to set our own polling day it is essential to get it right. Great timing means being neither too late nor too soon. As we will discuss in Chapter 4, the ending is the most important part of the story. In a campaign the ending has to be compelling, we want action as a result, so the final elements need to be timed well and come together brilliantly. A story that runs on for too long is as frustrating to the audience as one that stops too soon. If the most important page in a novel is the last one, the most important day in our campaigning life is polling day. According to Stan Greenberg:

'A campaign is about life and death... On polling day you live or die. In the minds of the audience you are clever (and right) if you win and stupid (and wrong) if you lose.'

Whilst Dr Greenberg goes on to point out that this type of audience perception might not always be true the bottom line is that, come polling day, the audience will make the final decision.

A focus on the inevitability of polling day acts as a powerful motivating force throughout the campaign. Whether our campaign lasts for one day or one year, we know there will come a time when we can do no more and the audience will make their decision. This is one of the reasons why we believe in the value of reverse planning, of working backwards from polling day. Time is the one resource we can never hope to replenish. No matter how we choose to address and manage it, the purpose is always to fill the time available as comprehensively as possible. Reverse planning enables this whilst also ensuring that everything we do leads in the desired direction.

Whilst reverse planning is an integral part of the *Campaign It!* approach, successful time management, like so many aspects of successful campaigning, is also dependent to a great extent upon that powerful mix of high levels of motivation coupled with acute awareness and self control. The emotional commitment generated by our cause must be controlled and directed in a timely manner. The emotionally intelligent campaigner demonstrates this through their ability to manage time or, to be more accurate perhaps, through their ability to manage the development and delivery of their campaign well within the timeframe allotted.

Just as the success of many businesses is dependent upon the number, quality and appropriateness of their distribution channels, so the success of a campaign is dependent on the number, quality and appropriateness of the communication channels by which the narrative and associated messages can be shared with the audience. Our research must help us to identify these as well as the individuals and/or groups who already influence our audience or segments of it. Just as there is no point in writing the best story in the world if you can't get it to a publisher, so there is no value in researching your audience and determining the most engaging narrative if you cannot access the most relevant communication channels. That is a waste of effort and time. Simply put:

Being right × Not being heard = Being irrelevant

Creating the right narrative, accessing the best communication channels and being heard as and when you intended are also dependent on having the right people working with you. These include the people in your campaign team and those beyond it whom you need on your side. The value of the people working with you is determined by any combination of their skills, attitudes, network, or status in the eyes of your audience. Whatever the source of their value, the most obvious prerequisite is that they are committed to your cause. There is value in thinking of your campaign team as an audience in their own right.

The audience within

When leading a campaign team, your understanding of the individuals involved and the social dynamic that exists between them needs to be as accurate and detailed as that of the external audience(s) you are seeking to gain permission from. Understanding the team members communication patterns and preferences as well as their motivations, personal agendas and skill sets is essential if you are to be an effective leader. The team needs to be understood before it can be developed as a unit and before the individuals within it can be assigned the most relevant tasks, motivated appropriately, encouraged, controlled or guided. The campaign team is not just at the heart of creating and implementing the campaign, it is also an audience, needing to be analysed as rigorously as any other audience we need to influence. Indeed, in one sense, for our campaign to be a success, we need to earn the permission of the campaign team just as much as we do that of our external audience. After all, without the support of the team we might be incapable of delivering the campaign. And, as with our external audience, our analysis of the team needs to continue throughout the duration of the campaign.

The other audience within is even closer to home. It is yourself. Understanding self often presents even more challenges than understanding others, primarily because it is difficult to create the emotional distance needed to undertake an objective assessment. However, to be an effective campaigner, an accurate understanding of one's own strengths and weaknesses is vital. This understanding should include your psychological tendencies as well as your innate communication preferences and campaigning-related skills. Again, feedback from significant and appropriate

> The more we understand others, the more capable we are of creating a story that reflects the drama of their lives.

others is a core part of this analysis. It is essential too, to be as honest and rigorous in your assessment of your self as you are with all other audiences and to then use the results gathered to create narratives that are meaningful and motivational to both audiences within.

LEARNING POINTS

- We need to be really, really curious about those we seek to influence.
- We need to learn how to ask great questions and to resist the temptation to jump to conclusions.
- There are a range of research methods we can use and we need to select and sequence them appropriately.
- We need to identify and manage the barriers that face us.

ACTIVITY!

How are you actually going to analyse your audience(s)?
Create a plan and implement it.

Final thoughts

'The audience is the best judge of everything. They cannot be lied to. Truth brings them closer. A moment that lags – they're gonna cough.'

Barbra Streisand

Theatrical performers often talk about audience responses that indicate how well the show is going, that reflect signs of support, enjoyment or even apathy. Too much coughing, it seems, often suggests a growing sense of boredom and an increasing disassociation from the performer, rather than a roomful of people with the first signs of a winter cold.

Audience analysis is an ongoing, iterative process that informs you of the best ways to appeal to your audience, develop your influence and, when appropriate, change their behaviour as your campaign story moves towards its conclusion.

The process is based on the following loop:

The audience analysis loop

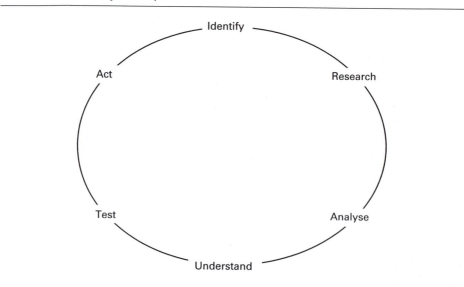

Just as in the theatre, there can be no successful campaign without audience support. The best way to gain, develop and keep that support is by basing your delivery on an understanding of how the audience are feeling right now. When data has been gathered and analysed and conclusions drawn, it is essential to test their validity before taking obvious action. Interestingly, this is another of one of the principles that is common to both AB's macro-campaigning and CP's micro-communications work. The desire for action cannot over-ride the need for thoroughness. Whether working to influence a society or an individual, challenge the rigour and accuracy of your research and analysis, and control and expose any presumptions, by testing your findings. Curiosity is a precursor to accuracy, providing we are curious at every stage of the process.

Only when you have tested your understanding and found it to be accurate can you use the insights gained from your research to make the audience laugh when you want them to laugh, cry when you need to them to cry, gasp with shock or surprise whenever you introduce an unexpected twist to the story and offer a standing ovation when the time is right. And, if you hear too many of them coughing, work on the principle that they are clearing their throats to tell you something you don't want to hear, so change what you are doing and the way you are doing it. According to AB,

'Feedback is the lifeblood of a campaign!'

As his following, brief examples indicate:

membership that the union had been promoting was in relation to negotiating terms and conditions of service for its members – collective bargaining, if you like, for pay and the associated packages of extras.

Our research led to the union defining itself as being akin to an insurance policy for work, there just in case because 'you never know when you might need us, especially in this day and age'. It was the start of a campaign of communications to grow the size and influence of the union and make it more effective for its members. Of course, we planned to keep in touch with the target audiences in case their views changed; a desire for collective bargaining could return as a motivator some time in the future.

Earlier in this chapter we mentioned that the Latin word '*audire*' meaning 'to hear' was the root of our word 'audience'. Public audiences, large gatherings of the populace, were not allowed in England until the thirteenth century when the Magna Carta granted a range of new freedoms, including freedom of speech and freedom of assembly. From that point on people began to congregate. Speakers were able to address audiences directly. In the following centuries, the nature and number of audiences grew and changed dramatically. If Shakespeare were alive today he might feel obliged to write:

'All the world is an audience.'

Now if we have access to media we are all encouraged to listen and decide about the value of a whole range of moral issues, business products, political views, individual talents, figureheads, designs and fashions. We are becoming as accustomed to voting for the next media superstar as we are for the next Prime Minister or President. Indeed, arguably, many of us are more likely to vote for the superstar than the politician, which raises a variety of questions about the nature and appropriateness of current political campaigning. None of which we will consider in this book.

We will, however, share the thought that the availability of social media, and the ever-increasing development of new channels of communication through which individuals can share their views with immediacy to substantial audiences is a significant shift in communication behaviour. Now audiences know the power they have in sharing both information and their personal views. They understand the role they play in determining what happens next and, if we are to influence them positively above the clamour of our modern world and the countless urgent invitations they hear to 'press the red button' or to 'call in and vote for your favourite', we have to become more than just campaigners who research, analyse and understand others. We have to remember the root from which the word 'audience' comes. We have to, in part, become an audience ourselves. As Stan Greenberg told CP, when seeking to analyse and understand your audience you have got to be curious enough to ask great questions and then:

'You've really got to listen.'

Finance, focus and feedback

In late 2010 I was asked to work with the Law Society on their campaign to stop the £350million of cuts to the Legal Aid budget being proposed by the Ministry of Justice. They already had an idea about the campaign messaging but I persuaded them to hold some focus groups to get a sense of the public's view about Legal Aid and its place in their lives.

Two interesting insights came from the research that changed the nature of the campaign being run.

The first was that there was very little support for lawyers. They were perceived as 'fat cats' who earned a very good salary.

The second insight was that whilst there was support for the principle of Legal Aid being there as a safety net to make sure that everyone had access to justice irrespective of their wealth, there was very little support for a campaign simply to oppose cuts. At the time the Coalition Government in the UK were faced with a dire economic situation following from the credit crunch and the banking crisis and much of the public sector was facing swingeing cuts, driven both by the ideology of the government and economic necessity. When teachers, nurses, police and much more were being cut it was felt that no area of spending should be held sacred.

I reported my findings. Firstly I told them that the public were very unlikely to go to the barricades on behalf of lawyers. The campaign had to make a distinction between Legal Aid lawyers, who earned very little (similar salaries to newly qualified teachers or nurses), and general lawyers who did indeed earn decent wages. We had to make education about legal aid part of our story and show what was being lost to society and individuals.

Secondly, I advised that they had to come up with alternatives to simply saying 'no' to cuts. The Law Society got on to the case, and soon found new and imaginative ways than the proposed £350 million in cuts. They promoted their alternative as reforms to bring Legal Aid into the twenty-first century whilst still retaining the essential principles that underpin Legal Aid in our country. Accepting that Legal Aid could be improved, and that they couldn't be immune to the financial realities of life in 2011, meant that they could build the support of public, charities and politicians behind their cause.

At around the same time I had also been advising a trade union working in the banking sector. It operated in a competitive environment, with another union making overtures to its members. The union my company was helping wanted to increase its membership from amongst those who weren't in a union already as well as making sure it retained its existing members who were being wooed by the other union.

The union agreed to a programme of research, a mixture of focus groups and in-depth interviews, so that we could learn what banking staff thought about them and trade unions in general. We spoke to a mix of union activists, ordinary members and non-union members. Our learning informed the communications plan we put together for the union.

Interestingly, we learnt new insights that allowed us to advise it to change its messaging and activities.

Key amongst them was that banking staff wanted help within their working environment and protection from unfair policies and poor management. This was a reflection of the environment. At the time of the research, in 2011, we were operating in financially straitened times as we were going through the aftermath of the credit crunch. Until we carried out our research the main benefit of

The narrative

04

> *I like a good story well told. That is the reason
> I am sometimes forced to tell them myself.* MARK TWAIN

> *Change the name and it is about you, that story.* HORACE

The purpose of this chapter is to:

1 Justify the importance of the narrative and storytelling in campaigning.
2 Explain how to create an influential narrative.
3 Explain how to deliver the narrative in ways that are engaging, meaningful and memorable.

In this chapter we:

- Define and explain what is meant by a campaign narrative.
- Discuss why stories are so appealing and influential.
- Identify and discuss the essential principles, techniques and skills for creating and delivering a narrative.
- Discuss how to develop strategies, milestones, messages, lines to take and flagship policies out of the narrative.
- Explain why the narrative is the heartbeat of the campaign.

A note from AB before we begin

'I just want to make clear what we mean by the *campaign narrative*. It is a story derived from a cause based on facts and evidence designed and delivered to gain permission for our desired end outcome. It is a story that is delivered through a series of integrated activities, which might include some written material and yet which are usually far more extensive than this. The nature and extent of these activities and the communication channels used are determined to a great extent by the nature and purpose of the campaign, the cause that has sparked it, the audience we are seeking to influence, and the context within which we are operating.

'The campaign narrative develops the understanding we need our target audience to have by the end of the campaign, or sooner, so that they are willing to give us permission to succeed.

'This understanding is created through sharing influential stories that explain to others why they should give us that permission, and to connect with them in ways that make clear the benefits and value of our cause to them. Thus the narrative guides all of the campaign activities. Everything that we do has to communicate at least one element or theme of the narrative to the target audiences.

'The story at the heart of the campaign does not want to be as complex as those contained in most novels. It needs to be simple enough for us to be able to tell it all in the early stages of our campaign and persuasive enough to create an emotional compulsion in our audience. However, there is much we can learn from traditional storytelling.

'With that said, if you are sitting comfortably, it is time now to get on with the chapter.'

Once upon a time and other ways to begin

'Once upon a time there were no stories.' That was how a wise man once began to enter-tain and teach the audience that had gathered around the campfire to hear him speak.[1] 'Can you imagine that?' The wise man asked. 'Can you imagine a time before stories?'

He paused, giving his audience chance to engage with his question. He watched as they frowned, deep in thought. He listened as they whispered to each other. He waited until they were all in agreement.

'Surely there can have never been such a time,' a grey-haired man said finally.

'I assure you that there was,' the wise man replied. 'It was the time before people and before communication. We cannot imagine that time because people have shared stories for as long as they have been able to communicate. Our ancestors shared stories through actions and pictures before they could speak or write about them. They shared stories about their environment, the weather and the journeys they had taken, about animals and hunting, about their enemies and the battles they had fought in.

'Of course,' the wise man continued, looking pointedly at a young man and woman who had been getting on exceptionally well together ever since they had first met that morning, 'Our ancestors also learnt very quickly that there were some stories that it is best to never share.' His audience chuckled. Well, all but two of them. 'Now,' said the wise man, 'before we go any further, let us take a few moments to do the following activity.'

---

[1] No, it is not the wise man with the 18th camel. This is a different wise man. This one doesn't have a camel. He has a Range Rover and a yacht and a holiday home in the South of France. This wise man uses his wisdom to tell some very well-known and influential stories and makes a lot of money in the process. The people gathered around the campfire are all busi-ness executives and they have each paid a lot of money just to be there. The campfire is in the grounds of a very posh hotel in Berkshire. Everyone is wearing designer clothes and more than a few of the executives are thinking of misbehaving with each other during the course of this three-day workshop. Where did you think we were – in a land far, far away and in a time long forgotten?

> ### ACTIVITY!
>
> Review your day yesterday and identify:
>
> - all the different stories you heard or saw;
> - all the different stories you told.
>
> Consider the different forms of media you experienced and the roles these played in both.

The phrase 'Once upon a time' operates like the word 'because' as a form of 'click-whirr'. We hear it and automatically know that a story is about to begin and, as long as we have the time to engage, we become the audience, the viewer, the reader. The storyteller then has the first of very many decisions to make. Their story is almost certainly going to contain some things that are new to their audience, things that might include places, experiences, or problems, and yet the storyteller needs to find some way to make their story relevant to their audience. There has to be something that is recognisable or understandable. There has to be some common ground established before the storyteller can lead their audience comfortably into newness. It might all happen in a land far, far away and in a time long forgotten (although the latter does beg the question, 'How has the storyteller managed to remember it when no one else has?') and yet, as the audience, we must be able to relate to it in some important ways if we are going to stay with the story to the very end.

The storyteller also has to decide how much to describe, how much detail to offer, about what and how soon. If the story is being delivered through words, spoken or written, the storyteller needs to empower the audience to visualize the characters and scenes. This draws the audience into the story and prevents them from imagining something very different from what the storyteller intended.

There is a part of every story that is always more important than the beginning, and we will identify and discuss that part later. Now, though, we will stay with the beginning for just a little while longer, until, in fact, it has eased its way into the main body of the chapter.

The most important thing to realize about the beginning of a story is that it has to engage our audience very quickly or their attention will be taken away from us and drawn towards a story that does start well. The award winning and hugely successful novelist Baroness Ruth Rendell stressed the importance of a great beginning in an interview with CP. She said:

> 'A very important thing is a good opening line. You want to engage the reader immediately, make them want to find out more.'

You probably realized that there are many stories that do start well when you reviewed all the stories that filled your day yesterday. For example, people constantly share stories with us at work. Sometimes they are about events that have happened, or things people have said and, inevitably, if several people tell us about the same happening their stories will be different in some significant ways. Of course, these are not the only stories we hear and are influenced by. We can access purely fictional stories in books, magazines, on television or at the cinema. The news is presented as a series of stories in a variety of media. We even make up stories in our own heads whenever we imagine something that we have to do.

Stories are everywhere. They are as much a part of our personal histories as they are our present and future. Actually, it is because of the ever-increasing proliferation of stories offered in a seemingly endless array of formats and media that we need to become great at campaigning communications. If we want our story to be heard, engage and influence, we have to:

- Tell it well.
- Get the structure, sequencing and timing of it right.
- Use the most suitable delivery channels.
- Know how we want your audience to be thinking or feeling at any given point.
- Have a great story to begin with.

And, to begin with, the beginning has to be brilliant. After the discussion around the campfire about how important stories are in every aspect our lives the wise man said, 'There is one object that will remind you always of the need to start your story brilliantly and of the challenges you face in keeping the attention of your audience fixed only on you. It is an everyday object, one that poses the greatest threat to the storyteller and yet, at the same time, can be the source of their inspiration and effort. It is, quite simply...'

The wise man paused again, knowing that the question he had raised in the minds of his audience would engage them just as his very first question had done earlier. He knew that if people are asked a question, however subtly, they have to engage with it. He knew that was as true for a person reading a book as for one sat around a campfire. He knew, also, that by pausing before he identified the object he was increasing the curiosity of his audience and he wanted them to be curious. Curiosity, he knew, was only bad for cats.

The wise man used his silence deliberately, building the need within his audience to know the answer. Silence, he had been taught once by a man even wiser than he, was a powerful influencer. However, like all methods of influence, it had to be delivered well and, in this case, it meant getting his timing just right. And now was the time to end his silence and reward their interest.

'...The remote control for the television,' he said, smiling. 'Please, just take a moment to think about how easy it is for us to move from one programme to another, one news story to the next. I suggest that, whenever you have a story to tell, you imagine your audience holding a remote control in their hands. If your story does not start brilliantly they will switch you off in an instant. If you story fails to maintain and develop their interest, they will do the same. You have to earn the attention and support of your audience. The remote control throws down the greatest of challenges to every storyteller. The challenge is:

> Start brilliantly and then get even better, because there is a world of stories out there, all just one click away.

'Remember, having a story to tell does not mean that you can call yourself a story-teller. You can only do that when you have the attention of an audience. That title is their gift, and their gift alone. Now, let's move on and consider why stories are so appealing and influential...'

Little Red Riding Hood and the power of storytelling

Storytelling is the oldest form of education. As we have already noted, stories have been used throughout the world as a way of passing down beliefs, lessons, traditions, culture and history from one generation to the next for as long as people have lived together.

We remember stories because they appeal to our brain's innate capability to create associations and meanings, to find connections between people and events. Stories are also more memorable than just lists of facts because they are invariably multi-sensory in nature, they stimulate our imaginations on every level and this, again, reflects the way the human brain works.

John Braggins, a man AB refers to as a giant of political campaigning with over 40 years' experience of helping and advising politicians about their campaigns of communications, observes,

> 'If I had been told a story as a six-year-old about a child being attacked by a wolf and how the wolf was then killed by a woodcutter, I would probably have been terrified and I would almost certainly have then forgotten it. However, the story of Little Red Riding Hood is with me to this day.'

Stories engage us emotionally and, because just about everyone enjoys a good story well told, they make learning enjoyable. Stories also contain humanity. No matter what the content or the characters involved, they remind us of, and reinforce, what it means to be human, of good and bad, right and wrong, of the inevitability of influence and change. Stories bring us together around a shared need, principle, challenge or opportunity. Stories are communal. They encourage us to consider the perspectives of others, to pursue our social responsibilities, and to value the power of communication.

Stories also help us to make sense of, remember and organize information. They engage our imagination and affect our attitude and emotional state. They encourage us to associate with the people and events within the story and they can be used to highlight role models, examples of desired behaviour, and likely consequences. Stories have played and continue to play a vital role in every country and every culture on the planet. They are at the core of what makes us human, which is why they are at the core of every campaign.

Stories are not only an essential teaching tool, they are an essential part of what it means to be human.

ACTIVITY!

At school you were almost certainly taught the names of the nine planets in the solar system. Take a moment now to see if you can remember them, starting with the planet closest to the sun and ending with the one furthest away.

How did you do? If not very well it is probably because:

- the information is no longer relevant to you;

- you were taught it originally as a list (and lists don't stimulate the brain naturally).

We have written the same information as the following story. If you do choose to read it you will never again forget either the names or the order of the planets in our solar system, even if the information is irrelevant to you. Stories that are told well really are this memorable.

'Imagine now that you are floating in the darkness of space. You are floating close to the sun. You are so close that you can see great flames and you can feel the heat although, wonderfully, you are safe. As you look you see fountains of silvery-grey liquid shooting up into the air, soaring across the blackness of space. You realize that these are fountains of Mercury, which is the planet closest to the sun.

'As you watch this amazing sight a beautiful woman soars past you, her arm outstretched. This woman is Venus, the second planet from the sun. Venus catches the Mercury in her hand and then hurls it across the dark sky. You watch as it flies through space before landing with an almighty crash in the Earth of your very own garden. Earth, of course, is the third planet from the sun. The ground shakes so much from the impact that your new neighbour comes out and angrily blames you for what has happened. He is very threatening. He is Mars, god of war, and the fourth planet from the sun. Just when you are certain that Mars is going to attack you, a giant steps into your garden and scares him away.

'The giant is wearing red wellington boots, long yellow shorts and a black t-shirt. He has a large, black beard and red, ruddy cheeks. He is Jupiter, the fifth planet from the sun. As you stare up at him, you see that he has the word *SUN* in large yellow letters embroidered across the chest of his t-shirt. You realize that this word represents the next three planets, Saturn, Uranus and Neptune. Looking up at his face, you see a small cartoon dog sitting on his head. This is Pluto, the ninth planet from the sun.'

Having read that just once test your recall by just beginning the story again in your mind's eye and seeing what happens. The likelihood is that you will remember it all. Stories that are well sequenced, that stimulate our imaginations and yet contain at least some elements of our own reality stay with us.

LEARNING POINTS

- A campaign narrative is a story derived from a cause based on facts and evidence designed and delivered to gain permission for our desired end outcome.
- The narrative is delivered through a series of integrated activities.
- The campaign narrative develops the understanding we need our target audience to have by the end of the campaign, or sooner.
- We live in a world filled with stories.
- Stories are powerful learning tools.
- Stories encourage and enable us to create associations and meaning.
- A story needs to start brilliantly and keep getting better.
- Stories are an essential part of our life experience.

Creating the campaign narrative

Creating the narrative reinforces the fact that campaigning is an iterative process. It requires a bringing together of everything we do and know, from our audience analysis and understanding of our opposition through to the clarity of our desired end outcome. Prior to writing the narrative we have to:

- Identify the cause.
- Ensure clarity of the desired end outcome.
- Understand our client (if we are working for a client).
- Identify and analyse our opposition.
- Identify and analyse the audience (and sometimes the environments within which we are operating).

Identifying the cause

The process begins, as every campaign does, with a clear understanding of cause. Most simply, we have to know what benefits our campaign seeks to create or maintain and what negative outcomes it seeks to prevent. Charles Dunstone talked to CP about the value of creating what he calls a *'grudge book'* for reminding yourself, team or business what it is you stand against and, more importantly, what it is you stand for.

Whether or not we choose to write and update a grudge book, we do all have to believe in the goodness of our cause before we can believe in the power and relevance of the associated story. To be sure that we have identified all of the benefits our campaign offers, and all of the negative effects if we are unsuccessful, we have to conduct a thorough ecology check. This combines a recognition and understanding of the environments we are working in and which are going to be influenced by the outcome of the campaign, whilst repeatedly asking the 'What if?' questions that underpin scenario planning.

Due to the interconnected nature of communities and cultures, every change has a knock-on effect to some degree or other. John Donne wrote:

'No man is an island'

as a way of reminding us that we do not operate in a vacuum. It is for this reason that campaigns often create ripples of influence beyond their immediate sphere of operation. By identifying the associated environments and by asking, '*What will happen if...?*' as we consider each desired milestone as well as the end outcome, we can identify the most likely effects and evaluate their appropriateness.

AB often stresses the fact that campaigners have to balance their desire for complete success with an acceptance of the inevitability of '*trade-offs*'. This takes us back to one of our earliest points. We only ever need to campaign a cause because there will be either apathy or opposition to it. If everyone were in complete agreement and willing to take action there would be no need to seek permission. The fact that we are campaigning means, by definition, that people are not motivated to act or are proposing an alternative view and are seeking or have acceptance for their standpoint. Winning in such a situation inevitably comes at a price, a trade-off. It is essential, of course, that these trade-offs do not outweigh the primary benefits. The most likely, and/or acceptable, trade-offs can be determined as part of this overall ecology check.

Ensuring clarity of the desired end outcome

In Chapter 1 we asked you the question: *What are you prepared to do to win?* Now the question has changed to: *How will you recognize the win?*

The ultimate purpose of your narrative is to persuade your audience that your desired end outcome is the best of all possible alternatives. To create a narrative that accomplishes this, you need to have a very clear vision of just what this end outcome will be. This vision needs to be shared with both your audience and your campaign team.

Sharing a vision requires:

- the ability to visualize it in detail;
- the ability to communicate it in ways that provide clarity and motivation.

Sometimes the desired end outcome contains layers of complexity and requires more than just gaining permission. Sometimes there are additional measures of success. For example, the end outcome you are aiming for might be simply to get your candidate elected, or your proposal approved, or your product bought by a particular chain of stores. However, there are times when it needs to be more than this. It might be, for example, that your candidate is almost certain to win and the desired end outcome incorporates the aim of engaging and mobilizing a greater percentage of the audience than ever before. It might be that you want your proposal approved and championed by particular individuals, or that you are aiming for a specific margin when selling your product. Sometimes the desired end outcome is to create change and sometimes it is to defend or protect something of value. Sometimes it might be determined by, or need to be agreed with, your client.

Understanding our client

The client can be an individual, an organization or a specific individual or team representing an organization. In the latter cases there is a need to understand both the culture of the organization and any associated internal politics. Organizational cultures are a powerful determinant of behaviours, including the nature and purpose of planning and the systems used to achieve outputs. Identifying the ways in which the corporate culture acts as a boundary or support to the development and sharing of a narrative is an essential part of analysis. There is also a requirement to gain the client's trust and, often, to educate them about the campaigning process and what it actually entails to share a narrative effectively.

Stan Greenberg told CP that his starting point was always his understanding of his client. He talked about the importance of determining the motivation and mission that forges the personal desire to campaign, saying that, to a great extent, his role was about:

> 'Trying to understand the decision, the choices, people made... What really motivates someone.'

John Braggins makes the same point when he says,

> 'I would always begin by asking (them), "Why do you want to be an MP?" The answer would often help start the process of creating the narrative.'

This is, of course, as relevant when seeking to understand a client as it is when seeking to understand an audience. Sometimes a client will have a personality, a history, a story, that makes them a natural figurehead and puts them square and centre at the heart of the narrative and the campaign. Sometimes, this is not the case and the narrative will be built around other aspects of the campaign and the benefits it offers. This is not to suggest that one approach has more value than the other. Not every story has to have the name of the lead character in the title to be successful. We don't all need to be a version of Little Red Riding Hood when we set out to campaign a cause, nor would we want to be.

Identifying and analysing the opposition

Sun Tzu, the sixth century BC Chinese military strategist, proclaimed:

> 'It is said that if you know your enemies and know yourself, you will not be imperiled in a hundred battles; if you do not know your enemies but do know yourself, you will win one and lose one; if you do not know your enemies nor yourself, you will be imperilled in every single battle.'

Whilst our campaigns are hopefully much less bloody than those Sun Tzu was preparing for, we do still need to identify those who will oppose us and understand their motives, resources, perceptions and arguments. Having said that, we would caution against spending too much time studying and analysing the opposition, especially at the expense of creating and progressing the quality and delivery of our own narrative. Whilst we do need continually to be aware of what is happening and be able to respond to feedback when necessary, if we spend too much time worrying about what the opposition is doing, or might do, we risk losing our own direction and momentum and dancing instead to the tune of others.

This is a point that was reiterated by Charles Dunstone, who, when talking to us about ways to gain competitive advantage, emphasized the need for the focus to be primarily on improving what 'we' do and less on implementing strategies based on the behaviours of our competitors.

Often an analysis of our own strengths and weaknesses will help us determine the most likely strategies and tactics of our opposition. After all, if we have an obvious weakness, or two, it would be reasonable to presume that our opposition will seek to expose these. The challenge in undertaking accurate self-analysis relates back to one that we have mentioned on several occasions. It requires the emotional intelligence necessary to take an objective, somewhat detached, appraisal of both our capability and our situation. It is as risky to underestimate our starting point and our potential, as it is to overestimate them. Knowing who we are in terms of our campaign capability is a prerequisite for planning, enabling us to build on our strengths whilst defending our weaknesses.

Equally we need to analyse our opposition's strengths and weaknesses so we can minimize one and exploit the other. It is always the aim of any campaign to set the agenda and for the opposition to respond to it.

When it comes to responding to threats, challenges or setbacks, Charles Dunstone offers advice that is at once humorous and strategically sensible. He says quite simply:

'I have two rules. They are: 1) never panic; and 2) if you do panic, panic first!'

Charles' thoughts about how best to manage panic reinforce two *Campaign It!* principles. They are:

1 Focus on developing and initiating your own plan rather than just responding to the actions of your opposition.

2 Go first!

The first of these two principles relates back to the importance of being the best we can be, of building our own positives and emphasizing those, rather than reacting only to the arguments and activities of those who oppose us. In the same pragmatic vein, Charles also argues that, no matter what the situation, we should always seek to find and tell the good value story that highlights the benefits of what we are doing and offering compared to our opposition.

The second principle further highlights the value of proactivity. Sometimes an individual needs to go first to actually begin a campaign and, if necessary, build a campaign team to support them. Often through a campaign there will be times when it is necessary to seize the initiative. Either way, campaigners are inevitably people who are willing to go first, even in the face of doubt, disinterest or opposition. They know that even if a narrative is to be told and reinforced through a hundred activities, it always begins with the first one and that somebody has to make that happen.

> Focus primarily on being the best you can be throughout your campaign, rather than responding to the opposition.

Identifying and analysing our audience and relevant environments

As we have already said a basic principle in creating influence whether on a macro or a micro level, is to understand and then begin from the starting point of those you are seeking to influence. This is as relevant when communicating with a community as it is when communicating with an individual, although, obviously, there tends to be more complexity when dealing with greater numbers. We will discuss this idea in more detail in the next chapter, Influencing conversations. The basic question we seek to answer though through our audience analysis is:

'How does the situation look and what does it mean from their perspective?'

Whilst writing the narrative is, in part, a creative activity, answering this question is not. The ability to see things from the audience's perspective is a prerequisite for developing a relevant narrative. It is this understanding that helps determine the beginning of the story, the key messages, the nature of the progression and the language, imagery and communication channels to use.

For some campaigns, analysis stretches beyond just the audience and into a consideration of the environment(s) within which we are operating. This might include developing an understanding of local resources, buildings, route ways, and even the history of the area. Ruth Rendell explained to CP how important an understanding of environments and context is when developing a novel:

'I have begun my research for a novel,' she said, 'with an area, a district, of London.'

Her research included a study of both places and people, developing an understanding of daily routines and patterns, and of the history of the area.

For campaigners analysis can also include internal environments and contexts. AB has plenty of experience in setting up campaigns for clients only to find that there is internal opposition to it. Often this necessitates an internal campaign to be run to gain the support needed to ensure the success of the original campaign. Again, an understanding of the existing organizational culture and associated power bases underpins the development of this campaign plan.

The purpose of our analysis is, simply, to identify and understand every aspect of both our audience and the environment that is relevant to create the narrative. As we deliver and reinforce the narrative throughout the campaign, the purpose of our analysis shifts to provide an understanding of the impact we are having as we move towards polling day. Our narrative has to gain agreement, it has to

> The campaign narrative has to do more than just engage our audience – it has to mobilize them!

create energy within the audience that will be made manifest through their active support.

Creating and sharing the narrative

In some campaigns the story is obvious and in others the story has to be deliberately created. Either way, the information and understanding gathered from the preceding steps is used to ensure that the narrative is both factually correct and influential. Unlike conventional storytelling in which the development of the story occurs throughout the duration of the piece, building towards the final revelation and resolution, the campaign narrative is often told in full from the very beginning. Sometimes, though, the narrative is complicated and has to be told in small sections, with the story growing as the understanding of the audience develops and, with it, their willingness to demonstrate their support.

One such example was in the referendum in the UK in May 2011. AB and John Braggins were called in to help the No to AV campaign. The campaign didn't have a coherent message and was seemingly unable to get started. The Yes campaign on the other hand was able to take on the mantle of 'newness, future and reform', especially when set against the recent scandal about MPs' expenses. AB recalls:

A silver bullet, the last chamber, and the golden rules

John and I had been hired to come up with the campaign narrative and the messaging that would bring it to life and then to advise on the tactical executions. In order to learn we conducted several focus groups. We'd been given the arguments currently being used by NO, and we'd checked out the YES messaging. We wanted to test some ideas of our own, but above all else we wanted to find out what would motivate someone to bother to go out and vote just to maintain the status quo.

We knew that the arguments weren't simple so each pair of focus groups was used to develop new ideas for testing in subsequent pairs of focus groups. We needed to track the development of a story and find the simpler executions that told our version in the quickest and easiest way. To encourage discussion amongst the participants, we introduced concepts and lines/arguments as appropriate and allowed them to use the ones they found to be more persuasive with each other. As such the topic guide evolved for each pair of groups. However, each followed the same structure:

- Start by chatting about current affairs leading into politics and politicians to get respondents used to each other and the style of the evening. Help them to discuss with each other by using appropriate questions.

- Introduce into discussion changes to politics and voting.

- Introduce referendum and explain AV.

- Test arguments in favour and against during explanation of AV.

- Show and discuss materials.

- Develop, test and refine lines that engage, inform and persuade.

We realized that awareness was low, and that we'd have to do something eye-catching to break through. We would have to follow PT Barnum's maxim that if you wanted to draw a crowd, you should start a fight. More importantly though, we learnt that we had to have a more reasoned conversation with the voters. We had to unpick the Yes campaign's arguments for change, demonstrating that AV wouldn't work, or wasn't fair, or wasn't right. We developed a plan and tested it in our groups. We learnt that there was a way it would work. And then, once we had exposed their arguments, we could come in with our final pay-off line about keeping voting fair and simple.

And even more importantly, we knew that before we could do any of that we had to define the positive nature of our campaign. There was a simple and very emotive line to deploy that John came up with and which worked in all the groups: The winner should be the one who came first. That line gave us our cause, and our emotion. It was our positive, and it is an example of one of the golden rules of campaigning. Which is:

'Define your own positive before you define your opponent's negative.'

We had to establish this concept first. Then we had to unpick the Yes arguments. This was going to take time. We had to undo them one by one. The most powerful was the cost argument. No one in the groups thought that it was the right time to spend £250 million on changing the voting system given the recent credit crunch. However, it didn't stand up on its own. It only worked once the other six parts of their argument had been unpicked. Because if AV was a truly astounding system, then it would be worth the money; as one of the participants said at the start, 'So if not now, when?'

We had a tricky messaging path to follow. We had to get our positive out there first, followed by any of the six negatives and then the cost of change. And all this before we even got on to our final call to action to defend equal votes. The No campaign had been looking for the one thing they could say to win. They had watched the campaigns of the nineties and still yearned for the simplicity of messaging. Fifteen years on, the public were in a different place towards politicians, and especially on this particular issue they were either going to vote Yes with their gut, or be educated into the No camp. Yes had the instinctive emotion of sticking it to the politicians, whilst, at its simplest, No could be defined as defending the old regime of MPs fiddling their expenses. We weren't going to win on emotion. As John said, 'These days, in a barrel of six bullets, the silver one is often in the last chamber'.

However, the No campaign was the client and they latched on to the cost argument as the potential silver bullet. (It was, but it wasn't in the first chamber.) Admittedly we were short on time but it was the wrong order. We hadn't got our positive definition out there before we deployed the Barnum principle; to good effect, I might add. Our ads about the £250 million cost of the referendum certainly caused a stir and got some wider interest in the campaign. It meant, though, that we nearly got derailed as we became vulnerable to charges of only running a negative campaign. We had to regroup and share the first part of our narrative, that the winner should be the one who comes first.

In hindsight, I can see benefits of using the money argument to get the first cut-through, but it was a problem that we hadn't got our positive out there. Luckily the opposition were also still stuck in the nineties with their campaign thinking, so that helped. The real breakthrough came when we persuaded Lord John Reid, ex-Labour Home Secretary, to join Conservative Prime Minister David Cameron in a joint appeal to reassert our positive message that all votes should be equal. After that it became much harder for the Yes campaign to get traction. We could get through to enough people with our range of arguments once we had got that positive, values message out.

Whilst there is a very deliberate sequencing and layering of messages and activities throughout any campaign, the story itself is always told as quickly as possible and then reinforced continually. It is another one of those golden rules. Whether the story is about a figurehead, the history of the environment, the benefits you are offering to create or defend, or, indeed, some other central focus, the essential approach to using the narrative to develop momentum is to:

Share, Remind, Reinforce!

In a world that is filled with, and fuelled by, myriad stories the campaign narrative has to be shared repeatedly using all relevant communication channels if it is to hold its place in peoples' thinking. To share the story once and expect people both to re-member it and be motivated to take action is to forget the number and variety of stories our audience has to choose from, including those beyond the perimeters of our campaign. Our story has to be more influential, memorable and acceptable than that told by our opposition. It also has to compete with the all the other stories, interests, and influencing factors that make up the daily lives of our audience. If we fail to remind the audience continually of our narrative and reinforce the value and appropriateness of it, we create a gap that will be filled sooner or later by a different story. Having said that, once we have established our story in peoples' minds we don't necessarily need to keep repeating it in full – a simple aide memoire will do by then.

Sometimes the media we use, be it, for example, a poster or a flyer, is intended purely to remind people of our narrative and the key points of it. Once we know the story of Little Red Riding Hood we only need to hear or see the title to be reminded of the contents and it can be the same with a campaign narrative. At other times the media used will just highlight and explain one or two elements, or themes, of the narrative. The skill in sharing the story lies in knowing how, when and where to communicate it and what our purpose is with each communication.

AB ensures, when writing the complete narrative, that it is never longer than two sides of A4. If it can be told fully in fewer words then so much the better. It has to be simple enough for it to be told swiftly and yet powerful enough for it to remembered and acted upon. As John Braggins says:

'If Little Red Riding Hood had been 300 pages long, I wouldn't have read it.'

So the campaign story needs to be an example of detailed brevity. It needs a begin-ning, a middle section, and an ending just as any other story. It needs to be easily understood, connect powerfully with the audience and their current situation, and be emotionally compelling. It needs to be a story that grabs the attention of the audience, gains their support and makes them forget the intellectual and emotional 'remote control' they possess. If the story is too long or too complicated, if it lacks the power of supporting facts, if it has no obvious and immediate relevance and offers no recognizable benefits, the audience will switch off to it and turn their atten-tion to a more appealing story.

Everyone remembers a great ending

It is true that every part of our narrative must have an obvious and specific purpose. The No to AV story demonstrates that. We need to be able to justify every detail. Given that, the most significant aspect is the ending. Every part of a story is designed to lead towards a memorable ending. No matter how good the story is, no matter how relevant the narrative, or how influential the facts, the audience will remember the conclusion beyond all else.

This is true for all forms of communication, simply because the ending is the last thing that happens and, therefore, the first and easiest thing to remember afterwards. The success of a conversation in a corridor, an email, a phone call, a business presentation and every type of entertainment is determined significantly by the quality and power of the ending. Imagine a joke that grabs your attention and imagination only to have a poor punch line. Think of a business meeting that appears to have being going well only to end with a sentence or two that makes you doubtful or concerned. Remember your favourite novel or film. It has a great ending, doesn't it? It has to, because if it didn't you would have felt let down by a story that had so engaged you only to fall at the final, and most important, fence. For Ruth Rendell, the ending is so significant that, whilst it is planned, she only begins to write it when she has edited the rest of the novel and is confident that everything is in place.

CP places the same importance on endings when providing presentation skills training. As he explains below, he begins by identifying the story that needs to be told through the presentation and then determining the very best way to end it.

Welcome to my world

Too often people confuse giving a presentation with just information-sharing. One of the most common reasons for this in my experience is that people usually fail to realize that they have a story to tell. And they inevitably do. It is just that they have not been given the encouragement and help to identify and shape it.

Actually, if you don't know what story to tell through your presentation, I recommend not doing the presentation at all! By telling a story we create a new world and draw our audience into it. If, for example, you are making a business presentation, you need to make your corporate world and the benefits it offers clear. If you are presenting alone to get the job of your dreams, you need to realize that you are your own personal brand and ensure that your audience recognizes the qualities you offer. You need to show how your world can mesh successfully with the audience's taken-for-granted world and so meet their needs.

In one sense, then, if you don't have a story you don't have a world to share, a world that offers something of value to those you are presenting to. And if you cannot draw them, for a time at least, into a believable world, they will inevitably become distracted and your messages will be lost.

Even if a presentation is one activity within a much larger campaign, it needs to be treated as a type of mini-campaign in its own right. It needs to be driven by a cause, be based on key themes, share messages and include the facts and figures that prove the claims being made. Importantly, too, it needs to be performed, with the realization being that the most important visual aids in the room are the people presenting and not the screen behind them.

As with the planning of an entire campaign, once I know the story that needs to be shared through the presentation, I decide the desired ending and work backwards from that. As with every other type of storytelling, the audience will only remember and value it if the story itself has both great content and is told well, and if the ending is then brilliant. It is so easy to become embroiled in the development of our own presentation we can forget that the ending is the last experience the audience will have of it before moving away from the world we have created and on to all the other stories vying for their attention.

There is an important difference, though, between the ending of a fictional story and that of a campaign narrative. It is the difference in the purpose of the two types of story. Fiction is designed to engage, entertain and distract. The ending of a fictional story needs to draw all of the key elements together, provide the final answers, suggest a possible future, and be either emotionally satisfying or emotionally challenging. The ending of a campaign narrative is designed to compel the audience to take a specific action. The ending of both types of story is dependent upon what has gone before, the way it has been sequenced and the understandings it has created. However, the campaign narrative is seeking always to establish and develop an emotional compulsion within the audience to act. Conventional storytellers only need to get permission to tell their story in its entirety. Campaigners tell their story to get permission to achieve something else. The campaign narrative is a means of affecting the actual reality of the audience's world. Its purpose is neither entertainment nor distraction. The ending of a campaign narrative has to motivate the audience to do something they would not necessarily have done otherwise. It is essentially a call to arms.

Whilst the campaign narrative needs to be appropriately brief, it must be convincing. The final part of the narrative brings together the key elements in a persuasive and conclusive manner, highlighting the goodness that will be available if the audience act in our favour. Ours is a story rooted in the realities of a current situation designed to create agreement about the future. Our purpose is to create within our audience the realization that our proposed future is the most beneficial and then to turn that realization into an overwhelming desire to act.

Ultimately, we measure the success of our narrative by the level of active support it generates. What began, perhaps, as a dream, has been turned into a clear and engaging desired end outcome that is shared and justified through a story. It is a story that compels significant others to give us their permission once they have recognized the truth of it and have come to see the situation from our perspective.

The bubble of fiction and the frame of perception

All novelists face a very specific challenge that has to be overcome if their stories are to be both enjoyable and believable. The challenge is to create what is referred to as a 'bubble of fiction' that will not burst under scrutiny. A novelist, by definition, is making many things up. The people, the events, and sometimes even the places in their stories are a product of their imagination and yet there has to be enough realism within the pages to convince the reader to care. Often, of course, the settings in a novel, either geographical or historical, are real and then the bubble of fiction is at even greater risk of bursting. If the author gets just one detail wrong and the reader recognizes the error, the bubble pops. The fictional world that the reader has agreed to enter and believe in has suddenly been shattered by a detail that is flawed. And, as with any other type of bubble, once it has burst it is all-but impossible to make it whole again. This is why research forms such an integral part of most novelists' work. The fiction has to exist within a reality that is both accurate and detailed. The bubble depends upon it. Ruth Rendell stressed:

> 'Every aspect of your story must be believable. You never want your reader, or listener, to say, "I don't believe that."'

Now, whilst we need to be very clear that our campaign story is never a work of fiction and is always built on, and incorporates, important information and facts, we do still need to create a bubble that is as strong and resilient as the greatest fictional versions created by the very best writers. Our campaign narrative, like every story, needs to be self-contained, capable of withstanding any form of scrutiny, and enticing. Whilst readers of fiction give novelists permission to draw them into their fictional world and, therefore, do not want a factual error to burst the fantasy, in our campaign world there will be those who will actively search for flaws in our story and do everything they can to pop the power of our argument.

To repeat the point made earlier, every campaign story will be scrutinized and challenged because our opposition is obliged, and have the right, to do so. We need to remember that our story loses its believability and, therefore, its appeal if we get just one detail wrong. Even worse than that, if our bubble of believability is burst there is an increased likelihood that the opposition's story will gain ground. Essentially, then, our story has to be rigorous enough to withstand any scrutiny and sustainable in the face of opposition, whilst also directing the thoughts, beliefs and perception of our audience. Simply, it has to persuade people to see things our way and then to give their support.

Arguably, there is no more powerful form of messaging than word of mouth and our narrative needs to get people talking about the topics we want and in the ways we desire. Before that happens the validity of our narrative must be accepted and the perspective we offer regarded as the most accurate viewpoint. We share our narrative to frame the perception of our audience. We create this frame by defining the context of our campaign and then gaining recognition of it and support for it. People will only give us permission if they view things from the same perspective as us. The power of likeness is at play here again. It is easier to understand and then support someone who shares your view on things than it is someone who has a very different perspective.

Our narrative must reinforce the connections we share with those who already support us and persuade those who are as yet undecided that our definition and/or explanation of the context and proposed solution are both the most accurate and the most valuable. Sometimes this means that we have to change peoples' frame of reference. And, again, there is nothing more powerful in this regard than a well-delivered narrative. Stories have been used for centuries as powerful reframing tools.

Richard Curtis and Emma Freud highlighted the power of a compelling narrative in gathering support and forging alliances in their conversation with AB. Richard said:

'"Make Poverty History" is a really interesting example because there was a sixteen month narrative and a proper deadline because of the Gleneagles conference... The moment you said to people "That's our story" they said "Oh, I'll do my extra bit for this then". And I think that's what allowed us to have the astonishing alliance between people who fundamentally disagreed about everything.'

If you have ever purchased an unframed painting, you will appreciate the effect different types of frame can have on your picture. Even a beautiful painting produced by a brilliant artist is dependent on the right frame if it is to be seen at its best. The frame does more than simply surround and support the picture, it draws the eye in in

Stories can change the way people view the world and how they behave. Stories are transformative.

a particular way, it either adds or detracts from the quality and content of the picture itself. The frame tells us something about the work and influences our thinking about it.

Peoples' beliefs and values act as perception filters, as psychological frames, for the way they view and interpret their experiences. Using a narrative to offer a reframe of a situation is to encourage and enable parts of our audience to consider a different perspective and so come to a different conclusion than they otherwise might. There are two main types of reframe: context reframing and content reframing.

Context reframing is based on the principle that most behaviours are useful somewhere, in a certain context. If necessary, we might, for example, use our narrative to demonstrate how an individual's experiences in a previous context have enabled them to develop attitudes or skills that are most beneficial in this or in a future context.

Content reframing focuses on the meanings given to a certain experience, or situation. The underlying principle is that we all have a choice about how we interpret our experiences and the value we place on them. It is the ability to reframe what something means that enables people to debate the meaning and/or value of precisely the same data or event. Again, it is through our narrative that we are able to provide our meanings and interpretations in ways that encourage a shift in perspective.

The ability to create accepted frames, or reframes, of perception is dependent also on the language we use, the examples we adopt, the way we sequence our story and the values it reflects. We need to ensure that our story is about people, places or issues that are important to our target audience. We also have to tell the story in language that is easily understood. We will discuss this in more detail in the next chapter; for now, though, we just need to remember that every story can be told from a variety of different perspectives and in a variety of different ways. When creating and delivering a narrative we need to be clear about:

- what type of story it is;
- the perspective, or perspectives, from which we are going to tell it;

- the most appropriate style of delivery, including media and length of story;
- the essential themes and the supporting facts;
- the time we have in which to tell the story;
- the appropriateness and purpose of the characters involved.

A convincing narrative needs a congruency, an essential alignment, running through it that brings together those different aspects to create a seamless whole. This relates back to the novelist's need to create a bubble of fiction. Our story has to speak to people, to mean something to them and to influence them, and for this to happen we have to present it using their language. This makes our story more easily engaging and it reinforces the fact that we both understand and are like our audience. After all, we are more likely to share things, to communicate, accurately and effectively if we are all speaking the same language.

Our narrative also needs to include powerful and relevant examples to support and prove its worth. Gaining permission from others invariably involves convincing them of the validity of our claims. To do this we have to be able to provide examples, facts or figures. We use this evidence to support and justify our argument and conclusion. As we have discussed previously, data alone does not persuade people to change or guarantee their support. However, relevant information, given in the best order and repeated, is an essential thread that runs through every convincing story. Without it, there is no congruency or persuasiveness and we are left with a narrative that can do nothing more than ask the audience to take an unsubstantiated leap of faith.

The structure, size and sequencing of a story is inevitably influenced by the time available to the storyteller. Polling day effects the creation and delivery of our narrative. Whilst the length of our story is never elongated unnecessarily it is always condensed to fit the boundaries within which we have to operate. In storytelling, as in so many aspects of our lives, timing is everything. We can be too soon, just as we can be too late. We can be too quick, just as we can be too slow. The delivery of any story needs to be appropriately paced. And that means knowing how and when to change the pace throughout. It is one important way in which the storyteller can engage, control and direct the interest and attention of the audience. The effective telling of a story requires the creation and management of rhythm. Increasing the rhythm creates a sense of increased urgency and is usually used to create a compelling rush towards the ending. Ruth Rendell talked of how sequencing, timing and pacing are important elements in growing her readers' interest and developing momentum throughout the story:

> 'You have to let your narrative grow out of what has gone before,' she said. 'The story should tell itself through dialogue, conversation and the things people do. There should be some big events in which all sort of things happen and can develop from. You can deliberately build up to things; have the reader looking forward to something.'

The deliberate sequencing of information to create maximum effect is as important as the deliberate sequencing of the narrative itself. Simply put, the order in which we deliver the information and/or story determines the response of the audience. A storyteller shares the events that run throughout their tale in a sequence that is designed to engage and lead the thoughts and emotions of their audience in a particular way.

The storyteller supports this sequencing with a careful mix of specific and artfully vague language. Specific language is the language of detail, of facts and figures, of supporting examples and clear descriptions. We use specific language to paint a very clear picture in the minds of our audience, to direct their thinking precisely, and to limit the possibilities of misunderstanding. Artfully vague language lacks this detail and is used whenever we want to encourage the audience to imagine, to fill in the gaps for themselves. There are times in every story when specific language is essential and there are times when only artfully vague language can create the desired effect in our audience. Our task through our campaign narrative is to sequence data giving and these language patterns appropriately to create our desired outcome.

The narrative becomes even more powerful if we incorporate significant shared values. Values are those behaviours, practices or principles that are important to us. They are the aspects of our lives we deem to be valuable. They are supported by our beliefs and, like these, they are developed through our personal experiences, cultural influences, and our choice of role models. Values are directly related to our sense of identity on both a personal and social level. They are a source of motivation and, because they are such an inherent part of who we are, they tend to influence us subconsciously. Values can be divided into two types: means values and ends values.

Means values provide the motivation to achieve goals. They precede and feed end values, which, in turn, reflect the ultimate reasons why we seek to achieve these goals in the first place. As campaigners actively seeking to promote a cause and achieve a specific, desired end outcome we are demonstrating very clear end values. As ethical campaigners with an agreed set of guidelines determining precisely how we will act throughout the campaign we are demonstrating our means values.

The way we sequence our story determines the audience's response to it.

All stories require a degree of dramatic tension and change within them. Without some form of conflict there is no story, in much the same way that without opposition there is no need for a campaign. By the end of a good story, beliefs, values and associated perceptions will have changed in the light of experience and learning. Through the drama of the story, at least some characters will learn to reframe situations or people and some means values or end values will have evolved. Hitchcock wrote:

'What is drama but life with the dull bits cut out.'

In the same way, our campaign narrative needs to be condensed, rich and valuable. It shares the truth of a situation from our perspective by directing the audience's attention to those aspects we deem to be most meaningful. It is a story with all the dull and irrelevant bits cut out.

LEARNING POINTS

- When campaigning for a client understand their motivation first.
- Analyse and understand your opposition without letting them dominate your thought processes and planning.
- Aim to tell your story quickly and then reinforce it continually.
- The ending is the most important part of every story.
- Word of mouth is the most powerful from of messaging.
- Share the story in the audience's language, not your own.

ACTIVITY!

Consider how the following letter, written by a young female student at the end of her second year of study, plays on the power of likeness, sequences information sharing, combines specific and artfully vague language, and makes use of several shared values to create a conclusion and a reframe that are powerful and irresistible.

Dear Mum and Dad,

I am sorry that I have not been in touch with you for the last six months. An awful lot has happened in that time and I am now able to share it with you.

I was involved in a terrible car crash that left me trapped in the wreckage for nearly four hours. The fireman who stayed without me throughout that time was very kind and caring. He even visited me repeatedly during my two months in hospital. I had never met anyone like him before and we fell in love.

We have decided to get married and are planning our wedding for next month. I know that might seem sudden, but we both feel it is important that we get married before our baby is born. Dad, I am sure you will be pleased to know that he is much older than me (obviously he has been married before) and that I will benefit from his greater experience and wisdom. The fact that he is an atheist and we are Anglicans is, I believe, another blessing in our modern, multi-cultural society. Our child will be able to understand his viewpoint as well as our religious beliefs and be able to learn from two very different approaches. I cannot begin to tell you how excited I am and I so want you both to share in my happiness!

There is just one more thing that I need you both to know. None of the above is true. I was not involved in a car crash. There is no fireman. I am not in love with an older man. I am not planning to get married and I am not pregnant. I just failed my end of year exams and I will have to re-sit the year. I wanted you to get that in perspective.

Your loving daughter,

Katy.

Well-packaged honesty

We are not offering Katy's letter as a good example of campaigning media, only as an example of how the sequencing of key elements leads to a desired outcome. Whilst Katy certainly found a way to create a powerful reframe for her parents, her use of deliberate falsehoods means that, in one very significant sense, it represents an approach that is unacceptable as part of a campaign narrative. Our campaign story is built on a series of demonstrative truths that are also carefully and deliberately sequenced. In an interview with CP, entrepreneur Christopher Ward talked of the need for

'well-packaged honesty'

when communicating with customers and potential customers. And that is as good a summary of a campaign narrative as you will hear. Having said that, the positive learning points within Katy's story are clear and, hopefully, it brought a smile to your face as it did to her parents.

As well as influential sequencing, the inclusion of relevant data, and the use of common language and shared values, the campaign narrative also incorporates:

- key themes,
- flagship policies,
- messages,
- lines to take,
- a slogan.

Key themes

These are sub-divisions of the narrative. They provide a way of shortening our story, breaking it down into easily understood and remembered elements. Themes are an inherent part of every type of story. Little Red Riding Hood, for example, is about far more than a girl, a wolf and a woodcutter. It is, like most children's stories, primarily a vehicle for the delivery of themes related to personal and social development and understanding. The themes within our campaign narrative summarize and highlight the key components of our argument. Every communication should explain at least one of the key themes to the audience. They are essential links in the chain designed to connect where we are currently with where we desire to be.

Flagship policies

These are specific examples of each of our themes. Flagship policies become metaphors for each theme and enable us to demonstrate to our audience precisely how our themes can be applied into, and how they can impact upon, their world. Originally, a flagship was the vessel used by the commanding officer of a group of ships. It would be distinguished from the others usually by the flag it carried. Over the years the term flagship has come to mean the highest profile or best known.

Our flagship policies, then, are the clearly marked practical examples of just what we stand for. They are shared in the specific language that is far removed from the artfully vague prose that encourages people to create their own vision or conclusion.

Messages

Messages are the understanding we want our audience to take from our different communications with them. The best messages bring parts of our story to life and encourage and help mobilize our audience. Information is used to support the messages we deliver. Information is never a message in its own right. We sequence the giving of information because we sequence the delivery of our messages. When creating the campaign narrative we are planning the most influential order in which to present our messages to the audience. Again, this can be worked out most effectively by starting with the desired end outcome, the totality of the learning we need our audience to have within the time available, and working backwards asking ourself, 'What do they need to know and understand before they can understand this next part of the story?' The success of our messaging is dependent upon this sequencing combined with a delivery that uses the language of our audience and the communication channels that reach them most frequently. An essential underlying principle is simply this:

> 'People do things for their reasons, not ours.'

Given that, our messages have to reflect an accurate understanding of our audience's needs, want and likes. And we have to remember always that the responsibility for developing our audience's understanding and turning that into active support for our cause lies with us. If those parts of our audience that we expect to understand us fail to do so, it means that we have made errors in our communication. Ultimately, campaigners take responsibility for the messages they share, the order in which they share them, and the outcomes they create. Messages should never be repeated word-for-word. They provide guidance for all campaign communications. The words to be repeated frequently are called:

Lines to take

These are the answers and explanations we can agree and prepare in advance as responses to the most likely questions or challenges, or when making statements or in written communications. Lines to take can be used to justify, clarify or explain the different parts of our story. They will be 'on-message'. They ensure consistency of response and take away the need for having to repeatedly reinvent the wheel as we progress the campaign. The lines we agree to take are the apparently impromptu remarks that Winston Churchill confessed to spending so much time preparing. They offer our perspective and the rationale for our argument in the language of our audience. They are the phrases we want people to remember to help them understand both our messaging and the development of our narrative.

A slogan

This is our strapline. It is a simple and easy reminder of our cause and campaign story that encapsulates what our campaign is all about. The fact that a slogan is a reminder presupposes that both our audience and our campaign team already know and understand our cause and desired end outcome, the key themes, the messages and so on. The trap to avoid is confusing the slogan with a message and using it too frequently when answering questions or producing influential media. The slogan is not a substitute for the other essential ways we create influence. An effective slogan is short and memorable, and often incorporates some clever word play, a pithy comment, or humour. Most important of all, it is easy for everyone to understand.

A rich reduction

No matter how we choose to sequence our story and argument, or what information, messages or flagship policies we offer, we need to be able to justify every word in our narrative. The writing and editing of the story is the process through which we reduce a lengthy narrative to something that can be written in less than two sides, or spoken in a minute or two, and is enriched by the reduction. The requirement to ensure that less truly is more, is a challenging one that has been acknowledged by many of the world's great writers and orators. We began this chapter with one of the greatest of them all, Mark Twain, and for the sake of circularity it seems most appropriate to let him remind us of the work needed to keep it brief and yet include everything. He said,

'I didn't have time to write a short letter, so I wrote a long one instead.'

However short our narrative, it needs an attention-grabbing beginning, an engaging and compelling middle, and a brilliant, memorable ending. To produce an influential story we have to write and edit with craft, care and rigour. To bring it to life, we have to tell it well.

ACTIVITY!

First, ensure that you have:

- identified your cause;
- understood your client's motivation (if necessary);
- identified and analysed your opposition and/or sources of apathy;
- have a clear and detailed desired end outcome;
- identified and analysed your audience and relevant environments.

Then develop your:

- key themes,
- flagship policies,
- messages,
- lines to take,
- slogan.

And write and edit your narrative.

LEARNING POINTS

- A campaign narrative needs to be perceived as relevant to our audience because people do things for their reasons not ours.
- Our narrative needs to enable the development and application of: key themes, messages, flagship policies, lines to take and a slogan.
- The narrative needs to be an inspiring example of well-packaged honesty.

Final thoughts

'A people are as healthy and confident as the stories they tell themselves... Stories can conquer fear, you know. They can make the heart larger.'

Ben Okri

The narrative is at the very centre of everything we do. It is through the narrative that we express ourselves and seek permission from our audience. It provides both freedom and boundaries for those within the campaign team. The freedom comes from being able to consider and develop new and ever-more appropriate ways to share the story. The boundary is, of course, the story itself. Whatever we say and however we say it, it has to be part of our agreed narrative. This needs to be supported by an integration of all our activities and the deliberate sequencing and layering of the details, messages and development of the story using the most relevant communication channels. All of this incorporates the identification and achievement of essential milestones that ensure the building of momentum towards the inevitable climax of polling day.

AB actually begins the process of creating the campaign narrative by imagining sitting down with a member of his audience and explaining to them why his cause should be supported and adopted. As he plays out this imaginary meeting he builds the story in his mind realizing what information or perspectives need to be presented, and in what order. By the end of this his narrative can be five or six pages in length rather than the required one or two. It is at this point that he begins the editing process, bringing the story down to a length that is quicker and easier to share whilst still maintaining the power and richness that make it persuasive. AB describes this as mixture of, *'creative thinking and engineering'*, a concept that was popularized by Walt Disney, but first named and publicly used by the American company Alcoa, who termed it, *'imagineering.'*

Indeed, the way Alcoa explained the word in a Time magazine advert in 1942 remains arguably the best way of describing the realistic creativity that is an integral part of campaigning. The advert said,

'Imagineering is letting your imagination soar, and then engineering it down to earth.'

There was once a time before stories. It is impossible now, though, to imagine a time without them. We owe it to ourselves and to those people, places and values that we care about to be able to create and share compelling stories of our own whenever we campaign.

Someone tells the stories that shape our lives, our societies, even our world. Someone tells the stories that become the accepted truths and the agreed ways of doing things. Someone tells the stories that are heard more clearly than others, that mean more than others, and that compel people to act. If you choose to *Campaign It!* that influential storyteller can be you.

Imagine that.

Influencing conversations

05

Each person's life is lived as a series of conversations. **DEBORAH TANNEN**

The true spirit of conversation consists in building on another man's observation, not overturning it. **EDWARD G. BULWER-LYTTON**

The purpose of this chapter is to:

1 Explain the importance of influencing conversations when seeking to gain the permission of others.
2 Explain why we need to identify and match the communication patterns and preferences of our audience, our campaign team and our client.
3 Discuss and demonstrate the relationship between micro- and macro-communication skills.

In this chapter we:

- Consider the power of words.
- Discuss the importance of micro-communication skills in all aspects of a campaign.
- Identify and discuss some essential micro-communication attributes and skills.
- Identify a range of decision-making strategies and motivational tendencies and show how to appeal to these.

Before the music plays

You don't have to imagine influencing conversations. We all began doing that before we were born and will continue doing that long after we have died. Unfortunately, we don't always do it in the ways that we would hope to. That is why we talked about the inevitability of influence in Chapter 1. It is why we discussed the difference between habit and skill and the frequency and effects of miscommunication in the same chapter. Incredibly, sometimes we influence conversations even when we are not there. We become part of stories that are told by others just because we exist. Our power to influence conversations is significant and unavoidable.

In one sense, everything we do through our campaign is designed to influence conversations in the ways that we intend to. In one sense, just a single conversation can become a form of micro-campaign. It can be in support of a cause, be based on our understanding of the other person or people, be built around a story that incorporates, for example, key themes and messages. Sometimes one conversation is all we need to achieve our desired end outcome. Often it is far more complex than that. Either way, we can learn to influence conversations deliberately, ethically and elegantly, or we can leave it up to chance.

Sticks and stones and all that jazz

The famous adage tells at most only half of the story. Sticks and stones can be used to cause harm, however they were also amongst our ancestors' earliest tools. They have played their part in the development of human capability and society. Ultimately, the value of sticks and stones has always been determined by the intention, skill and attitude of the people wielding them. And words *can* hurt us. They don't even need to be the words of others. Many of us would acknowledge that we have at times created self-doubt and fear, hindered our own performance, even made ourselves feel ill, through our internal self-chatter.

Words can make us feel confident and strong, or shiver and shake with nerves. They can make us wonder or provide certainty. They can make us cry or reduce us to tears of laughter. Words affect bodies because they affect our minds and mental state. Although words can be used to hurt, protect or build just as sticks and stones can, words have even more power. They have greater versatility. Words influence expectation, interpretation and performance. They are the building blocks of relationships and communities. A more positive rewriting of the adage would be,

Sticks and stones can build our homes, our words can make them loving.

This is dependent, of course, on the intention, skill and attitude of the people using the words and the conversations they create with them.

Conversations are to communication what improvised jazz is to music. Conversations are freeform. They flow. They share a common theme and yet there are often different interpretations being offered throughout. Conversations work best when there is a willingness to share and build off these differences, rather than when there is a desire to dominate or win. The best jazz musicians know how to work together, to complement rather than contradict. They know how to combine their skill, their passion and their commitment to create magic.

We can create magic through conversations, too. After all, they are, as Deborah Tannen observed the very fabric of our lives. They are central to the way we communicate. They play a significant role in determining the nature and quality of both our individual experiences and our communal ones. Whenever we engage in a conversation we are, to some degree or another, building and shaping our perceptions, our sense of self and our society. We influence ourself and each other through our conversations. The effects of our conversations and the stories we tell through them can be far-reaching. Conversations are passed on, albeit with variations. They spread meaning, interest, attention and interpretation. They are, in many respects, the building blocks of society: which is why a campaign aims to influence conversations. When we converse we are living in the moment, sharing with others just as the best jazz musicians do. Only they are highly trained and skilled and they practice their art rigorously and deliberately.

As we have noted there is a world of difference between the frequent repetition of a habit and the organized and structured development of a skill. To be able to influence the conversations we are engaged in deliberately and appropriately we need the same high level of skill that jazz musicians demonstrate; without it we risk making noise rather than music. To be able to influence the conversations of others, those conversations we are not directly a part of, requires the capability of the experienced and skilled campaigner. Indeed, many of the attitudes and attributes we have discussed in previous chapters are as relevant to the successful application of micro-communications as they are to macro-communications. The ability to achieve a short-term desired outcome through the immediacy of a conversation is based on:

- an understanding of the other person or people;
- a combination of respect and curiosity;
- the flexibility to adapt our style and content in response to feedback;
- the application of specific skills;
- knowing specifically what you need to achieve.

The challenge is to recognize and respond appropriately to the communication patterns, habits and preferences of individuals rather than to the social trends and views of groups or societies.

Whilst we can share the key themes of our narrative, or the messages and flagship policies, through carefully produced influential media, we also share them inevitably though conversations. The notion of having lines to take, for example, does not negate the need for great micro-communication skills. Rather, it emphasizes them. To presume that by simply repeating well-practised answers or arguments we will influence others positively is at best naive and, at worst, lazy and arrogant. Lines to take are an important part of the campaigning process, however to rely solely on these is to admit to a lack of curiosity, respect and understanding of others. The same is true for the sharing of messages or flagship policies.

Essentially, the quality of any communication is measured by the response it gets. As we said when discussing the creation and sharing of the narrative, as campaigners we have to take responsibility for the outcomes we create. Going first, committing to a cause and then seeking permission from others, requires more than personal courage and the belief in specific behaviours and values. It requires the application of excellent micro-communication skills within the big picture planning and the delivery of the campaign.

How well we manage and create conversations, both those we are engaged in and those of others, plays a crucial role in determining the eventual outcome. To return to one of our earlier stories, suits don't sell themselves because suits, like everything else, are sold ultimately through conversations.

Whenever AB advises politicians, he tells them to put doorstep conversations at the heart of all their work. And increasingly, as the following story shows, he is incorporating training on micro-communication skills as part of the help he gives.

AB's advice: doorstep conversations

I expect politicians to make phone calls to their constituents regularly so they keep in touch with local opinion, and these days electronic forms of communication are becoming important. But nothing is going to replace interacting personally, face-to-face with the people they seek to represent.

It's such a great symbol that someone cares – paying the respect of calling on constituents in their own home to ask their opinions. And it's exactly what politicians should do. I wish more of them did. I've always thought that an important part of a politician's role is to act on behalf of their constituents to improve their lives and the area they live in. You can't do that unless you know what the people you represent want. Once you know, you can take action. Then the politician should keep constituents informed about what they're doing and involve them as much as possible in solutions.

It's a communications loop: learning from local residents, taking action, informing them, involving them, creating a dialogue, learning as a result. And it all starts with a conversation.

Which, given their centrality to making improvements to the lives and neighbourhood of local people, means that those conversations should be conducted well.

Again, the politicians owe it to the people they represent. It's respectful. Even though the end result will be beneficial to all concerned, and they are done with the best of intentions, these kinds of visits from a politician start as an uninvited intrusion. The beneficial nature of the interaction has to be transmitted quickly and well, and the resident has to become comfortable chatting with a relative stranger on their doorstep. Then the politician can gain the insights that will enable them to take action to make improvements for the local community in an efficient amount of time whilst providing a positive experience for the resident.

Good micro-communications skills in areas such as building rapport, recognizing learning sides, using language preferences, motivational and decision-making tendencies and state management are vital if you want to make the interaction a good experience for the resident. And after all, why would a politician set out to get on the wrong side of a constituent with a vote by giving them a bad time when chatting on their own doorstep?

The purpose of the conversation is to find information that will lead to improvements for the benefit of that resident, the neighbourhood and the community. It's hard to argue with that as an intention. Yet too often we can make it hard work for all concerned by ignoring the need to have good micro-communications skills. That's why I've started to include it in my help for politicians. Conversations are too important to take a chance with.

As ethical and committed campaigners we are aiming to create an even more wonderful world than Louis Armstrong sang about. To achieve this, we have to know how to create and influence conversations and that, as ever, requires a specific skill set. Conversations, like jazz, don't mean a thing if they ain't got that swing. And to get permission from others, we have to begin by ensuring that our conversations are in tune.

Think of conversations as a form of music. And remember that words affect minds and bodies.

Being in tune

People sometimes use the phrase *being in tune* to describe a situation in which they feel completely at one with someone else. It is just one of the many ways we describe those times when we feel comfortable and understood, when there is a sense of close connection rather than distance and difference. As social beings we tend to place great value on this closeness. To be understood, to spend time with those we like and who seem to be like us, is fulfilling in many ways. We introduced this notion in Chapter 1 when we outlined some of the findings of Professor Robert Cialdini. We are going to develop it now by discussing:

- how we can create this sense of likeness deliberately during conversations by matching peoples' communication patterns;
- how we can apply the same skills and awareness throughout the 'big picture' elements of the campaign.

Matching communication patterns

Individuals tend to display patterns of preference when it comes to both intrapersonal and interpersonal communication. Our tendency towards habitual communication patterns probably stems from the fact that the adoption of successful habits frees us to concentrate on what we perceive to be the more pressing and important issues at any given time.

In a world filled with so much communication chatter, with so many people demanding our attention, and with so many stimuli bombarding us through every waking moment, we make rapid choices about what to ignore, what to focus on and how to remember it. We delete, distort and generalize our experiences and our communication of them even if, for the most part, we fail to realize that this is what we are doing. As individuals, families, societies, organizations and nations it is as if we have no choice within the complexity of our lives but to experience and then communicate selectively. The American comedian Jerry Seinfeld reminded us of this when he said,

'It's amazing that the amount of news that happens in the world every day always just exactly fits the newspaper.'

We delete, distort and generalize because:

- our conscious minds simply cannot cope with all the stimuli we experience every second of every day;
- we often have a particular purpose which directs our attention towards specific details and interpretations and away from others;
- our beliefs, values, assumptions and expectations act as perception filters.

Given this, we need to recognize the ways others delete, distort and generalize as well as their preferred communication habits if we are to begin our communication by meeting them on their terms. For our narrative to fit into and have relevancy in the world of our audience, it has to begin with, and address, these deletions, distortions and generalizations. Our interpersonal communication must be the same. When seeking to influence conversations, the process is:

- if ethically possible begin by matching the most powerful elements of the other person's communication, perceptions, experience and values;
- maintain the match until a sense of likeness is achieved clearly;
- then lead towards your desired conclusion.

Great teachers, who are, of course, amongst the very best communicators and campaigners, inevitably use a version of this approach. They do not, of course, match inappropriate behaviours or attitudes. They do, though, identify the student's starting point and begin from there. They also know that likeness can be developed whilst still asserting control and that this provides the foundation from which a genuine learning feedback loop can be created.

Basically we can create influence by either demonstrating our understanding and respect for others, or we can use force. Clearly, we are advocating the former.

To begin, here is one essential, underpinning principle when matching the communication of others:

Match with subtlety.

Remember, ethical communication is based on curiosity and respect. If we care enough to campaign then we need to do it well. This is as true for an executive running a campaign to create change within an organization as it for a counsellor working to create personal change in a client. In any social or professional setting in which individuals are communicating face-to-face we will see those who understand and respect each other instinctively matching both their postures and, often, their language choices. However, this very obvious matching is the natural result of a shared sense of likeness, of rapport. When we are seeking to understand and influence strangers quickly, we can appeal to their subconscious mind at least as much as we can to their conscious mind.

Just as we often delete, distort and generalize without consciously realizing it, so we can subconsciously recognize the communication tendencies of others and be influenced by them. You have probably had the experience of meeting someone for the first time and getting a sudden, intuitive sense of whether or not you like them or, even, could trust them. One way to think of this is that your subconscious mind has identified subtle ways in which you either naturally match or mismatch each other's communication habits. If we match, we subconsciously recognize the likeness and feel comfortable. If we mismatch, the opposite occurs.

Two other essential points to bear in mind throughout are:

1 People do things for their reasons, not ours.

2 People make decisions based on their criteria, not ours.

Our audience analysis, therefore, needs to identify these reasons and criteria and all associated intrapersonal and interpersonal communication patterns. If the audience is too large for this and/or if there are too many variations, the principle is to apply a scattergun approach, using a variety of communication patterns supported by a mixture of relevant supporting facts when delivering key messages.

The ability to identify an individual's intrapersonal and interpersonal communication preferences is based on our willingness to give them our attention. This alone, we would suggest, is a truly respectful thing to do. To give attention is to give a meaningful and powerful gift. Indeed, one could argue that there is little, if anything, of greater significance that one human being can give to another than their undivided attention.

> *Attention is a precious gift we can choose to give.*

Real attention giving can only happen when we remove our perception filters and accept that other peoples' patterns of communication are as valid as our own. Before we can give someone else our complete attention we first need to let go of our personal preferences and bias. This emptying out of our normal ways of doing things, putting to one side our preferred communication style and the assumption that has built up over the years within us that our way, if not the best way, is certainly as good as any, reminds us yet again of the need for the very highest levels of emotional intelligence. To give attention means, in one sense, to forget yourself and to prioritize the other. It means to give up, temporarily at least, important aspects of your world-view and associated behaviours, and to enter into and understand that of someone else.

Michael, our world traveller in Chapter 3, was incapable of giving genuine attention to others. He saw people only through the lens of his own beliefs, values and experiences. His casual glance was coloured by his sense of who he was and what was right. Michael visited many different places and met many different people without ever seeking to understand them. He did not know that, at the heart of giving attention, was the ability to truly listen and look and to do this we first have to silence our internal chatter. It is all-but impossible to get in tune with someone else if you are listening to the voice in your own head at the same time as you are trying to listen to them.

LEARNING POINTS

- Conversations are the building blocks of society.
- People delete, distort and generalize when they communicate.
- Use the communication preferences of the person you are talking to in order to create a sense of rapport and understanding.
- Match these preferences with subtlety.
- To really give someone else your attention, you have to temporarily forget yourself and your own world-view.

Hearing the music, reading the score

Micro-communication skills are essential when talking to our team, our client and our audience. They are as important in the creative process as they are in the sharing of the narrative. They are the mechanism through which we inform, motivate, delegate, persuade and engage. Micro-communication skills are the threads that hold the campaign suit together. They need to be elegant, consistent, and yet never eye-catching. The aim is for them to be ever-present and never noticed. When applied well micro-communication skills play a crucial role in creating influence without ever distracting from the matter at hand. Without great micro-communication skills our campaign would be, quite literally, threadbare.

In this introduction to matching communication patterns, we will focus on some simple and effective ways to match:

- language,
- body language,
- decision-making tendencies,
- motivational traits.

Language

Here is the one-minute-long micro-communications workshop:

'If you can only do one thing, it is this: use the language habits and preferences of the person you are communicating with right back at them always. If you are communicating to an audience share every one of your most important messages using a range of communication patterns. This increases the likelihood that each message will be understood as you require by each individual.'

ACTIVITY!

Select one email that you receive in the next few days and match the language
it contains in your reply.

Listen to the language used by individuals in conversation. Identify the
common phrases used. Consider how you would use these if replying.

Being able to speak a language is a sign of belonging. Different countries, communities, even professions, have their own language. It is one of the most powerful
ways of demonstrating likeness and, by definition, of also creating boundaries
around us. When we hear someone say of another,

'She speaks my language'

we know there is, on one level at least, a meaningful connection being acknowledged. To share the language patterns of another is to suggest commonality and
understanding. If we use the words of the other person, or people, and match also
the manner in which they say them, for example the tempo of their voice, their pace
and rhythm, then we are even more likely to create a sense of likeness and rapport.

Earning and then keeping the attention of others is a prerequisite for creating
both rapport and influence, and speaking in the language of others helps us to do
this. In an interview with CP, the actor Ross Kemp made the point that,

> 'You have got to make the audience want to listen to you. It's a mistake to think that all
> the audience members want to be there and listen. Good talkers know how to grab the
> attention of the people who don't want to be there.'

This point is as relevant for one-to-one conversations as it is for talking to an
assembled group. Ross went on to offer the following practical tips that, thankfully,
reinforce some of the points we have made earlier,

> 'You have to find the common ground between yourself and your audience. Grab their
> attention by saying something they were not expecting. Use humour if it is appropriate.
> Always personalize what you are talking about by making comparisons between your
> story and the audience and by giving examples that are relevant to them.
>
> 'One-to-one communications are all about gaining trust, about putting people at
> their ease, and with a large audience you should feel, ideally, that you are talking to
> everyone individually. It's important that you feel connected to them, and that they
> do to you.
>
> 'Remember, too, that the ending is the most important thing. Always reiterate what
> your message is, in simple terms, at the end. And lift them up, leave the audience with
> a positive, uplifting, motivational thought.'

Sharing language creates common ground between people and this, in turn, makes it
easier to personalize communication and to develop a feeling of trust. Alternatively,

a group can exclude others deliberately or unintentionally by using the common language that only they understand. The shared language of professionals and experts in different fields marks out their commonality as well as their exclusivity. Scientists, doctors, academics and engineers, are all examples of groups who can communicate amongst themselves in ways that would leave most of us wondering just what was being said! When needing to create rapport, to make it clear that someone is welcome, the specialist language of the group, has to be explained before it is used.

Whenever we are seeking to create influence, whether that is through a campaign of communications that will be complete within minutes or extend over years, we are committed to winning the hearts and minds of others. Sharing language plays a powerful part in bringing people to our cause and gaining their support. It increases the likelihood of us being understood as intended and of creating a positive emotional impact. Nelson Mandela understood this only too well. He said,

> 'If you talk to a man in a language he understands, that goes to his head. If you talk to him in his language, that goes to his heart.'

So, if you just want to be heard you only need to say something through a well-used communication channel in a way that will get peoples' attention, however briefly. However, if you want to be heard and understood, and create a positive emotional response and be remembered, you need to do that using the language preferences of the listener. Whenever a person has to use time and energy translating what they hear, there is a greater risk that they will misinterpret it and, even if they get it right, that they will not wish to keep investing the effort. When we think of people being multi-lingual, we think of individuals who can speak the languages of several different countries. As campaigners we do not necessarily need to be fluent in French, or Italian, or Spanish. We just need to identify and use the language preferences of others.

Body language

The point we made earlier that words affect bodies can be reversed because bodies also and equally affect words. There is a synergy between how our body is positioned, moves and feels and the words we are using either to ourselves or others and our emotional state. Sometimes we can change our state by changing our physiology first and sometimes we can do so by changing our internal or external talk. Knowing that, it is important that we match the body language of those we are sharing conversations with and that, if we take the lead during that conversation, we do so through our body language as well as our words.

Matching the body language of others during conversations is another powerful way to create a feeling of likeness and rapport. The need to be subtle is even more important when doing this than when matching language. For most people, most of the time, the topic being discussed and/or their personal agenda dominates their point of focus and prevents them from thinking about, or noticing, the deliberate matching of language patterns. The very obvious matching of body language, though, can be as clear, insulting and upsetting as a threatened punch to the head.

The bottom line is, we seek to create influence only because we genuinely believe we have something of value to offer to others. There is an essential ethical underpinning to campaigning communications and the use of the *Campaign It!* model because the macro- and micro-communication skills involved are so powerful. And power demands responsibility and care and respect for others. If we match with subtlety we are more likely to influence. If we are more likely to influence we need to be sure of the benefits we want to create. We need to ensure, therefore, that our process goals are as appropriate as our end goals.

Examples of subtle body language matching include:

Person A folds their arms.	Person B crosses one hand over the other.
Person A crosses their legs.	Person B crosses their ankles.
Person A leans forwards.	Person B angles their head forwards slightly.

The purpose of matching any communication pattern is not to simply mimic the other person, rather it is a genuine attempt to share their experience with them. It is one way of gaining entry into their world and coming to an understanding of things from their perspective. Interestingly, the more we match both the words and body movements of someone else, the more likely we are to gain an intuitive sense of what they are thinking and how they are feeling. The gut instinct we talked of earlier that enables experienced professionals to know what to do or say next can be developed through the application of micro-communication skills. Simply, the more we behave like someone else the more we come to understand them. The more we understand them the more we can subconsciously interpret and predict their behaviours and, wonderfully, the more likely they are to want to engage with us further.

Body language can be mirrored as well as matched. Mirroring body language means creating a mirror image of the other person. So, for example, if person A leans slightly to their left, person B responds by leaning slightly to their right.

The purpose of matching and mirroring is, ultimately, to gain permission to take the lead in the interaction. Teachers, healthcare professionals, managers, team leaders and parents are just some examples of people who ideally need to create rapport and trust before they influence by leading in a specific direction.

Whether matching or mirroring, there comes a point in the interaction when the other person, or people, will make a decision based on our communication with them. Engaging and then mobilizing an individual or an audience is an iterative process that can, by turns, be subtle or very obvious, supportive or challenging, apparently casual or clearly urgent. When all is, quite literally, said and done, the audience will decide.

LEARNING POINTS

- If a person has to translate what you are saying into their own preferred communication patterns the risk of being misunderstood is increased.
- By matching the body language of someone else we can develop our understanding of that person.
- We can match or mirror body language.

ACTIVITY!

Practise matching and mirroring the body language of others.
Be subtle in your approach.

Decision-making tendencies

According to Milan Zeleny,

'Man is a reluctant decision-maker, not a swiftly calculating machine.'

The concept of reluctance implies some sort of mental struggle, a sense of being pulled this way and that between two or more opposing options that might or might not include the possibility of choosing to do absolutely nothing at all, of refusing to engage. This dilemma is highlighted in the fable of Buridan's ass, which has its origins in Aristotle's De Caelo.

Jean Buridan was a fourteenth-century French philosopher who advocated the belief that individuals faced by alternative courses of action must always choose that which supports the greater good. He acknowledged that people faced with such a choice might delay their decision to give themselves time to assess the situation fully and to explore the possible outcomes of their choice. Subsequent writers satirized his position by describing an ass which, forced to choose between food and water equidistantly apart, must inevitably die of both hunger and thirst whilst spending too long considering which one to choose first.

This story reinforces one of the essential challenges we all experience when having to make a decision. It is the challenge of making a decision that leads to appropriate action within an appropriate timeframe. On a micro-level, CP has been experiencing and managing this challenge for over three decades.

CP has been studying the martial arts since 1973. As he explains, the ability to make appropriate and committed decisions, often very quickly, is an essential martial skill and, through his training, he has come to understand the difficulties we can all face in making decisions:

CP on the martial arts

As a martial artist I have had to develop the ability to decide on a course of action, specifically an attack or a defence or an evasion, and to commit to it without hesitation or doubt. As a martial arts teacher, I have to teach my students how to do the same. We frequently hear people tell us that they have made a decision, often as the result of many conversations with a number of others, only to discover some time later that they are still considering their options. Of course, there are situations in which we have a great deal of time to decide what to do and it makes sense to use that time wisely. Inevitably, though, the moment for decision arrives and, it seems to me, that when it does it catches many of us unprepared.

In the martial arts, when someone is attacking you or when you have the opportunity to initiate your own attack, decisions have to be made in fractions of a second. When I talk about decisions in this context, I mean decisions that spark committed action. I have learnt through my martial arts training what a decision means: it means that the time for further consideration has ended; it means that I have made a commitment to a certain course of action and it is no longer a question of 'if' that action will happen, it is only a question of 'when'. On many occasions I watch less experienced martial artists recognize a number of ways they can respond to their opponent only to spend so long deliberating over which is the best that they fail to do anything at all within the time available to them.

As a martial artist I seek to close the gap between analysis, thought and action, because, essentially, if I can do this more quickly and accurately than my opponent I am more likely to win and I will, at the very least, gain the first advantage. To do this, to close the gap effectively, I have to be able to recognize and focus on only the most relevant information with regard to the situation at hand. For example, I have to be able to distinguish between what is a genuine threat, or a genuine opening, and what is a feint. Once I am committed, I have to be impossible to distract.

Of course, beyond the immediacy of combat, in our normal day-to-day experiences we often have more time in which to make decisions. As I have already said this can be a benefit because we can use this time to gather as much relevant information as possible. It can also be a weakness, because an increased understanding of the different options available to us can limit our sense of urgency or increase our sense of confusion. At this point, we become, as Zeleny states, reluctant decision-makers.

In training, when one of my partners or students tries to punch me in the head they are giving me every possible reason to make an instantaneous decision followed by an immediate action. I have come to learn from AB that campaigners seeking to influence large audiences have to use communications to create that same urgency and commitment, that same irresistible desire to decide and act.

I have no hesitation in doing what is best for me whenever a fist is hurtling towards my nose. As campaigners we have to develop that same level of motivation and certainty in our audience. We have to ensure that they realize the absolute need for them to make a decision within a limited timeframe, and we have to do everything we can to encourage them to make the decision and take the action that we believe is best for all concerned.

All decisions no matter what timeframe they are made within, are made up of three stages: the pre-decision stage, the decision itself and the post-decision stage.

The pre-decision stage

This begins with a sense of conflict, of emotional or psychological discomfort. If we already have a preferred bias, a world-view or a skill set towards which we turn without deliberation or doubt, this stage is barely noticeable. In this situation, our existing perception filters show us that the solution is clear no matter how many options are apparently available and we make our decision without hesitation. It is for this reason that, as we mentioned earlier, we cannot persuade everyone to agree with us. If, however, that bias is missing, we are obliged to make sense of the options open to us and, usually, we realize that the perfect solution is neither readily available nor feasible. The situation is complicated further if the alternatives available to us are similar in their appeal and potential value. When faced with such a selection to choose from we inevitably seek out more and more information to help us distinguish between the options.

> Decision-making can involve a degree of psychological discomfort.

The internal conflict continues as we become increasingly aware of the gap between what is achievable and what is available. At this point we might make a number of partial decisions, which can include discarding those options which seem the furthest away from the ideal, reconsidering options that we had discarded previously and adding, or deleting, criteria against which to assess the choices available. The essential purpose, of course, is to determine the best alternative and, once that is clear in our mind's eye, to go in search of it or the one that is closest to it. Whilst it might be relatively easy in the early stages to discard certain options, as the process progresses and the number of choices being considered diminishes, the sense of cognitive dissonance can increase as it becomes more and more difficult to separate the relative values of those options that are 'still on the table'. Whether or not we do this consciously, we seek to reduce our sense of cognitive dissonance by asking ourselves, 'Which alternative will reduce our discomfort to an acceptable level?'

Researchers tell us that, from then on, our desire to reduce and/or eliminate the internal conflict we are experiencing means that we tend to focus on evaluating those options that are already known to us rather than continuing to search for new ones.

The implication of this for campaigners is clear:

1 Those people AB thinks of as 'floating voters' can be experiencing a degree of internal conflict arising from not knowing which option to choose.

2 Their level of cognitive dissonance might increase when they have whittled down their options to those that seem closest to their ideal (albeit in different ways) and which appear to offer some benefits (albeit different ones).

3 As the campaign moves towards its conclusion, as it gains momentum, key elements within the audience might, therefore, be experiencing their most significant levels of dissonance.

4 The focus, then, needs to be on helping these people reduce their discomfort whilst coming to the desired decision.

We believe that if you are convinced that what you offer is of value you have an obligation to:

1 Help your audience move through the pre-decision stage by presenting an irresistible and emotionally compelling option in ways that reflect your understanding of them and create powerful and positive associations for them.

2 Do this as quickly as possible.

Understanding peoples' decision-making tendencies and motivational traits can assist greatly in helping move your audience in the desired direction. Simply put, if you know what people need to experience, what they need to see or hear to be convinced, you can present your argument in ways that ensure these criteria are met and is therefore more persuasive. Some examples of decision-making tendencies and motivational traits follow. The operating principle is:

'If you know the tendencies or traits of those you are seeking to influence, communicate in ways that reflect these specifically; if you do not, or if the audience is too large and the mixture of approaches is too great, use a variety.'

> *The challenge is to make decision-making as easy as possible for the audience.*

Three decision-making tendencies

The three we will consider are: frequency; timeframe; and sensory preference. (We think of these tendencies as 'convincer modes'.)

Frequency

Have you ever asked yourself, 'How many times do I have to experience something before I accept its validity?'

In all likelihood this is probably not a question that has ever attracted your attention. And yet on a subconscious level at least you might well know the answer. Think of it this way:

Imagine that you have to do a task for the first time, something that you have never done before and that you have to prepare for. There might be a task in your workplace or at home that fits this bill. If so, just imagine that. If not, choose something else.

Now, imagine preparing to do this task and then actually carrying it out successfully. Run a film of it in your mind. See and hear the event unfolding. Having been successful once will you then be confident that you can always achieve the same result? If not, would you need to be successful two or three times, or more, before you were convinced? Perhaps, as you consider this, you are realizing that you would never believe in the certainty of the outcome because you instinctively regard each attempt as a unique activity, the result of which cannot be assumed just because of your previous experiences?

Many of us have an instinctive sense of how many times we need to do, see or hear something before we are convinced. For some a single example is sufficient, for others there needs to be a specific degree of repetition, whilst for the rest of us every example is considered as a separate, individual experience and is judged therefore on its own merits.

For us, as campaigners, this particular tendency has implications in terms of how many times we need to share an important message or how many examples we need to give in order to convince others of the value and truth of our cause.

It is also often connected to the next:

Timeframe

The next question to ask yourself about your imaginary task is, 'Over what timeframe do I need to experience these successful experiences before I am convinced of my ability?'

Again, now that you have asked the question you might find yourself offering an instinctive answer or, instead, you might be reviewing situations from your past when you needed to be convinced about your own personal capability or the appropriateness of a cause of action.

Obviously, if you are convinced by the first successful example the timeframe is short, almost immediate. If, on the other hand, you need a number of common experiences before you are persuaded, do consider the impact the timeframe has on your decision-making. Shifting context from the imaginary example you have been focusing on, just answer this question: 'Do you believe in love at first sight?'

Whether your answer was 'Yes' or 'No', just consider your reasons for it and the way they reflect the importance of the timeframe and frequency in your approach to decision-making.

We cannot always create campaigns that are based on the timeframes our audience prefer. When polling day is set by significant others we have no choice but to make clear to our audience, and justify, the schedule in operation and persuade them of the need for us all to function within it. When we can set our own polling day it is worth determining what timeframe, if any, the majority of our audience do prefer and, if possible, creating a campaign that reflects this.

Sensory preference

Going back to our imaginary task, the final question to ask your self is, 'By which mode am I most readily convinced?'

Are you more easily persuaded if you see something, or hear about it, or if you actually do it yourself? And if you can be persuaded by just being told something, who are you most likely to be persuaded by? Which person, or type of person, or group of people are you most willing to believe?

Obviously, the answer to these questions depends to a great extent on context. We prioritize and use different senses in different situations and value the opinion of different people according to their perceived level of relevant experience or expertise.

Again, if we know the preferences of our audience we can present our case in the ways that engage them most appropriately, whether that is by showing them compelling examples, creating hands-on experiences for them, through the testimony of persuasive figureheads, or through a combination of these. The fall-back position when seeking to influence an audience comprising an equal range of sensory preferences is to mix 'n' match.

LEARNING POINTS

- All decisions comprise the pre-decision stage, the decision stage and the post-decision stage.
- In the pre-decision stage people usually experience cognitive dissonance.
- Our campaign must help our audience move through this at the most appropriate pace.
- Three decision-making tendencies are: frequency; timeframe; and sensory preference.

Four motivational traits

The four we will consider are: proactive/reactive; towards/away from; external reference/internal reference; and general/specific.

Again, we need to bear in mind the fact, whilst many of us are creatures of habit and tend to demonstrate repetitive communication patterns, we are also the most adaptive of all species and we do often vary our responses according to the situation we are in. So, as with decision-making tendencies, these traits can be contextually driven. We will discuss them now by focusing on the extremes of each example, ie people at opposite ends of each continuum. Inevitably, of course, there are those who fit somewhere in-between.

Proactive/reactive

Some people like to seize the initiative whilst others only change when they are convinced that the situation is forcing them to. Proactive individuals are those who instinctively look for and create opportunities, they have a desire to make things happen and to stay 'ahead of the game'. If you ask a proactive person to 'Wait for a moment whilst you deliberate about the best approach to take', they will in all probability use that time to create and act upon a solution of their own. Reactive individuals on the other hand are more likely to give you all the time you need, whilst they consider whether or not it is actually necessary or appropriate to make a decision *now*.

Here are some ways you can identify and distinguish between proactive and reactive people:

- Determine their job roles and the associated attitudes and skills that are essential for success.

- Ask questions that reveal when and how they have made important decisions.
- Outline possible situations and ask how they would instinctively respond.
- Ask questions that reveal the process and behaviours they value.

To appeal to and motivate proactive people use any or all of the following:

- Demonstrate that your campaign is proactive, that you are seizing the initiative.
- Highlight the reactive nature of your opposition.
- Emphasize the fact that you support peoples' right to choose, to shape their own destiny, to come to a decision of their own making.
- Use language, images and examples that reflect and encourage proactive thinking and behaviour, that shows why something has to be done *now*.
- Use words like '*do*', '*now*', '*opportunity*', and '*choice*'.
- Use phrases like '*Your choice*', '*Your decision*' and '*Your right to...*'.

To appeal to and motivate reactive people use any or all of these approaches:

- Highlight the fact that your campaign is the consequence of a careful, thoughtful, appropriately lengthy process, based on an analysis of all options.
- Demonstrate that you are reacting to circumstance.
- Encourage your audience to give thoughtful consideration to the situation and to avoid making hasty decisions.
- Use language, images and examples that reflect and encourage a reactive approach.
- Use words like '*because*', '*must*', '*consequently*' and '*inevitably*'.
- Use phrases like '*As the result of...*', '*In response to...*' and '*As a consequence of...*'.

Towards/away from

It is important to realize that people can make the same decision and demonstrate the same behaviours, working to achieve the same outcome, for very different reasons. People who are motivated by a desire to move towards a particular goal and those who are motivated by a desire to move away from their current situation can both behave in precisely the same ways whilst seeking to achieve precisely the same outcome. However, they cannot be motivated to do so in the same way. It is an error to presume that people who are behaving in the same way to achieve the same goal can automatically be motivated in the same ways.

To create influence we need to understand the motives of others, not just the behaviours of others. People with a 'towards' motivation are instinctively goal-oriented, they are motivated by targets and outcomes. They seek the reward, the gold at the end of the rainbow. People with an 'away from' motivation are driven by a desire to escape from the perceived problems of their current situation. Sometimes these very different motives result in apparently identical behaviours and the valuing of identical goals. To influence both groups we must firstly distinguish between them and secondly communicate differently.

> *We can use the word 'motivation' to remind us that we need to identify peoples' motives for action.*

Here are some ways you can identify and distinguish between people who are motivated by achieving targets and those who are motivated by moving away from a current problem:

- Determine the extent to which their job role is based on achieving targets or solving problems.
- Ask questions that reveal how and why they have made important decisions.
- Outline possible situations that encourage or require goal-seeking or problem-solving and determine their preference.
- Ask questions that reveal how they feel about their current situation and what they are doing, or planning to do, about it.

To appeal to and motivate people with a 'towards' motivation use any or all of the following:

- Demonstrate that you and your campaign are goal-oriented.
- Highlight the fact that your opposition is not.
- Emphasize the fact that you value accomplishment, the ability to set and achieve targets.
- Use language, images and examples that reinforce the above.
- Use words like *'goals', 'targets', 'benefits'* and *'aims'*.
- Use phrases like *'Our goal is to achieve...', 'Our purpose is to accomplish...'* and *'The benefits we are aiming for are...'*.

To appeal to and motivate people with an 'away from' motivation use any, or all, of the following:

- Demonstrate that you and your campaign are leading people away from a problematic situation.
- Highlight the fact that your opposition is not.
- Encourage your audience to appreciate how bad the current situation is and how and why it must become a 'thing of the past'.
- Use language, images and examples that reinforce the above.
- Use words like *'away', 'release', 'escape'* and *'freedom'*.
- Use phrases like *'We must move away from...', 'This situation cannot be tolerated any more...'* and *'It is time to escape from...'*.

External reference/internal reference

One of the many challenges when seeking to influence others, when needing to gain their permission, is the fact that whilst some people habitually turn towards others for confirmation and affirmation, others are more comfortable trusting their own innate sense of what is best, of how well they have performed and what they should do next.

People with a totally external frame of reference need others to either validate the quality of their performance or to confirm and support the appropriateness of their decision-making. They need the assurance of others to give them confidence in the value of their behaviours. Obviously, this tends to be the assurance of those people they regard as appropriately significant others. These might be people they acknowledge as experts in the given field, or those they have become socially conditioned to turn to for advice and support. Sometimes, when needing to make a decision between competing options, individuals who operate with an external reference can also be influenced by the words or example of celebrities they trust, respect or wish to be like.

People with a totally internal frame of reference feel no need to ask for the judgement or advice of others. They set and work to their own standards, they trust in their own ability to assess the quality of their performance, and they will interpret the value of your campaign against their own criteria.

Here are some ways you can identify and distinguish between people who are externally motivated and those who are internally motivated:

- Determine to what extent their job role is dependent upon their willingness and capability to set and measure standards, to create targets for themselves and/or others or to work independently on projects.
- Ask questions that reveal how they know when they have 'done a good job'.
- Outline possible situations that encourage or require the need for independent assessment or external validation and determine their preference.
- Ask questions that reveal how they would feel when either given full responsibility for completing a task to a required standard or when required to let someone else judge their work.

To appeal to and motivate people with an external reference use any or all of the following:

- Demonstrate that you and your campaign, and your champions, have the authority and the capability to determine what is right and to evaluate both situations and performances accurately.
- Highlight the fact that your opposition do not.
- Encourage your audience to recognize the current need for external support and validation and ensure that your figurehead and champions are individuals your audience will turn to willingly for assurance or support.

- Use language, images and examples that reinforce the above.
- Use words relating to your capability like *'judgement'*, *'assessment'*, *'experience'* and *'understanding'*.
- Use them in phrases like, *'Based on our extensive experience, our understanding of the situation is...'*, *'It is our considered judgement that when assessing this...'* and *'You can trust us to set the highest standards and ensure they are met...'*.

To appeal to and motivate people with an internal reference use any combination of these approaches:

- Demonstrate that you and your campaign believe in the value of letting people come to their own conclusions and set their own targets – and that you do this also.
- Highlight the fact that your opposition do not.
- Encourage your audience to judge the arguments for themselves, to apply their own criteria and make their decision based on what feels right to them.
- Use language, images and examples that reinforce the above.
- Use words like *'you'*, *'yourself'*, *'personal'* and *'self'*.
- Use phrases like *'Your decision...'*, *'Do what feels right...'* and *'We all know when something is right.'*

General/specific

This descriptor distinguishes between those people who are instinctively drawn to identify and focus on the 'big picture' or the general sense of any situation and those who feel the need to initially identify and understand the various details of a particular context.

Those with a general motivational frame focus on the 'big picture'. They need to determine the overall purpose and complexity of a situation they are in or need to assess. They want to know how the different elements interact and the effect any change will have on the totality of the situation. They are driven by a desire to understand how every relevant element connects and works together and they need to be convinced that 'every piece in the jigsaw fits'. Consequently, these people might find it relatively easy to focus on a variety of inter-related topics at the same time and to think systemically, to consider how systems, structures, processes and philosophies combine to create a valuable totality. Given their focus on, and acceptance of, a level of dynamic interaction between the variety of elements that comprise any situation, they will compromise on certain details if they believe that is the only way to create an acceptable 'big picture'. These are individuals you would want to develop a strategic plan with broad aims and a clear over-arching vision.

Those with a specific motivational frame are drawn to detail. They naturally question, value and evaluate the specifics of a situation. They will explore and, if necessary, correct minutia without necessarily considering the effects that any changes might have on the overall picture. They will automatically notice those details that appear to lack validity, purpose or fullness and/or appear to contradict each other.

These are the people you would want to check every aspect of your plan, or design your home, or proofread your manuscript.

Here are some ways you can identify and distinguish between those people who are naturally drawn to seeing and understanding the 'big picture' and those who are attracted towards details:

- Determine to what extent their job role is determined by their ability to create a strategic vision and purpose or to recognize, manage or create detail.
- Ask questions that reveal how they instinctively view situations – is it the 'big picture' or is through details?
- Outline possible situations that encourage or require the ability to think about, manage and create an over-arching plan or to identify and manage details and determine their preference.
- Ask questions that reveal how they would feel when given either the task of creating a strategic plan or determining the tactics that would need to be applied to make the plan work.

To appeal to and motivate people with a 'general' motivational frame use any or all of the following:

- Demonstrate that you and your campaign understand and are motivated by the current 'big picture' and are offering a positive and powerful 'big picture' of your own.
- Highlight the fact that your opposition are not and/or that their alternative is either fragmented or flawed.
- Encourage your audience to consider the 'big picture' and to resist the temptation to be distracted by isolated details or examples.
- Use language, images and examples that reinforce the above.
- Use words like *'overall'*, *'totality'*, *'community'* and *'interaction'*.
- Use phrases like *'The inevitability of cause and effect means...'*, *'The big picture is...'* and *'Our vision is to create...'*.

To appeal to and motivate people with a 'specific' motivational frame the following examples apply:

- Demonstrate that you and your campaign understand the importance of paying attention to details and that your proposals are fully detailed.
- Highlight the fact that your opposition are not and that their alternative cannot be trusted because it lacks 'substance'.
- Encourage your audience to focus on the details of your proposal and that of your opposition in light of the current situation.
- Use language, images and examples that reinforce the above.
- Use words like *'specific'*, *'detail'*, *'facts'* and *'attention'*.
- Use phrases like *'Attention to detail shows...'*, *'The facts of the matter are...'* and *'Let us consider these specific examples...'*.

Remember, the ability to appeal to decision-making tendencies and motivational traits is based on an understanding of others developed through our audience analysis. It reflects our desire to communicate with them in their ways rather than ours, to help them make sense of and evaluate arguments, process information and reach decisions in the easiest ways possible. Inevitably when addressing a large audience we need to use a mixture of approaches to ensure that our style and, therefore, our messages are understood by, appeal to and influence, as many people as possible. Ultimately, this is one powerful way of using audience analysis to create a sense of likeness.

ACTIVITY!

Review the section about motivational traits.
Use the guidelines and examples provided to identify your own personal traits.

The decision stage

Once a decision has been made it is no longer viewed as a partial decision. In other words, all impartiality or, indeed, objectivity has been put to one side. The most obvious way for us to overcome the feelings of cognitive dissonance is to commit to the choice we have made. After all, if we were still to acknowledge the doubt, we would still be making a partial decision. Inevitably, then, the more we commit to a decision, the more we ignore or deny the value of alternatives.

As campaigners we are seeking ways in which to encourage our audience to affirm, and then re-affirm, their decision. As we discussed in Chapter 1, people are more likely to act consistently once they feel they have made a commitment. As human beings we have to create meanings that, in turn, give us a sense of power, purpose and worth. This desire stems, in part, from the need to avoid the sense of cognitive dissonance. The more we are sure of the value of specific attitudes, behaviours or goals, the more we are likely to work towards them, and to support those who value them equally. We campaign communication to gain commitment and then consistency from our audience. We develop momentum throughout the campaign to grow that commitment.

The post-decision stage

Reducing dissonance by making a decision is, essentially, a process of evaluation and reassurance. However, it is inevitably directional. Meaning we choose to go towards the option that appears to be the most beneficial and attractive. And, once we have committed to our choice, we tend to notice and give attention only to those things that support the appropriateness of our decision. Given this it is important that we, as campaigners, ensure that our audience have many opportunities to see, hear and experience things that support and justify their decision. As AB is fond of reminding everyone:

'Campaigns never end; the day after our polling day we just clean the whiteboard and start again.'

LEARNING POINTS

- Four motivation traits are: proactive/reactive; towards/away from; external/internal; general/specific.
- Audience analysis can enable us to identify these.
- We can use this understanding to structure our communications.
- Once a decision is made objectivity is put to one side, at least for a period of time.
- People then tend to notice and prioritize only the evidence that supports their decision.
- Campaigners need to ensure that such evidence is clearly available.
- This encourages the audience to make a commitment and then act consistently.

Our own words

It is all well and good being able to recognize the word patterns of others and so communicate in ways that match their tendencies. We also need to own our words. For what we say to have real value and to demonstrate a congruent identity we have to match our words with our behaviours. Words are the glue that hold our life together. Words bind us. As Meher Baba, the Indian spiritualist wrote:

'You have asked for and been given enough words – it is now time to live them.'

Words have an inevitable power. We control the nature, direction and degree of that power, in part, by making our words and actions indivisible. We can also manage the power of words by remembering that words themselves act upon the recipient. And we all know this to be true. We have all heard words that have changed our emotional state. We have all felt the power of words. Haven't we?

Final thoughts

'There is no such thing as a worthless conversation, provided you know what to listen for. And questions are the breath of life for a conversation.'

James Nathan Miller

We will end this chapter by returning to a topic we discussed in relation to audience analysis. It is the importance of asking great questions. Primarily we develop our understanding of others by looking, listening and asking great questions. We need to do this because every conversation and, indeed, every other form of communication, include numerous deletions, distortions and generalizations. We ask questions to uncover the missing information and insights. We ask questions to challenge or educate. We ask questions of ourself and others because what we learn will inform and improve our actions.

Questions are the keys that unlock our thinking. If words have the power to affect minds and bodies, then questions have a special power. They need to be constructed and used with the greatest of care and for very specific reasons. Great questions respectfully asked can breathe life into conversation and develop understanding and respect between people. If misused, questions can hurt individuals, damage relationships and anger communities. Questions connect most obviously to two very significant words. They are: 'but' and 'and'.

Whenever we hear someone's answer to a question our immediate response tends to hinge around one of those two words. The choice we make is crucial to the way in which we then influence the conversation.

'But' is a word that is used primarily to signal disagreement. It appears midway through a sentence and it marks the start of the counter argument. 'But' is a word that lacks subtlety, creativity and harmony. And, most of the time, we hear it coming. There is an obvious and inevitable shift in the tone of voice when the word 'but' is just a few syllables away. It does not matter how much the other person appears to be agreeing with us, or acknowledging our point of view, when we hear that tone we know instinctively that they were just marking time before telling us why we are wrong. 'But' can lead to nothing other than disagreement. It emphasizes the gap between different perspectives. It is a point-scoring word, most at home in a conversation in which one party at least is concerned with proving the other party wrong. The most likely effect of the word 'but' is to entrench people within their initial position and create a claim and counter-claim argument. In a garden, the word 'but' would be a weed, growing quickly if not treated in the first instance, choking plants nearest to it and leaving little space for the growth of others.

In contrast, the word 'and' is the foundation for shared understanding, the creative development of new solutions and agreements, and respectful communication. It reflects the *'true spirit of conversation'* that Edward G. Bulwer-Lytton made reference to in one of our opening quotes.

In the first part of this chapter we compared conversations with jazz. We talked of the free-flowing, freeform nature of both. In the world of drama, the first rule of improvisation is to accept whatever the other actor gives you and build from it. Improvisations, like jazz and conversations, cannot grow from denial. The starting point is to say, 'Yes, and...' rather than 'No, but...'.

Conversations that have as their purpose the sharing of ideas and insights follow the same rule. When we use the word 'and' in the midpoint of a sentence, what follows it is inevitably very different from what tracks the word 'but'. 'And' is a building word. It is used to acknowledge and then develop from the current situation, rather than to dismiss it. 'And' has a special power. It is an essential part of the creative process. Often by using it we challenge our own thinking as well as challenging the thinking of others. The use of the word 'and' does not necessarily imply that we agree with the other person or people. However, it does force us to seek connections between our view and theirs, to find ways to match before we can move forwards. 'And' dares us to understand and share, rather than to dismiss or dominate.

Florence Scovel Shinn, the American writer and artist, wrote,

'Your word is your wand.'

'And' and 'but' emphasize the different types of power our words possess. The question we have to ask ourself and each other is,

'What kind of magic do we plan to use?'

And if we want to create magic we do need to plan. Which is why the next chapter is about how to map the campaign.

Mapping the campaign

06

> *A good plan is like a road map: it shows the final destination and usually the best way to get there.* H. STANLEY JUDD

> *Map out your future – but do it in pencil.* JON BON JOVI

The purpose of this chapter is to:

1 Demonstrate how to map the campaign.
2 Discuss the nature of creativity and its role in the campaign process.
3 Introduce and discuss the inevitability of uncertainty when campaigning.
4 Introduce the concept of a Campaign Grid.

In this chapter we:

- Discuss the importance of, and challenges involved in, establishing an initial overview of the way forwards – the map.
- Identify the principles and processes that underpin the creation of the campaign map.
- Discuss the importance of creative thinking and provide practical models and techniques.
- Consider how best to manage uncertainty.
- Discuss the role that feedback plays in the creation of timelines and targets.
- Consider how to manage resources and create a great team culture.
- Highlight the importance of building momentum.

Maps, models and the courage to go first

This is a chapter about how to plan, or map, your campaign. The campaign map begins as a rough idea of what you are going to do and develops over time into a detailed and specific grid that lists all activities and the sequence in which they will happen. However, before we get into detail about maps, models and the courage to go first, we need to make one really important point. It is this:

> 'A map is a map whether anyone uses it or not.
> A plan is no more than imagination on a page until our actions bring it to life.'

So whilst we might refer to our map as a plan, we are clear in our minds that this is a working document. For some, a map is a detailed and beautiful overview of an environment that serves purely as a decoration. Our campaign map is never for decoration. When we talk about mapping, or planning, we are talking about the process by which we:

- Prepare the initial structure, timing and sequencing of the campaign.
- Implement this.
- Monitor, manage and develop it throughout the lifetime of the campaign.

The campaign map is created when the narrative is written and agreed. Mapping the campaign requires far more than just creating a proposed route from point 'a' to point 'b'. It involves creating the route, gaining support for it and then leading the way along it. To plan is to make a commitment to act. The map that we are going to create will reflect our strategy and tactics, be shaped by the timeframe we have to operate within, our understanding of our audience(s) and any opposition we might encounter, and the resources we have at our disposal. Mapping successfully requires both strategic and creative thinking. It needs the courage to go first and the ability to take others with you. It is dependent upon a willingness to adapt the plan if necessary in response to feedback and the ability to monitor, interpret and manage our environments and any barriers or boundaries that exist within them.

Traditional maps are an age-old form of picture communication. Human beings have always wanted to know how to find their way from one place to another. Our ancestors produced maps of the stars to help them navigate long before they began to produce maps of the Earth. As societies and cultures developed and spread, maps took on an additional and equally significant role. When Churchill said, 'History is written by the victors' he might just as well have added 'For they draw the maps'. The political power that comes from being able to establish and define geographical boundaries and to claim control of the natural and strategic resources contained has been fought over for millennia.[1] Over the centuries, maps came to identify power bases as much as they did scaled-down interpretations of our environments.

Now maps exist in a multitude of formats. In our modern world, it is almost impossible to get through a day without coming into contact with, or making use of, a map of one form or another. Weather maps appear in our newspapers and on the

---

[1] Interestingly, countries will also fight to gain control over anothers' mental models and maps as well as their geographical ones.

television. We have maps for all the various types of travel we can take, including road maps, underground maps and train timetable maps. We can access satellite and aerial photography in ways that, not too long ago, most of us would never have imagined. Now, if we want to find a shop or a hotel or restaurant we can almost certainly check out the location using a Google map on its website.

Maps, then, have played, and continue to play, an important role in human existence and development. We know instinctively that maps will provide us with a range of information about an environment and associated conditions and that, if we know how to read them, we can identify the best ways for us to travel and the milestones we will reach along the way.

The key here is that, as travellers, we need to know only how to read a map, whilst as campaigners we have to be able to create, share and, when necessary, update our map. Mapping a campaign is not like using a geographical map, because it is driven by our need to establish our own route rather than simply following in the footsteps of others. Writing in 1933 in his work *Science and Sanity*, Alfred Korzybski, the founder of General Semantics, wrote, 'The map is not the territory.' His point was that a map is only a model, a representation, of specific phenomena. He argued that, whilst we live in communities based on a multitude of models and maps that we and those around us create to help make sense of our world, they are inevitably only an abstraction, or approximation, of the actual experiences that make up our lives.

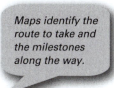

Maps identify the route to take and the milestones along the way.

The maps that Korzybski was referring to are psychological, emotional and perceptual. In one sense they would seem to be far removed from the practical, strategic purpose of our campaign map. In an important way, though, they have a vital part to play. The ability to develop and then act upon, the campaign map is dependent to a great extent on those mental maps that have been created by, or are reflected through, our acceptance of the cause.

Our campaign map plays a crucial role in helping to develop the campaign team and the culture that binds it. The map shows the agreed way forwards. It provides a focus for our initial research and analysis and its production creates the initial impetus for movement. It is of great significance precisely because we are all going to work together to implement it. And it requires from the campaign leader the courage to go first.

There comes a time when the relative safety of planning has to give way to the challenge of action and we have to be willing to take the lead even though our map might not yet be perfect. Indeed, to be more accurate, we have to be willing to begin the campaign in the absolute certainty that the plan is not yet perfect and in the realization that it does not need to be – any more than the narrative needs to be. The principle when sharing a narrative whether in film, theatre or a book, is that if the storyteller and/or performers make it as good as they can, getting as close to perfection as they know how, the audience will do the rest, instinctively filling in the spaces to make the story complete from their perspective. In the same way, if our cause is shared, agreed and established and our vision is clear, those working with us will help to develop the plan, filling in the spaces as they progress it.

The oft-used phrase, 'paralysis through analysis' reflects the danger of spending so much time researching and planning that we lose the will and/or the time to act.

Of course, as we have already made clear, campaigns are built on an understanding of audiences, contexts and resources that grows out of analysis and yet, as we have also made clear, campaigning is a verb. We cannot wait until we believe the plan is perfect before we begin to share our narrative, for if we do we will never be heard. There is a time for planning and a time for action. The two are not mutually exclusive. Neither are they independent of each other. We plan to encourage and empower action. We analyse the results of our action to help us measure the appropriateness of the plan. We act once again on the results of that analysis. And so it goes on.

How do we know when to stop planning and let action commence? Sometimes external factors will determine it for us. An opportunity will present itself. A threat will appear that we had not expected. A change in the environment will require us to act. Often, though, it will be our intuition, our gut instinct, that tells us. As campaigners we need to be willing to use all of the resources at our disposal, and that includes combining our intellectual and intuitive capabilities. Albert Einstein wrote:

'I never discovered anything of value with my rational mind.'

And there is a growing body of research that supports the notion that much of our decision-making is influenced and directed by our unconscious rather than our conscious mind. The unconscious recognizes and interprets both internal and external cues far more accurately and quickly than our conscious mind. In what seems to be an apparent paradox, researchers are suggesting that it is the unconscious that will often first make sense of whatever stimuli we are experiencing, and will then pass it on to the conscious for rational consideration. Whilst it is also true that the more experience an individual has in a particular field the more likely they are to make accurate intuitive decisions, three facts remain:

1 Regardless of our level of experience, we are all processing the world at an unconscious level.

2 At some point we have to put our plan into action – and we need to get the timing right.

3 We should learn to listen to our gut.[2]

We live in a world that is drawn, defined and dependent upon the detail, accuracy and relevance of an endless array of maps. No matter what the gradation of cause, our campaign map marks the way forward and challenges us to begin the journey towards our desired end outcome.

Creating a campaign map: from fiction to reality

The campaign map comprises all elements of our eventual campaign. This includes the narrative, the possible activities, the targets and a growing sense of the order in which the story will be developed, messages will be shared and things will happen.

---

[2] Margaret McDonagh will reinforce this point shortly.

Before any of these can begin to be planned, we need to be very clear of our desired end outcome and to work backwards from this.

The starting point, then, for creating our map is to know precisely:

- what we are aiming to achieve;
- who we need to gain permission from;
- when *polling day* is.

In Chapter 2, when considering cause, we asked you to write down your desired end outcome and, most importantly, how you will know when you have achieved it. This needed to be a thorough and detailed description of what you will see or hear, of what will have changed or been maintained once your campaign has been successful.

ACTIVITY!

Review your response to this activity in Chapter 2.

Consider if there are more details you can add.

How clearly have you identified those you need to gain permission from?

Ask yourself, 'What else do I need to know about my desired end outcome?'

Polling day

Polling day, the time when the audience makes their final decision, can be either fixed or flexible. If it appears to be fixed, the first thing to do is check that it absolutely is. Once you are sure that this is the case, use the certainty it brings to focus your mind and the minds of your campaign team. Develop your map using reverse planning. Begin with your detailed vision of accomplishment, your success on polling day, and ask yourself:

'What needs to happen the day before to ensure that everything is in place?'

Then repeat this process, clarifying what things need to have happened several days, or a week, before each event throughout the campaign. Although this approach is best suited to the development of a detailed and accurate plan, you can still expect to be buffeted en route by your opposition and by those every day unexpected happenings that Harold Macmillan called simply, 'Events, dear boy, events.'

And of course, different types of campaigns have different lengths. At the Labour Party, AB was involved in a series of four-year election campaigns as well as many shorter ones, such as parliamentary by-elections that can last anything from four weeks to eight months. In his later role as Head of Campaigns and Research for The Football Association he had hoped to instigate a five-year change programme at The Football Association in England.

In his personal life, away from work, he ran a three-month campaign to influence his local council to extend a parking zone,[3] an eight-month campaign to buy the house he wanted and an eleven-month campaign to get a job of his dreams. (Interestingly that was supposed to be at Chelsea FC and turned out to be a role that was just as inspirational at the FA. The end outcome changed along the way, although the cause remained true throughout the campaign.)

And in AB's current work as a campaign consultant his company has, amongst other things, run an 18-month campaign to influence the government to alter a piece of legislation, a 12-month campaign to influence Ofcom to change a regulation, resulting in cheaper mobile phone costs for everyone, and a campaign of indeterminate length to grow the membership of a trade union.

CP is involved in a campaign every time he works with one of his university students. For undergraduates he has nested campaigns of different lengths, all within the three-year campaign that ends with their graduation. For his martial arts students he works to a polling day that is unknown. It depends on the student's commitment to learn and his willingness to teach them. The day it ends is subject to many influences. Some of CP's campaigns to help individuals with their problems in his therapeutic work can last months, weeks, hours or even minutes.

If CP is giving a workshop in communications skills, ostensibly the campaign lasts for as long as the workshop and ends when he leaves the stage. However, CP often operates to the principle of stretching out his polling days, after all, he is in complete control of the ending, and continues to help with his clients' learning long after the workshop has finished. He will stretch things the other way, too, by starting work with them before the actual workshop begins.

Jan Stimpson, an expert in parenting and co-author of *Raising Happy Children* and *Raising Happy Brothers and Sisters*, says the campaign to raise a child lasts a lifetime, with significant milestones at 3 hours, 3 months, 3 years, 13 years, and 18 years. 'Pregnancy normally leads to an overemphasis on the birth of the baby,' she told AB. 'But once the birth is done, things really begin!

'The mum is no longer an expectant parent, however wonderful or overwhelming that may have felt. She is now a parent for real, for sure and forever. It's a long haul. Nothing will ever be more important to do well. And actually at the point of the baby's arrival I defy anyone to know for sure how it's going to go.

'It's true that raising a child is one of the many areas of life that effort does not necessarily equal reward or success. We need more than effort. We need good luck, good fortune for all the areas we have no control over at all and we need a fabulous well thought-out, strong, emotional campaign and strategy for the rest. And we do need that effort – buckets of it; work, patience, love, on very little sleep and often with not much support.

'Parenting is an extraordinary journey full of such contrasts. It challenges us like nothing else on earth – every bit of us; our emotions, our history, our personalities, our resources, our self-belief, our self-control, our hopes and fears. And yes, some of it comes naturally, but how we approach it can make an extraordinary difference to

---

[3]   More on this story in Chapter 8.

the enjoyment of our relationships and the children becoming adults in our care and under our watch. Having a rough campaign and strategy mapped out helps enormously and then being responsive within that campaign plan is key.'

And think of other examples, too. A community fundraising campaign, putting on an event, such as a conference, a dinner or a wedding, selling a suit to a customer or securing planning consent for a new conservatory or a multi-million pound development, are all campaigns with different lengths.

A short campaign influences the type of narrative and increases the pressure on getting the narrative understood quickly. A longer campaign gives more time to explain the narrative, to repeat and reinforce it, yet at the same time allows more time for others to influence the outcome, and for those unexpected 'events' to play a part. Longer campaigns often require more resources, and over a sustained period. Shorter campaigns will require different activities to longer ones, and will have a different pattern of resource use. Longer campaigns enable more time for feedback and modification whereas shorter campaigns rely more on getting it right from the start.

Uncertainty

The length of a campaign creates different demands on resources, differences in activities, different impacts on pace and speed and the ability to use feedback. The narrative will be different, the effects of external factors will be different and the audience have different amounts of time to change their opinions, beliefs and understanding. And, no matter what the cause, the campaign, or its duration, some degree of uncertainty is inevitable.

Campaigns are always uncertain because we cannot always prevent or control those events that go on around us. Of course, not all will present a threat, or a distraction, or be damaging to our campaign. Some of them might provide unexpected support or opportunities. Whatever their nature and potential effect, they do all need to be managed and this begins with an acceptance of the inevitability of uncertainty.

Campaigns do not follow well-established paths, they do not build momentum within the security of a safe, well-signed route into the future. Rather, the campaign map charts unknown territory. Campaigners are explorers rather than weekend ramblers. The complexities of our world and the uncertainties of the future combine to challenge every campaign. It is why campaigners need to be both creative and courageous. They have to bring life, strength, acceptance and momentum to a story and a process. To do this they have to create communication space for their campaign in a world that is already crammed.

So, when mapping a campaign identify the best channels of communications, those which are cost effective for the size of audience and which will create cut-through and get noticed. These will be your primary channels for creating space. Identify also the most appropriate supporting channels, occasional channels and those channels that are unlikely to be used. With that done, map out a rough sequence of communications using mostly the primary channels, with some secondary and the possible tactical use of others.

Bear in mind, too, that the different sizes of audience will place different demands on resources and the use of different channels. For example, when AB was involved in the AV referendum the electorate was 43 million people. This meant that leaflets and other printed communications were prohibitively expensive and would have limited impact, especially given that it was not possible to segment the electorate any further. The primary channels, therefore, became free and bought media.

Conversely, in a constituency of 70,000 voters, advertising would not be cost effective. It simply costs too much to produce bespoke adverts for such a relatively small number of people. To reach an audience of this size the use of free media and leaflets, flyers, direct mail letters, supported by events, phone calls and home visits would be a more effective way of getting attention and creating space.

If polling day is flexible levels of uncertainty increase. Without a fixed end-date to work back from we can never be sure that we are on schedule and this brings a greater sense of urgency to our operation. Whilst we are always planning to tell our narrative as soon as possible so that we can repeat it as many times as we can, when polling day is unknown we have to apply more of our campaign more quickly just in case our audience is asked to decide at the very earliest opportunity. However, we also have to guard against the desire to cram too much into our campaign at any one time, because by doing so we risk confusing or alienating our audience. No matter how great our concern about a sudden, unpredicted polling day, we still have to follow the basic principles of basing our actions on the lessons we are learning from audience feedback and the current nature of the environment and context we are operating within.

Given this, one of the very important facts to ascertain as soon as possible is:

'Who determines polling day?'

If we identify these influencers or decision-makers, we have a chance of influencing them or of identifying the factors, or indicators, they will focus on when setting the date. Armed with this information we might be able to guess the most likely time they will choose. Or we might be able to narrow down the possibilities by working out the earliest and latest parameters such as 'not before', 'some time before' or 'by this date at the latest' and then operating within those. Alternatively, we might seek to force their hand by implementing a strategy that encourages them to select the time that is most beneficial to our cause.

ACTIVITY!

When is your polling day?

Is it fixed or flexible?

Who influences or determines it?

Can you influence them?

If so, how?

Facing the whiteboard

During this early stage the campaign plan and, therefore, our vision of success, live only in our imagination. We start by creating what AB refers to as a *'fictional campaign'*, which is simply his way of reminding himself and his team that everything we create begins as fiction. Nothing exists in reality until we create it and then make it happen.

The map we are building does not describe either a context or a process that exists currently; rather it is the shape and direction of things to come. In the first instance we have only AB's 'clean whiteboard', a blank canvas upon which we can draw our plan. This 'clean whiteboard' offers both opportunities and challenges. It invites our analytical, strategic and creative thinking. It dares us to be comfortable with uncertainty. The whiteboard begins as an arena for ideas and becomes the platform for progress. By choosing to campaign we are choosing to create something new, a process designed to influence others that was not in existence until we felt the need to promote our cause.

Inevitably, when we commit to our campaign there is much that we don't know. We have an emotional compulsion to act, an understanding that we need to sequence our communications appropriately using the most relevant and powerful communication channels and, perhaps, an instinct about the attitudes, views and possible responses of some of our audience. The research and analysis, however, still needs to be done and the creative, yet realistic, plan is still to be developed. To be able to welcome and use this time of unknowing, we have to recognize the opportunities it offers to gain new insights. We have to believe in the value of uncertainty, of the importance of this time when we don't yet know the best questions to ask let alone have the best answers to them. We have to believe in our ability to step into this situation and create something of worth out of it. AB says:

> 'There are times I don't know what to do – and that's when the creativity and learning truly starts and when the map can begin to take shape. I have to take a deep breath and start by doing what I believe is best and then alter it accordingly as I learn more.'

We will talk about creativity in a moment and, in keeping with the content of this chapter, we will offer you a practical model that you can apply when facing the 'blank whiteboard' and throughout the creation and implementation of the plan. First, though, there is a point to make about the danger of imagining a fictional campaign. It is a point connected to creative thinking and the use of our imagination and it is simply this:

> The fiction we design must have a realistic and practical application.

Too often, when imagining what might be, people forget the boundaries and barriers created by the reality of what is. Whilst our map might well need to challenge or stretch current realities, there are inevitably forces at play that we cannot simply ignore and some, perhaps, that we cannot change, so we need to plan for these accordingly. Our aim is the application of what we think of as *realistic creativity* – the ability to create a desired end outcome that is bold and new, when appropriate, and relevant and worthwhile always.

Fictional planning is never an excuse to forget the practical demands and requirements of running a successful campaign. Neither, though, can so-called practicality be a reason for limiting our vision. If a plan can never be implemented it is worthless, no matter how great it looks on the whiteboard. If a plan does not push some boundaries, it may not be bold enough.

Establishing and maintaining this balance between fiction and reality, between creativity and practicality, requires the levels of personal awareness and emotional control we introduced in Chapter 2. Connected to this, we also have to manage our emotional commitment to our own ideas. The basic principle is:

> It is quite normal to fall in love with your own idea or plan – just be willing to recognize and fall in love with a more appropriate one if it is presented to you.

Every campaign begins as a work of fiction.

ACTIVITY!

Use reverse planning to create a first, rough campaign map by working from your polling day backwards.

Notice how you feel about and manage the uncertainties that are an inevitable part of this activity.

LEARNING POINTS

- A campaign map begins as a rough idea of the narrative and activities that will comprise your campaign and develops into a detailed and specific, timeframed grid.
- Before you can begin to map your campaign you need to know what you are aiming to achieve, who needs to give you permission, and by when.
- Create your map by working from your polling day backwards.
- Polling days are either fixed or flexible.
- Be comfortable with uncertainty.
- Your fictional plan must work well in the real world.
- The world as it currently is must not act as a brake on ideas. Our campaign must make new things a reality.
- Be willing to put your plan into action – and get the timing right.
- Learn to work intuitively as well as strategically and rationally.

Creativity

Dr Kenichi Ohmae, a business and corporate strategist who was for many years a senior partner in McKinsey and Company, the international management consulting firm, observed that:

> 'Strategic success cannot be reduced to a formula...there are habits of mind and modes of thinking that can be acquired through practice to help you free the creative power of your subconscious and improve your odds of coming up with winning strategic concepts.'

Creativity is an essential trait for campaigners. And, much like campaigning itself, it reflects a mindset as well as a skill set. Simply put, creativity is the ability to think of and develop something new whether that is an idea, a process or a product. However, as we have already suggested, creativity does not just happen inside a person's conscious mind. It is not a purely rational and logical process. Rather, it occurs through the interaction between a person's conscious thoughts, their unconscious processing of stimuli as they search for meanings and then create associations at a speed and in ways that are often beyond their conscious awareness, and the socio-cultural context within which they are operating.

In one sense, then, the very process of campaigning with its mix of audience and environmental scanning and analysis, time and other resource constraints, narrative development and delivery, activities, and varying levels of uncertainty and competition, requires and encourages creativity in equal measure. The intuition that can provoke action can also uncover solutions or inspire initiatives.

According to Professor Mihalyi Csikszentmihalyi, famous for his theory about the importance of 'flow' in the creative process, there are 10 core traits common to the most creative of people. Interestingly, these traits tend to combine the following apparent opposites:

1 Physical energy and a recognition of the need to rest and recuperate
2 Smartness and naivety
3 Playfulness and discipline
4 A highly developed imagination and a very clear sense of reality
5 A combination of both extroversion and introversion
6 Humility and pride
7 Masculinity and femininity
8 Rebelliousness and tradition
9 Passion and objectivity
10 Joy and suffering.

Physical energy and relaxation

Creative individuals demonstrate great physical energy whilst also being willing to rest wherever they feel they need to. Creative campaigners have the ability to focus their energy with great power and intent on the project at hand and, as soon as the opportunity presents itself, they will take time to recharge their batteries.

Smartness and naivety

Smartness here does not imply an outstandingly high IQ, more a high level of general intelligence. Naivety refers to a childishness that is often reflected through the willingness to play and an occasional sense of mental immaturity. These qualities often enable creative individuals to be able to use two very different ways of thinking, known as divergent and convergent. Divergent thinking is based on the mental flexibility and originality in perception that many children demonstrate through play. Convergent thinking requires an intellectual ability to evaluate the worth of the ideas created through divergent thinking. This mixture of smartness and naivety, divergent and convergent thinking, is of value throughout a campaign as we respond to audience feedback and develop influential media.

Playfulness and discipline

The desire to play is a common quality of creative people. When faced with a problem they are able to create a wide variety of possible solutions, many of which appear to lack an acceptance of the realities of the situation. This detachment from reality is a necessary, and yet temporary, part of the creative process. Once a sufficient number of ideas are in the bag, play time ends and a rigorous evaluation ensues. There is little, if any, benefit in being able to create lots of ideas before and during your campaign if you cannot tell a good one from a bad one.

Imagination and reality

As well as being able to switch between fantasy and reality, creative campaigners can do so in ways that connect the two. Paradoxically, a very realistic and thorough understanding of the realities of a situation is often a prerequisite for the flight of fancy that will lead to a creative and practical solution. Imagination is the vehicle in which we escape from both the present and the past, to return with something that is, as Csikszentmihalyi describes it:

'original without being bizarre.'[4]

It is the ability to recognize and manage these two apparent extremes, as if living in the present and the future at the same time, which enables a campaigner to create a fictional campaign that can become a meaningful reality.

Extroversion and introversion

Many people tend to think of themselves as either extrovert or introvert. Creative individuals, though, are more likely to demonstrate both traits. They are as comfortable interacting with other people, seeing them, hearing and talking to them,

---

[4] Csikszentmihalyi, M. 1996. *Creativity, Flow And The Psychology of Discovery And Invention*. HarperPerennial, New York.

understanding their attitudes and desires and so on, as they are being alone to think, plan or write. Campaigns, of course, are dependent upon both sets of behaviours.

Humility and pride

Creative individuals tend to be respectful of those who have gone before them, paved the way and provided inspiration. They are quick to focus ahead, looking for the next project as soon as the current one is complete. They often acknowledge the role that luck has played in their success and are their own greatest critic. This combination usually ensures a modesty that can belie the significance of their accomplishments. However, creative individuals do also realize that, compared to many others, they have achieved much. They believe that they can accomplish whatever they set out to and, if the situation demands it, they can be aggressive in they way they progress their project. This mixture of humility and security, or pride, makes it relatively easy for such people to prioritize their work over their own personal gain or comfort. They will demonstrate what Margaret McDonagh refers to as:

'the somewhat obsessive nature that great campaigners tend to have'.

Masculinity and femininity

Creative individuals tend to be innately resistant to the many social and cultural influences evident in all societies that encourage boys and girls to develop certain traits and ignore others. Research shows that the most creative people avoid the confines of rigid gender stereotyping and, by doing so, effectively double their perceptual ability and therefore the number of responses they can make. This psychological androgeny enables the individual to access a range of states that traditionally would be regarded as either predominantly masculine or feminine. For example, they can be aggressive or caring, dominant or submissive, sensitive or stubborn. Essentially, they bring to the campaign the combined strengths of both genders.

Rebelliousness and tradition

In the way that campaigners need to believe in a cause before they can create a campaign, so creative individuals have to understand and value a particular domain before they can seek to change it. However, the change they seek has to enhance the domain; creating something new for its own sake is never the purpose. The rebellious person is often independent in nature – a necessary trait when challenging some aspect of accepted behaviour or thinking – and yet their rebelliousness grows from their understanding of, and concern for, the context within which they are operating. Campaigners seeking to create change need to create and demonstrate a balance between their spirit for something new and their care and respect for what currently is.

Passion and objectivity

This duality relates back to our previous comment about the willingness to disregard your own idea in favour of one that offers more. In conversation with CP, the great chef Raymond Blanc talked at length about the importance of:

'finding your passion'

before committing to a particular career or lifestyle. The most creative individuals shift from attachment to detachment at will, using the energy this creates to maintain and grow their enthusiasm for the task whilst also ensuring the quality of their output. As we discussed in the previous chapters, campaigners are driven by the emotional compulsion of their cause and are wedded to the need for ongoing analysis and strategic thinking. Passion and objectivity are paradoxical soulmates in the campaign process.

Joy and suffering

Inevitably, the more one is emotionally drawn to a cause and the greater the level of emotional commitment to a desired end outcome, the more susceptible one is to the often associated emotions of joy and suffering. *'I care therefore I cry'*, would be the admission of many writers, artists, inventors, leaders and creative thinkers, coupled, thankfully, with, *'I cry often with joy'*, as they

> Creativity grows out of a range of seemingly opposing traits and is rooted in a thorough understanding of the context within which we are operating.

move toward and achieve their goal. The suffering experienced by creative individuals has two sources. It stems from the negative or challenging responses of others and from their own sense of inadequacy. However much they might add to a domain, creative people feel that they always fall short of their innate potential. For them, the joy of creation is often scarred by the sharp edge of perceived under-achievement. It is a trait that helps drive the creative process and yet needs to be managed carefully to avoid harm.

Although creativity is an essential part of the campaigner's armoury, it is important to stress here that individual campaigners do not need to possess all of the traits outlined above in order to be successful. An understanding of our own creative strengths and weaknesses enables us to enlist the help of people with complimentary traits and skills. The aim is to get the balance of the campaign team right, rather than expect that the campaign leader should be extraordinarily multi-talented.[5]

---

[5] This is true for all the skills required within the campaign team. The leader has to ensure that the mix is appropriate for the campaign they have mapped out.

ACTIVITY!

Assess your current level for each of the traits outlined above. A score of 1 indicates the lowest possible level and a score of 10 reflects the highest:

- Physical energy and a recognition of the need to rest and recuperate

- Smartness and naivety

- Playfulness and discipline

- A highly developed imagination and a very clear sense of reality

- Extroversion and introversion

- Humility and pride

- Masculinity and femininity

- Rebelliousness and tradition

- Passion and objectivity

- Joy and suffering.

The 7I creativity wheel

Developed by CP through his work on creativity and innovation with a range of organizations, the 7I creativity wheel reflects many of the creative traits previously identified. It also highlights the key aspects of the creative process, reinforces the notion that courage is a prerequisite of going first, and reminds us that we are never operating in a vacuum.

There are seven aspects of the 7I creativity wheel. Although each of those seven follow on sequentially, for example we have to identify a problem, an opportunity, or a cause before we can begin to imagine how to address it, it is important to realize too that each aspect can be applied at any stage of the process. We can, for example, imagine a range of options and interpret their value whilst at the inventing stage. We can identify problems that might occur during the implementation phase and so start the wheel turning again within that particular part of the process.

The 7I creativity wheel

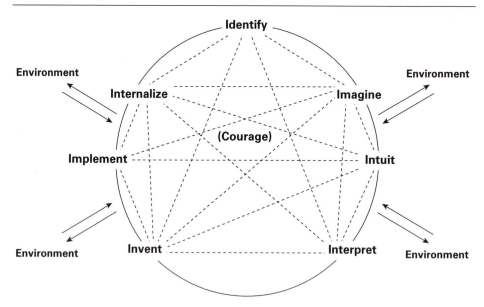

The following brief overview outlines the nature and purpose of the 7I's:

Identify

This focuses on the ability to draw the current picture, to identify accurately the threats, opportunities, strengths or weaknesses that require our attention. As campaigners, we need to identify our cause and the nature of the environment and those forces within it that we need to utilize, defend against or seek permission from. We also need to be aware of the limitations of our own perception filters and biases and do everything we can to ensure clarity and completeness of vision. Again, whilst this is the starting point for both creativity and campaigning, the environmental awareness that enables the accurate identification of key points of leverage and drivers of change is an ongoing and essential part of the process.

We might remind ourselves too at this point that there are two environments we need to observe and understand. These are the external environment within which we seek to either create change or maintain the status quo, and the internal environment within our own campaign team. Our aim is to be able to accurately draw the current picture of both at any given time.

Imagine

For campaigners this is initially the ability to imagine the desired end outcome with ever-increasing clarity. As mentioned previously, both this and the associated campaign map begin as a product of the imagination. We can also use our imagination to conjure up possible improvements as well as possible questions and doubts, or objections and resistance, to whatever we are doing. Such imaginings are then best tested through a well-planned and executed analysis before they are acted upon.

Many people tend to make the mistake of presuming that imagining is the core, if not the only, creative skill. The truth, though, is that it is only one part of a more complex process and that there is no value in whatever we imagine until, and unless, we bring it to life and then demonstrate its worth.

Intuit

The French actress Juliet Binoche, when asked how she selects the films she appears in said:

> 'When I choose a film I need to believe in it and believe I can do something special with it, and after a while that means not trying to judge or analyse why I should do it. You have to follow this intuition thing, which is a mystery to me.'

Creative theorists and practitioners alike emphasize the importance of intuition in the creative and decision-making process. According to researchers this mystery within tends to be more powerful, obvious and accurate when individuals have significant experience of the context they are operating in.

Gary Klein, an American research psychologist, has spent several decades researching the ways individuals make decisions and has concluded that the most critical decisions we make are often based on intuition. His studies of people experienced in those fields in which complex and often time-pressured judgements are required – think of fire fighters for example – reveal that up to 90 per cent of their decisions are based on gut instinct. Perhaps even more interestingly, he and many of his peers operate on the belief that a person's intuition can be explicitly trained and developed.

It is an attribute that is as relevant to the campaigner as it is to any other creative individual. Margaret McDonagh observed:

> 'The things that I've been most annoyed with in my life have always been when I knew in my stomach that something was wrong and I didn't speak up. I just went along with something and, particularly in campaigning, you get a sense of right and wrong. Even though you can't articulate it, you just know "Oh my god this is going to lead to trouble!" You get a smell, you know...'

Interpret

This is the ability to evaluate the options that have been imagined against the realities of the situation and then to select the most appropriate one(s) to act upon. In creative campaigning, this requires finding the best fit between the needs and demands of the environment, and the stories and messages shared and the media used at any given time. This, in turn, is based on accurate analyses of the feedback being received and a realistic understanding of resource availability, including timeframe.

Interpretation is the stage in the creative process when fiction is measured against current and desired realities. It is the time when what we imagine, know and intuit comes together to provide the foundation upon which we build. Campaigning, like all forms of creativity and every type of communication, depends upon an accurate interpretation of feedback, capability and possibilities. Interpretation underpins the creation of the campaign map and the development of the narrative. It is the basis for invention.

Invent

This is, quite simply, the stage at which something tangible is created. For us, as campaigners, this can include the map, the grid, the narrative, or a piece of influential media. This is the stage beyond simply thinking, analysing, and talking about what we need to do. Now we begin to make our commitment manifest as, more clearly than ever before, we begin to *'walk the talk'*.

The challenge here, as AB made clear earlier, is that we can never be absolutely certain that our campaigning inventions, particularly the earlier ones in the campaign, are the best possible. We would argue, of course, that the more fully we imagine our desired end outcome and all associated possibilities, the more rigorously we analyse and interpret feedback and the more we exercise our intuition, the more likely we are to be right. However, campaigning, like every creative endeavour, is about shaping the future and so ultimately there are no guarantees. Which is why, perhaps, more than any other, this part of the creative process reminds us of the need to have the emotional drive and commitment, the belief in the value of our cause and what we are seeking to create, which enables us to be courageous.

In an interview with AB, Gerd Leipold, the former Executive Director of Greenpeace International, talked about the importance of this belief and how it fires the willingness to commit:

> 'There's a limit to how useful wisdom alone is in campaigning, because you need this absolute belief that you can do it, that you can win against all odds. Or sometimes it's just that the cause is so important that you fight for it regardless of the outcome. It takes courage to go against more powerful forces. For example, when we campaigned against nuclear weapons, or nuclear weapons at sea, it was a bit ridiculous to assume we could win that but without that sense... When you try to stop a nuclear ship, that takes some courage....'

Implement

This is the introduction of the invention into the place or system for which it was intended. This is arguably the most obvious part of the change process and it can often be the most challenging. The first part of the challenge lies in persuading significant others to adopt the new way. The second lies in ensuring the adoption lasts and works.

Depending on the nature of the campaign, there are various types and numbers of adoptions that have to be made both along the way and on completion. One example is the campaign grid, arguably, the most essential tool for coordinating the campaign activities and managing some of its uncertainties.[6]

---

[6]   The campaign grid will be discussed more fully in Chapter 7.

Internalize

The ultimate aim of any form of creative endeavour, including campaigning, is to reach a point when the creation is accepted as a natural and essential part of the environment. This only happens when people stop either celebrating their success in the conflict or mourning their loss and internalize the result of the campaign, making it a part of their usual behaviour and thinking.

This internalizing of behaviours and thought leads to the development of habit and beyond that to the creation of instinct and intuition which relates back to one of the previous elements of the creativity wheel, reinforcing the synergistic nature of both the creative, and the campaigning, process.

> *Creativity is a multi-sensory activity. You need to use your I's, listen to feedback, trust your gut instinct and recognize **that** smell.*

Creativity, like campaigning, is an iterative activity based on a number of ongoing feedback loops that feed our understanding and fuel our drive and sense of direction. Forces within the environment are at play at all times, requiring us to be aware, adaptable, pragmatic and practical. The fact that we are discussing campaigning through the medium of a book requires us to present the work in a linear fashion, Chapter 2 has to precede Chapter 3 and so forth. In reality, though, the creative campaign is more circular in nature, hence the use of a wheel supported by a series of interconnected spokes to represent it. To create value through a campaign, momentum has to be created and controlled. The initial challenge is the transition from inertia to movement and, once this is achieved, the task becomes that of increasing and directing the rate of progress. In the *Campaign It!* model this is accomplished by transforming the map into the grid.

ACTIVITY!

Assess your current level of ability for each of the 7I's. A score of 1 indicates the lowest possible level and a score of 10 reflects the highest:

- Identify

- Imagine

- Intuit

- Interpret

- Invent

- Implement

- Internalize

Repeat this activity on behalf of two people that you know.

Then consider the two I's in which you scored them most highly. How do they demonstrate their ability? What do they do and say (equally, what do they not do or say) that makes them so good?

> **LEARNING POINTS**
> - Creativity is an essential part of campaigning.
> - Creativity is a complex, iterative process that requires a range of skills and attitudes.
> - It is not the 'gift' of a chosen few.

Momentum

A campaign without momentum is a campaign without life. Actually, a campaign that lacks momentum is not really a campaign at all. It has more in common with a chat in a pub over a pint of beer than it does a planned sequence of communications that makes use of all appropriate channels to achieve defined outcomes in a specific timeframe by influencing the decision-makers who will allow success.

A campaign moves towards polling day. It travels. Sometimes, like an aeroplane on a long-distance flight, our campaign will face some turbulence and be knocked off course and then our job, from our campaign cockpit, is to make the necessary corrections and get back on target. The difference between our campaign and the long-distance flight is that the pilot slows the plane down to ensure a safe landing, whereas we seek to increase momentum as we close in on polling day. What began as awareness, grows into a commitment, is shared, gaining recognition, gathering support, developing power and energy, becoming a force to be reckoned with as its momentum builds. All of which requires:

- strategic planning and thinking;
- time management;
- resource management, including the identification and use of the most appropriate communication channels and the development of a powerful culture within the campaign team.

Strategic planning and thinking

At the core of this is the ability to combine two apparent opposites, 'big picture' assessment and planning with ongoing attention to detail. 'Big picture' awareness and understanding is essential because there is never a vacuum, because of the inevitability of 'events, dear boy, events', and because whenever we travel it always works out best if we plan ahead. To focus only on the 'big picture' though, is to forget where the Devil lives. For campaigners, the detail is recorded and updated on the campaign grid. And, as we have said, we will talk about this more in the next chapter. Time now, though, to talk about 'time'.

Time management

There are three aspects to this. They are the ability to live in the moment, to learn from the past and to imagine the future. From these three aspects, timelines can be drawn and our grid can begin to take shape. Living in the moment is a matter of focus and concentration. It is a prerequisite for giving attention to detail. It is the state from which we best interpret what is happening in the instant, or write or design some influential media, or understand those we are communicating with.

In one sense both the past and the future are subject to our creativity and imagination. The former exists only in our memory and the latter as a series of possible scenarios. We can draw useful lessons from the past only if we can be certain that we recall it accurately. We can mentally restructure the past, either deliberately or not, and we would do well to remember that accurate and detailed memory-management is a skill not a natural trait. There are many situations in which forgetting what has happened, or, even, mentally rewriting it, might be positive. Learning from the past, though, requires the same degree of accuracy and objectivity as audience analysis. For that reason it is often best done as a team activity, with the key players involved sharing their recollections and interpretations collectively.

Scenario planning requires an understanding of the environment and the significant forces operating within it. It is a game of the imagination based on the willingness to ask and then engage fully with a series of 'What if?' questions. The purpose of scenario planning is to identify likely future events and to estimate their impact. Should a particular scenario seem very likely and/or very significant, plans can be put in place. The following story from AB taken from his time as Head of Research and Campaigns at The Football Association is a great example of scenario planning.

Resigned to losing to Germany

I would often throw in a bit of my own imaginative thinking, based on speculation and 'what-ifs', into the focus groups I had organized to test the fans' attitudes and reactions to certain possibilities.

I knew that the FA had no succession planning for the England manager and would end up, again, being pushed around by the media in the event that the current manager, Kevin Keegan, left abruptly or, for that matter, came to the end of his actual contract. Keegan had a bit of a reputation as an emotional man who was liable to walk away from the job if he thought it was the right thing for him to do and I wanted the FA to be able to retain control of media and public opinion over a replacement if that happened.

When I assessed the likelihood of Keegan being replaced by another Englishman in the event of him resigning there were few credible candidates other than Terry Venables, and I knew the politics of the FA meant it would be unlikely that he could return yet. It seemed to me that we needed to expand our possibilities.

So I started including the topic of the FA appointing a non-English manager of the England team in the discussion guide for my research agency, TW Research, in early 2000 on the basis that we might need its findings come the summer when the European Championships were taking place in

Holland and Belgium. As it turned out, we didn't. Despite our dreadful performance, Keegan stayed. The report I had written advising David Davies and Adam Crozier how to manage public opinion if they were minded to look overseas for a new manager remained in my desk drawer. Because you never know....

On the tube on my way home from England's World Cup qualifying match against Germany in October that year I heard that Keegan had resigned. I know we had to act quickly or the media would. I called David and told him that I had a report that I wanted to get to him as quickly as possible. I gave him a brief overview and promised to fax it to him as soon as I got home. The gist of the report was as follows:

'It would be perfectly possible for the FA to appoint a foreigner as England manager. The public would support it as long as:

- We explained why there was no suitable Englishman available.

- We found a top-notch foreign manager with an obvious track record of success.

- We made it explicit that the person appointed would groom and train other possible English managers as part of his contract, and that he would eventually be succeeded by an Englishman.'

To their credit, the FA played a blinder. They were in charge of the media process the whole way through. They got their man, the first ever non-English manager of the England football team. (By the way, I hadn't mentioned any names in my report for David, nor had I researched any. The choice of Sven Goran Eriksson was theirs alone. I'm having no part of that on my CV!) The football public were completely behind the decision all the way, as I knew they would be if the FA communicated well.

Resource management

Externally, momentum is developed by the deliberate sequencing of the narrative delivered through those communication channels that enable us to connect most effectively and efficiently with our audience. This may include any or all of the following:

- increasing the speed and pace of the campaign communications;
- increasing the frequency of activities;
- changing the content, look or feel of the communications;
- increasing the numbers of events;
- increasing advertising spend;
- increasing the numbers of people visibly supporting the campaign.

Internally, momentum is created by a team of strategists, analysts and critical friends with the desired mix of personality types and levels of emotional intelligence, creative skills and attributes. It is one of the responsibilities of the campaign leader to build a team with the best possible mix of attributes and attitudes. The team culture, underpinned by shared beliefs and values relating to process goals and the desired end outcome, will be reflected as much through what it doesn't say on the campaign grid as by what it does.

Resources will be applied to build momentum only in ways that reflect these beliefs.

Whilst flexibility is a required trait in a campaigner, and the grid will change inevitably in the light of new learning, the core beliefs and values will remain constant throughout. The campaign is never left to its own devices. It is sculpted and directed by the culture of the campaign team as much as it is by external events. It is managed at all times. Its size, pace and intensity are made clear on the grid. Everything builds towards polling day. The day after, the grid can be removed. The whiteboard will be clear again.

> *To campaign is to plan and undertake a journey during which the generalized map becomes a series of detailed grids developed as we learn.*

LEARNING POINTS

- Campaigning is an iterative rather than a linear process.
- The aim is to create ever-increasing momentum as you move towards your polling day.
- Strategy, resources and time all need to be managed.
- The campaign team needs to be built to ensure a complimentary mix of skills and attitudes, held together by shared beliefs and values.

Final thoughts

'If your position is everywhere, your momentum is zero.'

William N. Lipscomb Jnr

Campaigns and the campaigners who bring them to life stand for something. They have a commitment both to the desired end outcome and the ways in which it will be achieved. They also, inevitably, stand against something. To campaign is to take a position. It is to make clear what we believe is right or wrong, to argue for what should be created, sought out or avoided, and to act proactively in support of that argument.

This is why opposition can be expected. As we have already discussed, no single campaign can appeal to all people. Audience analysis enables us to target those whose support and permission we need and who are also open to persuasion. It also allows us to ignore those we cannot influence and to understand our opposition. The campaign map charts our starting position and the way forwards. As we progress through our map we differentiate ourselves more and more clearly from those who are taking a different route in pursuit of a different outcome. We have to make our position clear before we can attract others to it. Just as we need to know our identity before we can introduce our self with accuracy so, as campaigners, we need to take a position, determine our desired outcome and then map out a way of achieving it before we even consider building momentum.

Indeed, if we have not taken a position based on a commitment to a cause there is no need for momentum. We are going nowhere and we have nowhere to go to. As the American Nobel Prize winning chemist William N. Lipscomb Jnr observed, momentum is dependent upon positioning. We have to know where we are and where we are going before we can develop and direct the energy needed to move effectively and efficiently in a specific direction. We can no more hope to be everywhere at once than we can appeal to everyone at the same time.

Essentially, there are two types of position we experience when campaigning. The first position is that which we choose to promote. It is the one we feel compelled to take in support of our cause. It is the one we seek to define to others and which, in turn, defines us. The second type of position is strategic. It reflects where the campaign is on a daily basis. This is determined by the appropriateness of the plan we are implementing, the ways we are using the resources we have at our disposal, the influence of our opposition and the response of our audience. To seek competitive advantage, we have to recognize accurately what position we are in at any moment of the campaign and then determine the best way to move on to the next. It is through the development and management of momentum that we make these transitions.

Actually, when we said that campaigners *'stand for something'*, that was only half of the truth. Once they have identified something worth standing up for, campaigners *move*.

Momentum is not separate from us. It is the energy we build and share that creates change, that defends the status quo, through which we influence others.

Integrating activities

07

"The quality of life is determined by its activities. **ARISTOTLE**

"Theatre is a verb before it is a noun,
an act before it is a place. **MARTHA GRAHAM**

The purpose of this chapter is to:

1 Demonstrate and discuss how to put together the communications that will explain our narrative and persuade our audience to give us permission.
2 Introduce different activities and communication tools that we can use to progress our campaign.

In this chapter we:

- Reinforce the point that campaigning is an active, practical process.
- Identify a range of activities and communication tools we can employ.
- Make clear the importance of matching the right content with the right activities at the right time.
- Show how to create and manage the campaign grid and associated frameworks.
- Highlight the role and associated attributes of the campaign team leader.
- Explain how to manage the final part of the campaign.

Bringing the campaign to life

Let us just take a moment to review everything we have done so far. We have:

- identified our cause;
- defined our desired end outcome;

- analysed and understood our client's motivation (presuming we have one);
- analysed our audience and identified their starting point, their needs, beliefs, values, fears, the people who influence them, and the best communication channels to use to reach them;
- identified and analysed sources of opposition;
- written a narrative and key themes, flagship policies, messages and lines to take;
- assembled our supporting information, facts and figures;
- written a slogan;
- created our initial campaign map.

All of which is well and good, and an essential way to start presuming we have the time in which to do it all.[1] However, so far we haven't actually done any campaigning! We haven't shared any of our narrative with our audience and, therefore, we haven't started to influence them. So far we have planned, prepared, written and discussed. We have been motivated by a cause, realized what we need to achieve, developed an understanding of all the key players and aspects of the context within which we will be operating, and created the story we feel best meets our needs. And if we stop at this point it will all have been a complete waste of time. Not a single audience member will have been motivated to act. We will have mobilized our brain cells only. The audience will be doing what it would always have been doing without us. Our level of influence will be zero. Time will not have been lost, it will continue regardless. We will have lost. The English essayist and poet, Austin Dobson wrote,

> 'Time goes, you say? Ah, no! Alas, Time stays, we go.'

If all we do is plan our campaign, it would be fair to say that in one sense we didn't even start. The need for campaigners to move on from planning to action was emphasized by Emma Freud and Richard Curtis in their conversation with AB. They said:

> 'Someone has got to act. But when you open the door everyone is waiting to come through, because they secretly know that it is true... Somehow it needs to have one obsessed person to say, "Act on it!"'

Our purpose is, and always has been, to create reasons for people to do something. The nature and number of the activities we integrate throughout our campaign is determined by the quality of our imagineering and the availability of the required resources. There is no more important resource than time.

Whatever else we have said about time management, the bottom line is that time is the one resource we cannot recoup. Everyone in a campaign, including our opposition, is operating within the same time lines. Polling day is inevitable if occasionally flexible. A campaign is a finite activity, a project with a specific beginning and end. It is time-bound. When the time for just planning is over, the time for activity-led

---

[1] Sometimes we don't. Sometimes the timeframe means that we just have to take a deep breath and actively begin without the support of this detailed analysis and preparation, using feedback and flexibility to adapt and improve the campaign as we go.

planning begins. From then on, we act, learn from feedback, adjust our plan if necessary, and then act some more. This iterative feedback loop creates the momentum that drives our campaign. The creative wheel is now turning. The campaign is being brought to life. Now we have to earn our right to influence. And we do this through a carefully coordinated series of integrated activities through which we aim to tell our story in a timely, engaging and memorable way.

> *The campaign narrative is shared through a series of integrated activities.*

Activity management

The obvious and important point to make here is this:

> We have to create the activities just as we had to create the narrative.

And we can create and then execute any type of activity as long as it shares part of our story and is in keeping with the nature of our cause and overall campaign. This means that there is inevitable and ongoing work to be done throughout the life of the campaign. Activities are not self-creating. Whether or not Aristotle was right when he said that the quality of our lives is determined by the nature and quality of the activities we undertake, we can say for certain that the quality and impact of any campaign is related directly to the quality and integration of the campaign activities.

Our challenge at the beginning of this book was:

> 'If you care enough, Campaign It!'

It is a challenge simply because it is a call to action. And in our busy, multi-layered, story-filled world it can be all too easy to believe that we have neither the time nor energy to undertake a thorough and rigorous campaign or that, as we discussed in Chapter 1, we don't need to do anything differently because we are excellent communicators already. One of CP's academic friends and colleagues, a sport psychologist, observed to him once:

> 'When I tell people about my area of study, most people nod and tell me that they know all about motivation and goal setting. It makes me smile because, if that is the case, why are so many of them unhappy with the lives they have created?'

What is certain is that our life, like a campaign, will be filled with activities. As campaigners we not only need to be willing to create, manage and learn from them, we also have to know how to integrate them fully. Individuals within the team will inevitably need to take responsibility for specific activities and, whilst doing so, will need to understand how each activity fits into the big picture of the campaign.

Integration means far more than just getting the sequencing right. Integration is caused primarily by the need to tell the narrative. It is the way in which we make our activities feed and build off each other, the way every activity lays the foundation for the one that follows. We integrate activities to ensure that our current activity connects with both what is to come and what has gone before, no matter what the channel used, to help build the overall picture. We create momentum through the appropriate integration of our activities.

There are two types of momentum. The first is created by the urgency of the activity itself. This can be determined by its relative importance in the progression of our campaign and the amount of time available to prepare for it and/or by the degree of audience expectation and motivation for it. The second type of momentum relates to the way in which we share and build messages, so that the totality of our story and the understanding it creates within our audience tumbles into place with increasing speed. We also need to bear in mind that different parts of our audience might come to our campaign and, therefore, our story at different times. This is another reason why some of our activities need to repeat and reinforce what has already been said. They serve to introduce the previous elements of our story to any new audience members, whilst reminding the others of what has gone before.

Momentum is created by integration.

Simply organizing a series of activities without integrating them fully severely limits the overall influence of a campaign. Resist the falsehood that a series of communications about a common theme automatically equals a narrative. Integration is integral to the delivery of a persuasive narrative.

We campaign because we have a cause we care about. We create a narrative about our cause because we need a powerful and persuasive way to communicate with, and influence, our audience. We share our narrative through the number and variety of activities we organize and deliver because this is our manner of storytelling; this is our actual campaign. We integrate these activities because by doing so we create a connected, progressive argument that gains momentum as it moves towards polling day.

The best story in the world told badly will lose its audience. Likewise, the most compelling narrative delivered through disconnected, poorly organized activities that fail to produce the desired outcomes, will quickly become inconsequential. Our trustworthiness in the eyes and minds of our audience is determined by the relevance and quality of our narrative, the information we offer in support of it, and the way we deliver and manage all of our activities. As campaigners we understand the need to share emotive messages rather than just facts. Inevitably, we share messages through the quality of our organization and delivery. An activity that is badly organized, delivered poorly, or mistimed, will, in the eyes of some, cast doubt about the validity of our story and our right to win the support of our audience. Sometimes we doubt the messenger not because of what their message is but because of how they deliver it.

When jazz musicians Melvin 'Sy' Oliver and James 'Trummy' Young wrote their famous song, 'It ain't what you do (It's the way that you do it)' in 1937 it is reasonable to assume that they did not realize they had created what could be regarded as the campaign theme for the ages. Congruency throughout the campaign is maintained as much by the continual quality of our activity management as it is by our commitment to our narrative. We share our story through a series of activities that are organized, presented and managed in a manner that strengthens our claim for legitimacy. Sy and Trummy, although great musicians, were not completely right with the first half of their claim, though. What we do does matter. Our activities have to be timely, effective and efficient mechanisms for reaching our audience. However, once we have decided what to do, then how we do it matters above all else.

The skills needed to plan and manage any activity depend, to a great extent, on the nature of the activity itself. To organize an event, for example, requires a different skill set than if researching, writing and publishing a report. Whatever the activity, the campaign leader needs to ensure that there are individuals within the team with the necessary skills for every type of activity planned and/or that such people are available through the team's immediate network. In previous chapters we have touched on the importance of the make-up of the campaign team. We will take a moment now to reinforce and develop that.

LEARNING POINTS

- Influence is created through activities not just planning.
- Activities have to be created.
- Unconnected activities do not constitute a campaign and are limited in their influence.
- Every activity should progress or reinforce the narrative.
- Momentum is created through the integration of activities.

The campaign team

A successful team is dependent on the best mixture of skills and attitudes, bound together in a common purpose that incorporates shared process and end outcomes. The American news writer and management specialist, Lloyd Dobens wrote:

'It is not a question of how well each process works; the question is how well they all work together.'

This, of course, is as true for our campaign activities as it is for the campaign team itself. The common purpose that binds the team together is the commitment to the cause. Common processes grow out of a commitment to share the narrative and the agreed ethical stance.

The starting point for the development of every team is selecting the team members. When putting together a campaign team it is important to know what specific skills and other attributes you need before beginning the selection process. This requires an understanding of the desired end outcome, the activities that will lead towards it, and the ways the team will need to operate, both internally and externally, to achieve it. Another golden rule of campaigning is this:

'Let the intended activities determine the capabilities of the team rather than the other way round.'

Ideally, knowing what you want to achieve and how you intend to do it precedes the building of the team. If at all possible, the rule is to create a plan first and then put together the team that can best implement it.

Irrespective of the precise nature of the campaign, it is certain[2] that some team members at least will need to be good at:

- defining the cause;
- writing a narrative;
- imagineering;
- research;
- managing feedback;
- planning.

However, we need to avoid the presumption that an individual can only be good at one thing. Some people might possess a variety, if not all, of the required skills and traits. The campaign leader simply needs to ensure that the right balance is created and that individual's workloads are manageable.

When managing a team that includes volunteers, there are additional issues that have to be addressed. Most obviously, volunteers can withdraw their services at a moment's notice and, particularly in large-scale campaigns, they are both an inevitable and essential part of the team. This dependency on people who are working often on a part-time basis and always solely because of their support for our cause, reminds us that we always need to gain permission internally from our team as well as our target audience. Volunteers join a team because of their internal motivation and their commitment to the cause. It should be recognized that their rewards can also include personal development, networking, an enhanced CV or the possibility of a future job. They can be an invaluable resource that we cannot afford to lose. The question, then, is,

'How do we keep them, and keep them motivated, throughout the process?'

The answer is one that is as applicable to the other members of the team as it is to our volunteers. It is this:

'We have to ensure that everyone has the best possible experience whilst working with us.'

The campaign leader does not need to possess all of the skills and attributes we identified previously. Their role is to provide leadership, to bring the best out of each individual, and to ensure that the campaign is coordinated and congruent, focused on its audience and end outcomes, and that all activities are integrated and on message.

> Get to know your campaign team as you do your external audience; create great experiences for all team members.

---

[2] And it is almost certain that you will need people to stuff envelopes at some point during your campaign!

Interestingly, many of the things we do to create, manage and motivate the campaign team mirror those things that we do to create and run a successful campaign. It is unlikely, for example, that all of our team members will be equally skilled and experienced and, just as we need to know our audience and understand their starting point, so we need to know and understand that of our team members. Just as we need to make clear the benefits on offer to our audience, so we need to with the individuals working with us. The identification of preferred motivational traits is as important when communicating to individuals within the team as it is when seeking to influence a much larger audience. Recognizing an individual's decision-making tendencies is as useful when needing to explain your thinking to them as it is when prompting an audience to choose. Talking to team members using their preferred language patterns shows them the respect and understanding that we aim to demonstrate to our audience, and is just as meaningful.

Whilst everyone in the team is inherently motivated by the cause and their desire to share the narrative and so create something of value for others, the team leader needs always to be searching for ways to win and keep their hearts and minds, just as the campaign seeks to win the hearts and minds of the audience. People work with and for other people just as surely as people buy from people. A cause, however right and justified, however necessary and needed, cannot sell itself any more than a suit can. People bring their cause to life through their campaigning activities, and campaign leaders seek continually to influence their team members just as they seek to influence their audience. It is the ability of the team leader to share information appropriately and use a wide range of micro-communication skills that is essential for the development of a high-performance team that is truly greater than the sum of its parts.

One final point to consider in this regard is the fact that leaders, by definition, are *of* the team rather than *in* the team. Leaders are at least one step removed from those they are leading. In the way that they combine big picture analysis of the campaign with attention to detail as and when required, so too they view and manage their team. To be able to observe the big picture within the team, the way it is operating and how individuals are interacting, and to recognize individual strengths and weaknesses and signs of inappropriate tension or fatigue, the leader has to keep their emotional distance from those around them. They have to do this whilst at the same time providing support and guidance and reinforcing the fact that they are sharing the experience with all involved. This is another test of their emotional intelligence.

Beyond this, the team leader is also ultimately responsible for managing the relationship between resource availability, the nature and detail of the plan and the creativity of the campaign team. This is an important and often challenging balancing act. No matter how creative the plan, it can only be brought to life if the required resources are readily available. Sometimes they are not. In such situations the campaign leader is faced with two choices:

1 to limit the plan and the associated activities; or
2 to acquire the resources required.

AB's personal preference is always to implement the best possible plan and, therefore, to explore ways of acquiring the needed resources. This inevitably necessitates additional degrees of creativity and persuasion, of work and commitment. This crucial aspect of resource management is another part of the imagineering process, of transforming an excellent idea into a practical and beneficial reality.

This relationship between the plan, the acquisition and management of resources and the challenges of a successful campaign was emphasized by Gerd Leipold, during his interview with AB when he said:

> 'If you don't have a plan, success kills you. You want to grow a campaign, you
> want more people and more people often requires more resources, and if you
> don't have an idea of how to get the resources as your campaign grows – success
> kills.'

Of course, the resources not only need to be available, they need to be managed well. If accessing resources is the first step, applying them effectively and efficiently is far more than just the second step. Resource management is central to the development of momentum and is an ongoing part of the campaign process. It determines the way that we do things and the impact that we have upon our audience.

Again, although our primary focus is on larger-scale campaigns, the principles, practices and processes we are discussing throughout can be applied to help us campaign successfully for any cause. Whether, for example, your purpose is to develop your career, share certain values with your children, prevent a housing development in a local park, or even persuade a publisher to publish your book, your ability to share your narrative persuasively through a series of integrated activities will be resource-dependent.

Sometimes the resources that are needed will be personal ones. They might be a new skill, a shift in attitude, or a schedule change to create more time. Sometimes they will be beyond our personal control or development and involve us joining forces with others, or acquiring something of a more tangible nature, money, for example. Whatever resources we need, identifying, accessing, maintaining and/or developing them is as important in the examples above as it is in campaigns that require an experienced team and the support of volunteers to implement.

We all have the right to campaign. And we can campaign for anything we care about. Literally, anything!

LEARNING POINTS

- Activities determine resources.
- Individuals can possess a range of valuable traits and skills.
- Ensure that all team members have the best possible experience.
- Motivate others by using their preferred decision-making, motivational and communication preference.
- Leaders are *of* the team, not *in* the team.

Tools, channels and an essential wiggle

Fortunately, we have a range of communication 'tools' that we can use and a range of communication channels through which we can make contact with our audience. Whatever activities we decide to create and whatever channels we choose to use, we need to be clear always about the following:

- how every activity progresses the sharing of the narrative;
- how each specific interaction sets up the following one;
- how many other communication activities we can create from every one that we actually do.

We also need to ensure that every activity is:

- 'on message',
- memorable,
- timely,
- appropriately sequenced.

Every activity has to share at least a part of the narrative and reflect one of the key themes or messages. This is what it means to be 'on message'. It is not often that we can share all of our narrative through one activity at the beginning of our campaign. If we can, of course, we will. However, usually our story is told as quickly as possible, progressively, through our initial activities. After which, our activities enables us to repeat, remind and reinforce the key messages and themes of our story for the duration of the campaign.

For AB some of the most important questions the campaign team can ask themselves whilst planning and delivering their narrative begin with the phrase, *'How can we...?'* The questions that follow tend to be either creative or pragmatic. They might include:

- How can we get the additional resources we need?
- How can we share this information in a more engaging way?
- How can we make this activity newsworthy?
- How can we build other activities from this one?
- How can we do this activity on a limited budget?
- How can we show this activity in ways that will grab peoples' attention?

AB is always looking for engaging and memorable ways to give the campaign life, to include a creative twist that makes an activity compelling. He refers to this as *'wiggle'* and he says that, whenever possible, a campaign has to wiggle. There are many ways campaigners can make their delivery wiggle. The use of powerful, unusual, emotive, active or humorous images is one example. So is the use of a memorable soundbite. Ultimately, though, the ability to create wiggle is determined by the campaigner's level of creativity combined with their understanding of the context they are operating in.

It is this willingness to constantly seek out memorable ways of delivering the narrative, of getting attention by doing something different, amusing or eye-catching, which creates wiggle. In a world filled with competing stories only those with movement, energy and life will stand out. And if you want your story to stand out, you have to find ways to make it stand up and wiggle.

In the by-election in Preston, England, in 2000, John Braggins brought his very last leaflet to life in a way designed both to raise and a smile and share the message that he, the campaign team and the candidate they were representing were sharing the audience's experience and responding to events on a daily basis. It had rained continuously for much of the campaign, and everyone involved had finished most days soaked to the skin having spent much of their time on doorsteps meeting and talking to the constituents. In acknowledgement of both this and the fact that it was almost certain to be raining on polling day, John sent out his final communication, reminding voters of why they should support his candidate and urging them to turn out and vote, in the form of a leaflet that could be turned into a paper hat. Alongside his final, obvious messages were instructions for folding and cutting the paper so that it could become a humorous defence against the downpour. It was the final wiggle in what proved to be a successful campaign.

ACTIVITY!

Select three stories that were newsworthy this week.

Identify what made them wiggle.

We can share our story and so influence conversations through the use of any, or all, of the following channels:

- free and bought media;
- events;
- written communications that we create;
- third party endorsements;
- conversations.

Media

Here, too, there is a range of possibilities. We might aim to engage the national press, the regional and local press, or online media. We might choose free media or bought media. We can, of course, use any combination. Free media includes newspapers, television and radio reporting, and the ever-increasing number of bloggers. Bought media is advertising in all its various forms. It is easy to think that the essential difference between the two is that we have to pay for one and not the other. However, in one sense, this is not strictly true. Even when using 'free' media, people have to make the stories happen; the stories have to be created, managed and shared. There has to be an investment of time, skill and energy. There is also another type of cost associated with the use of all free media and it is this:

> Whenever we use free media there comes a point, no matter how well we have structured, sequenced, timed and packaged our activity, when we lose control over how it is presented and reported.

When we engage the free media we have to accept the fact that we stop being the editor of our own story or the director of our own film. The final word and, therefore, the messages the audience receives, lies with the person in charge of that particular media outlet. It is for this reason that we have to understand both their agenda and their schedules and do everything in our power to present our activity to them in a way that limits the number of changes they might make.

The starting point is to know:

- which media you need to use and why;
- how to ensure that the activity is newsworthy.

The former is based on an understanding of the media preferences of your audience and the attitudes and agenda of the media available to you. The latter is achieved by getting the timing of the activity right and by creating some noteworthy wiggle and/or ensuring strong content.

Choosing the most appropriate media outlets is essential. There is little point trying to attract the attention of programmes or publications unless your activity and associated messaging is clearly something they will be interested in. Equally, there is no point having your activity reported through a channel that few of your audience access.

Timing activities to ensure maximum media coverage and impact involves:

- accurately calculating the planning and lead-in times for the activity itself;
- understanding and working around the production, publication, or filming schedules of the media outlets chosen;
- knowing how to make the activity newsworthy.

Understanding how to work within media schedules and to how provide good media copy is one essential part of this.[3]

Gerd Leipold made this point clearly when talking with AB. He then went on to explain the ground-breaking ways Greenpeace created images with wiggle. He said:

---

[3] This is only relevant, obviously, to those campaigns that need media coverage. Many of our personal campaigns, for example buying a house, probably won't.

Greenpeace creating images with wiggle

When it comes to certain types of campaigning the media play an important role. When people think of Greenpeace they don't think of books or of slogans they think of images and again that is now much more prevalent than it was 30–40 years ago. Because we were so mindful of the media and gave importance to it, we spent much more money on communications and technology compared to other organizations. Greenpeace was one of the first organizations, if not the first, who could transmit images from ships via satellite. We were the first to send video from it. The expense we went to would have shocked other organizations, but it was important that we got our message out.

You have to be acutely aware how important timing is in that respect. We were, and are, acutely aware that if you do the action at 5pm you are unlikely to make the evening news, so you have to time it with a view to the media.

We had one camera person with the skill to film the action whilst also thinking of the news footage we had to create. He did not deliver half an hour of footage. He delivered 3 minutes. It was not a full piece, but it had 40 seconds of the action itself and typically 40 seconds of action is more exciting than 10 minutes, because it's difficult to keep 10 minutes interesting. So we would pick the images with great care and we would combine them with a few key interviews and, maybe, a one-minute background piece.

I should say that there were three key elements that were typical of Greenpeace. Firstly, we were very conscious of the role of the media. Secondly, that you do symbolic actions. And you do the symbolic actions on the spot, but you do them also with a view of reaching a much larger audience. Thirdly, we recognized how important visual communication is.

Just because an activity takes place it does not mean that it is automatically newsworthy, and just because we have managed to make it newsworthy does not mean that it will automatically gain and then keep the attention of our audience. There are myriad stories reported in the news every day. Every audience member views them armed with their emotional remote control, ready to ignore them at first glance if the headline, or the lead image, or the topic, or the language does not appeal. They are equally ready to move on to the next story as soon as their interest wanes. This, again, is another reason why our activities need to be well prepared and delivered, and fully integrated, playing their part in grabbing the audience's attention, sharing something memorable and so influencing their subsequent conversations, whilst also preparing the way for the activity that is to follow.

> Being in the media does not guarantee that your target audience will see it.

Events

Events, like every other type of activity, range in scope, size and nature. They can include:

- meetings,
- speeches,
- question and answer sessions,
- launches,
- dinners,
- photo opportunities,
- conferences.

They are, like every other type of activity, vehicles for delivering the narrative and developing momentum and/or gathering insights into audience needs and attitudes. AB stresses the point continually that:

'An event is not a campaign!'

The question he asks when planning every event is:

'And then what?'

Event planning and management is just one more example of the need to combine big picture planning with attention to detail. Whilst the event itself has to be well organized, run smoothly and achieve the desired outcomes, it also has to play its part in progressing the overall campaign. Every event has to be a success in its own right and act as a stepping-stone to the next activity, the next part of the story, the building of momentum. The value of an event, as with every other type of activity, lies in the degree to which it helps to motivate and mobilize the audience. The question AB seeks to answer whenever organizing an event is,

'What do we do to ensure that those who attend go back and influence conversations on our behalf?

In order to achieve this, the event needs to be memorable, there needs to be a reason, or reasons, why the participants continue to think of it amidst the many constant and changing stories that make up their lives. AB will often provide a memento of the event, something that can only be associated with and will, therefore, always remind the participant of their experience.

This deliberate creation of associations in the minds of the audience is, in one sense, the very purpose of campaigning. Everything we do should remind people of the benefits of actively supporting us and, by extension, of the reasons why they should not support our opposition. In the face of apathy or opposition we are obliged to become involved in a form of comparative campaigning. Whenever people hear about, or engage with, any of our activities, whenever they hear any part of our narrative or recognize one of our messages, whenever they see or are reminded of any of the people involved in our campaign, they should associate that automatically with the positive value we offer and by doing so they should be reminded of the inappropriateness of the other options available.

As human beings we make sense of our world and develop a feeling of personal power and control through our ability to create meanings out of our experiences. The human brain is hard-wired to create neurological pathways that establish associations between experiences, objects and people and what they mean to us. Sometimes these associations are positive and sometimes they are negative. Hopefully we all have, for example, experiences, places or people that make us smile and feel good whenever we think of them, visit, or meet them. Sadly, we might also have those that create the opposite effect.

It is partly because of our brain's innate capability to create associations and establish meaning that we talked earlier about the inevitability of influence. If we exist we cannot be ignored. We cannot be ignored because at the very heart of peoples' ability to function effectively, to make decisions, to create relationships, to solve problems, is the need to establish, at least to their own satisfaction, what everything means. And once a particular meaning or association has been made, the likelihood is that possible alternatives will be ignored in favour of interpretations that support and reinforce the accepted perspective.

This basic and important fact reinforces yet again the significant relationship that exists between micro- and macro-communication skills. People will create associations, either positive or negative, with campaigns and the narrative they tell as naturally as they do with individuals. The power of associations in directing peoples' attitudes and behaviours, and the need to be able to create and manage these well, is as relevant in intrapersonal and interpersonal communication as it is in campaigning to much larger audiences. And, of course, throughout a campaign there will be many occasions when all involved will need to exercise their skills in intrapersonal and interpersonal communication to create or reinforce the desired associations.

So, from the very first moment that we make our audience aware of our campaign we are effectively encouraging them to determine the meanings they place on both us and on our opposition. Through the activities we create our aim is to define ourself, those who oppose us and the context within which we are all operating in ways that highlight, demonstrate and justify our right to be given permission. Stories have always played a vital role in helping and encouraging people to recognize, categorize and define. They have been used to promote values, solve problems, justify behaviours and create context. Cultures of all kinds, national, local and corporate, are based on shared and accepted stories. The campaign narrative and associated activities are the mechanisms by which we define, explain, justify and persuade. It is how, one way or the other, we create associations.

Once people are aware of our existence, they have to associate us with something and, once they do, they are unlikely to change their minds easily. Our task, then, is to ensure that enough of them make the positive associations and develop the understanding we desire, and so come to the conclusion that we are seeking to establish.

Sometimes events create their own cluster of activities around them. For example, a simple coffee morning requires advertising, which then also serves to remind the audience of the campaign. When organizing a coffee morning as part of an election campaign, AB would send letters of invitation to 2,000 people. Although only perhaps

50 of those would attend, he would then send a subsequent letter to all 2,000 informing them of the outcomes of the event. Thus one relatively small event created a reason for two different communications with a much larger audience that served to remind, reinforce and repeat the benefits of the campaign.

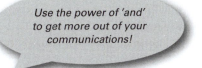

Use the power of 'and' to get more out of your communications!

AB's use of his *'And then what?'* question is a great example of the creative power of the word *'and'*, and the role it can play in creating a cohesive, interlinking sequence of communications. The question challenges everyone involved to build off the event, to use this one activity to add value to the campaign in as many ways as possible. Just as the use of the word *'and'* creates a dialogue, so, too, it creates value around and through every event.

LEARNING POINTS

- Activities need to be 'on message', memorable, timely and appropriately sequenced.
- Create activities that wiggle.
- Whenever you use free media you lose control over how your activity is presented and packaged.
- Free media rarely comes at no cost.
- Always explore how you can get more value from a single event.
- Make events memorable.
- Create positive association for your audience.

Written communications that we create

No matter what variety of events we create or media we use, all communication and, therefore, all influence, is ultimately the result of words, images, sounds or action. When all is said and done, there is no other way to exchange. It is all said or done. Written communications are an essential part of most campaigns and can be powerful sources of influence. They include:

- leaflets,
- flyers,
- letters,
- posters,

- newsletters,
- blogs,
- emails,
- text messages.

The primary difference between written and verbal communication is that the written word lacks the adaptability of the spoken word. Whilst written words can be edited during the writing process, once they are presented to the audience they are fixed. This means that the written word is unchanging and has only one chance to share your message successfully. Having said that, we do usually have time to craft the written word very deliberately and, when writing, are rarely engaged in the immediacy of conversation.

Key principles to follow when writing influential communications include:

- Know what role you are playing and what style best reflects this before you begin writing.
- Have clear desired outcomes.
- Avoid complex writing styles and structures.
- Remember the impact of the visual nature of the written word.
- Use the most appropriate organizational patterns.
- Edit your work based on the above.

Know your role and what style best reflects this

Your role and the style you use are determined to a great extent by your desired end outcomes, the language preferences and expectations of the audience and the nature of the overall campaign. Sometimes it is important that the writer of the communications is clearly identified to the audience. This is achieved at least as much through the writing style used and the deliberate creation of a 'voice' as it is through the inclusion of a name, a signature, or a photo. An understanding of the audience enables the writer to match shared experiences, concerns or goals, and common interests or aspirations, as well as linguistic preferences and habits and preferred decision-making and motivational strategies.

Unless the nature of your communication absolutely prohibits it, write in appropriate multi-sensory language that makes it easy for your readers to visualize situations that reflect your content, and that stirs their instinctive emotional response. Share your messages in an evocative way, supporting them with powerful examples, using specific, detailed language to prove your points and being artfully vague only when you are absolutely sure that the majority of your readers will fill in the gaps in the ways that you require them to.

Underpinning all of the above is the need to think of your audience as *people*. And, just like everyone else, they have needs, wants, likes, hopes and fears and will automatically seek to interpret the meanings of your communication through the blinkers of these perceptions. Given that, every piece of written communication needs to play its part in the integrated delivery of the narrative and in the achievement of the desired end outcome.

Avoid complex writing styles and structures

The Japanese have a phrase, *Bunbu Itchi*, which refers to the power of *the pen and sword in accord*. Most modern day campaigners do not carry a sword, nor would they want to. However, if you tell a story, share information, or deliver a message simply and clearly, words can have a power that a sword cannot. Words can cut through assumptions, ideas, even the perceived reality of everyday life. Complex writing styles and structures, however, lack that edge. Communication is a process of exchange that also directs peoples' attention. Once the reader focuses on the complexity of the writing style or structure, rather than on the story being told, their attention has been misdirected.

Remember the impact of the visual nature of the written word

Readers see documents, leaflets, letters, flyers and all other forms of written communication before they actually read them. The presentation, structure and style, sometimes even the *feel*, of the communication all reflect the nature and tone of your content and the values you stand for. Readers draw meanings from the visual impact of the written word just as they do from the actual words themselves.

Factors that determine the way the written words looks include:

- font type and size;
- the type of paper, its feel and weight;
- the pictures, images and colour schemes used;
- heading and sub-headings, their placement and the language used;
- the size of the document;
- the type of a cover or binding.

We support our verbal communication through the body language we use and the personal image we present. The aim being to create a congruency between what we are saying and the way we look when saying it. In just the same way, we need to remember that written communications inevitably create a visual impact that influences the state of the reader even before they turn their attention to the words in front of them. This is as true for an email as it for a campaign letter that is received through the letterbox. It is as true for a CV as it is for a poster in a window. How we dress reflects our mood, value and sense of self-identity. It reflects our role, purpose and, sometimes, even the expectations of others. We have to be clear whether our written communications need to be sent out dressed in jeans and a t-shirt or a business suit.

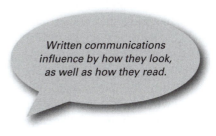

Written communications influence by how they look, as well as how they read.

Use the most appropriate organizational patterns

Whatever dress code you choose for your written communications, do also determine the most appropriate ways to order, organize and deliver your content. These patterns will be determined to a large extent by the nature of the role you are playing and the needs of your audience. Examples of organizational patterns include:

- **Concept, structure, use.** Much information sharing incorporates these three elements and many people have developed a subconscious preference for the order in which they are presented. CP is writing this and you might be able to guess his preference?[4]

  As we discussed in Chapter 5, Influencing conversations, the key here is to match the preference of the person we are seeking to influence. If you know that someone prefers to be told how something works and the value it offers before they are told how it is structured and the concepts and principles that underpin it, then meet their need and share the information that way. In written communications to more than one person incorporate a range of styles and preferences.

- **Sharing the big picture.** Ask yourself, 'Is it necessary in this communication to share the entirety of the situation with the readers?' If so, consider if there are obvious categories of information you can present sequentially to help define, explain and build the big picture. The basic premise is always to seek to simplify complexity without ever being patronizing or so simplistic that key information is withheld. We have to balance this with the awareness that a complex argument, explanation or justification risks being switched off by an audience with myriad, simpler stories demanding their attention.

- **Presenting small units of information.** Following on from the above, we can divide a mass of information into smaller, inter-related chunks. To do this, begin by considering to what extent the information can be:
  - classified/categorized;
  - compared or contrasted;
  - defined;
  - clarified through the use of analogy;
  - discussed within a cause and effect relationship.

  The primary benefit of breaking large amounts of information into smaller chunks is that it makes it easier for the audience to assimilate and remember. The examples offered above appeal because they support our desire to create meanings and manage complexity. Creating categories, for example, is a form of generalizing, whilst identifying cause and effect is to establish a pattern.

- **Sequencing your information.** When the sequence of events is a crucial factor in helping the reader to understand the situation, use it to help you structure your document. As Katy's letter to her parents reinforced, the manner in which you sequence information influences the nature of the conclusions others draw and, therefore, the responses you get.

- **The 5 Ws.** These are: What? When? Where? Who? Why? By identifying the relevant 5W questions you need to answer you can ensure that your content is appropriately detailed and sequenced and that you meet the

---

[4] It is the order in which it is written. CP only ever thinks of, or talks about, these three in this order. So, if you ever need to share information with him that incorporates these elements, just do it this way for maximum effect.

decision-making tendencies of your audience. When considering the latter you might, for example, ask yourself the following:

- What information will be most important to my reader?
- What are their sensory preferences?
- What timeframes will they apply?
- When is the best time to give them my written communication?
- What do I want them to do or understand as a result of this document?
- When are they likely to make their decision?
- Where are they likely to look for confirmation or a second opinion?
- Where can I direct them?
- Why will they be interested?
- Why do they need to be involved?
- Who influences them?
- Who can I refer to in my document to strengthen my case?

Edit your work

In the same way that it is easy, tempting and, possibly, natural, to fall in love with our own plan, so it is easy to be attracted to our written work. To edit effectively it is necessary to let go of any emotional attachment and to adopt a distanced, clinical, approach. Professional writers have editors who help enormously with this process, however as campaigners we might need to do this ourself and/or with the assistance of other members of the team. The challenge for all involved is to create a working state that demonstrates the same level of emotional intelligence as we discussed earlier in the book. This state can be thought of as, 'third position'.

As a writer there are three positions we operate from. These are:

1 **Yourself.** This includes your role, purpose, and skills as a writer.
2 **Your audience.** This includes understanding their needs, expectations, experiences and concerns.
3 **Third position.** This is the emotional state removed from the previous two, from which the writer evaluates how fully the work has met its purpose.

To help create this emotional shift you might consider using any, or all, of the following:

- editing in a different environment from that in which you wrote;
- delaying the editing process at least overnight and for several days if the campaign schedule allows it;
- using critical friends to evaluate the work against agreed, specific criteria;
- justifying every aspect of the work in a Q & A session with members of the campaign team.

Before undertaking the last option do ensure that, from third position, you have checked spelling and grammar and evaluated how well you have:

- Identified yourself, and your role, and established your 'voice'.
- Presented the communication.
- Used a simple, clear structure and style.
- Shown the big picture.

- Shared all relevant details.
- Used organizational patterns.
- Appealed to their decision-making and motivational tendencies.
- Used specific and artfully vague language.

Remember also that, if you are sharing work with the team, someone ultimately has to take responsibility and be the decision-maker.

As a final point about editing, do leave the editorial third position behind fully if and when you begin to rewrite parts of the communication. Intensity, passion, focus and a state of flow are qualities of the writing state. The editor is more removed and dispassionate. Sometimes writers and creators struggle to edit their own work effectively and sometimes editors cannot write creatively. The key, as with all the other skills and attributes needed, is to ensure that the most effective mixture exists within the campaign team.

LEARNING POINTS

- The written word lacks the adaptability of the spoken word.
- Every written communication has to play its part in progressing the integrated delivery of the narrative.
- People see written communications before they read them.
- Use appropriate organizational patterns.
- Edit from third position.

ACTIVITY!

Choose any three examples of written communications. You might, for example, select an email, a magazine advert, and a newspaper article.
   Evaluate their effectiveness in terms of:

- their visual impact;
- language style and use;
- clarity of purpose.

Third party endorsements

Gaining endorsements from others who are known and trusted by the audience we are targeting is a powerful way to develop support. The primary requirements when seeking third party endorsements are:

- They are people our audience will respond to positively.
- Their authority to comment is clear.
- They have something interesting and relevant to say.
- They have no history, associations, or views that will undermine the campaign narrative.
- Their involvement will add strength to our campaign.
- We are please to be associated with them.

Essentially, when gaining third party endorsements we are adding a part of someone else's brand to ours. And they, in turn, are probably adding a part of us to them. There needs to be a synergy therefore between the respective brand values. There might also be a need for some form of trade-off to be agreed in order to gain this support. Whilst some people might give their support without expecting anything in return, the likelihood is that those who choose to endorse our campaign do so because it suits their own agenda in some way. Given that, we can often expect to be asked to offer something in return. And we also need to be aware that, as with free media, we lose some control over our message delivery by handing part of it over to somebody else.

An alliance is a form of third party endorsement that almost certainly necessitates some degree of trade-off. Sometimes unlikely partnerships are formed in pursuit of a common cause. These relationships, whilst adding power to the overall campaign, also add to the complexity of managing the internal relationships within the campaign team. The precise nature of the alliance, the degree to which the partners work together, and the manner in which they create and share their public image, has to be agreed and managed in a mutually beneficial way. It can be as important to demonstrate some ideological distance over some issues as it is to show agreement over the campaign cause. Creating an alliance is just one more example of the many balancing acts that have to be managed throughout a campaign.

> Ensure there is synergy between yourself and any third party endorser.

Conversations

As we discussed in Chapter 5 the overall success of a campaign is determined by the degree to which it influences conversations in the desired manner. No matter what communication tool or channel we use, or what part of the narrative or message we are seeking to share, the eventual purpose of every activity is to lead people into talking and thinking about our story. And to keep them doing so. We integrate activities throughout the duration of the campaign in order to tell a cohesive story in ways that are persuasive and engaging. An activity that becomes newsworthy is new and worthy in the eyes of the media for only a limited period of time. Even the most originally shocking, exciting, inspiring or surprising event ceases to be new and, therefore, worthy of significant, ongoing media coverage as soon as the audience becomes used to it and other stories push their way to the fore. One extreme event can change the world forever. However, even that will not be forever newsworthy on a daily basis. Inevitably, it will become part of *what is* and *how things are* and, therefore, no longer new.

When John Braggins made reference to the tale of Little Red Riding Hood in Chapter 4, he was reminding us of a very old story. You probably know it. For many of us it is a part of our literary culture. It is unlikely, however, that you had thought about it, let alone had a conversation about it, recently. It is an old story that is currently not news. People tend to have conversations about what is current in their world. We do this partly because the news media focuses only on that which is new and, in their opinion, worthy of reporting. Given this, the word *newsworthy* provides both an instruction and a reminder about the two things we have to ensure we create with our activities. They have to be new and they have to be worthy of media attention. The BBC will never run a news programme called 'The 6 O'Clock Olds'.

In our modern world, stories become old surprisingly quickly. Which is why we have to keep sharing our narrative and repeating and reinforcing the key messages whilst creating as much wiggle as we can. We have to make our story 'new' every day if we are to have any chance of our audience talking about it repeatedly. We can only do this through a series of integrated activities that are in some way new and, according to others, worth giving their attention to.

Planning, unpredictability and trade-offs

Influencing conversations through newsworthy activities requires specificity of planning and application on every level and in every aspect. Later in this chapter we will show you how to construct and use a campaign grid and a range of associated schematics and charts to record and orchestrate your activities. Even using this detailed approach, however, we cannot hope to control everything that happens throughout the duration of our campaign.

Our plan is simply the best way forward today. Tomorrow something might happen within the context of our campaign, or, indeed, beyond it, that is of such significance that we have to adapt. Our activities are never the only ones taking place. When the context changes, we must be capable of changing with it if it is necessary to do so. One of the great challenges, as we have mentioned before, is to be totally committed to the implementation of the plan, whilst being willing and ready to adapt it whenever changing circumstances require us to.

Sometimes we might find ourselves facing an unexpected threat or an opportunity that simply has to be addressed. Sometimes an unconnected event of such magnitude occurs that the vast majority of people turn their attention to it and every other story is lost in its shadow for a period of time. Sometimes, changes in the environment mean that we have to make changes to the nature of our desired end outcome.

AB regards trade-offs as an inevitable part of many campaigns. He acknowledges that they can be the result of unexpected changes in the environment just as they can be the outcome of negotiations with third party endorsers and partners, or even opponents or the ultimate target audience. The chaos of our modern world with so many different stories being presented, so many different agendas being proposed and so many different choices on offer, is made even more chaotic by the number of random, unexpected events that affect us on an individual, social and, sometimes, even a global level. Every campaign attempts to create and maintain a pathway of order through this complexity and confusion.

There can be no absolute guarantee of success because there are too many variables beyond our control. It is precisely because of this complexity and unpredictability that we need to turn our rough campaign map into a detailed and up-to-date plan. We then need to have mechanisms for managing, monitoring and developing that plan.

Campaigns aim to shape the future. The extent to which they are successful is determined largely by the ability and willingness of the campaign team to apply a detailed approach throughout. And by the way they respond to unpredictability. Amongst the different tools that AB uses to ensure detail, cohesion, progression and the flexibility to adapt quickly are:

- the campaign narrative over time;
- the campaign grid;
- the media story planner;
- the target individual plan.

The campaign narrative over time

For AB, this is the first part of the detailed planning process. The aim is to determine the most influential ways to layer the narrative and associated key themes throughout the duration of the campaign. Whilst the goal is to share the entire narrative as quickly as possible the speed with which this can be done, and the time it will it take, is determined primarily by the complexity of the story and the nature and availability of the most effective communication channels. In campaigning, as in all things, speed is a relative term. It is important to realize that, although some narratives can be told in only a handful of communications, others will take far more. Quality and completeness of delivery must always take precedence over speed.

Layering the narrative, however, requires far more than simply telling the story once. Layering refers to the ways and number of times the key themes and messages, the essential concepts and sometimes even the entire narrative itself are repeated and reinforced in the days, weeks, months or years leading up to polling day. Layering the campaign narrative over time is dependent upon an understanding of the audience's starting position, a good sense of storytelling and, as ever, the ability to acquire and then respond to feedback. It requires the layers to be sequenced for best effect and for each layer to be rich with purpose. It is through the layering of the narrative that an audience develops an understanding of your cause and the benefits you offer. It is the process by which influence is achieved. Again, reverse planning is used to ensure that no details are missed and that all available time is used fully.

The example of a campaign narrative over time shown on the following pages is an early draft of a story sequence that AB produced for his work when he was advising the mobile phone company Three on their campaign to Terminate the Rate. This story sequence went through many subsequent iterations before the campaign was launched.

The story development, week-by-week

Week	w/c	Main story of the week
Pre launch		Planning and early briefings
1		Launch: a) Big Picture – What it's all about – 10x fixed to mobile than mobile to fixed b) BT + Three leading a wide campaign with partners c) We're asking people to help us and tell everyone how unfair it is, and for other orgs to join us too
2		Explain MTRs and that they are outdated now
3		Highlight cost of MTRs to us all: £900 million. Use pen pics of example phone users. Show how much each typology of user benefits with MTRs at a fair rate; link to credit crunch.
4		Ofcom's remit is to be on the side of the consumer. They're looking into this issue right now. Help us – tell others and tell Ofcom (others actions too).
5		Benefits to us all as phone users if MTRs set at equal level for all: Three all you can eat tariff BT tbc.
6		a) Announce new partners. b) Invite other mobile operators to join.
7		Highlight cost of MTRs to business. Show how those costs are passed on to us or eg may mean the difference between redundancy for staff or not; link to credit crunch. Make use of business partners.
8		Highlight cost of MTRs to third sector. Show alternative uses of that money for the people helped by charities and volorgs etc. Make use of third sector partners.
9		a) Announce new partners. b) Invite other mobile operators to join.

Week	w/c	Main story of the week
10		Highlight cost of MTRs to public sector and thus all of us through the taxes we pay. Show alternative uses of that money; link to credit crunch. Make use of public sector partners.
11		We can change it (reminder and explanation of what individuals and organizations can do).
12		Short campaign – Mobilize and action. Sign up to Terminate the Rate.
13		Short campaign – Mobilize and action. Tell Ofcom you care and pass it on to others as well.
14		Campaign finale.

ACTIVITY!

Plan and create your campaign narrative over time.

Once the campaign narrative over time is complete, the campaign grid can be created.

The campaign grid

AB sometimes refers to the grid as the 'campaign-wide web' because it contains, reflects and drives everything that happens throughout the campaign. He says:

'The grid is as much a concept as a tool – nothing is real on it until we invent and create it. The grid is a kind of web around which the campaign is woven.'

The grid is the embodiment of the plan. It is a day-by-day, week-by-week planning tool. It allows campaigners to structure, schedule, coordinate and integrate all aspects of their communication.

AB uses reverse planning to draw up the grid. He devises a different style of grid for each new campaign. They all tend to have time (ie dates and weeks) along the top and the various channels of communication available to the campaign down the side. And they will all incorporate an overt reference to the message, narrative and story sequence.

At the start of a 12-month long campaign, for example, AB's first grid would provide detail for all the events and associated timings, stories and messages for the first two weeks, whilst also identifying the person or people responsible for ensuring the delivery of each event. As the first week progresses this level of detail will move forwards into week three and so on. Beyond this, the grid will show what is planned for the first three–four months on a day-by-day basis, with a single page showing the plan for each week. It is important to note that AB plans for a seven-day campaigning week if the campaign calls for it. The next four months will be shown in less detail with one page reflecting what is planned for each month. The final months will be written only as a series of rough notes.

Over time these will turn into the detail required to enable the campaign to gain its full momentum as it closes in on polling day. The content in the grid, the planned sequencing of activities and increasing pace coupled with clear personal responsibilities, shows how the campaign team is working to build momentum in the final days and weeks before polling day. In the same way that a runner aims for a sprint finish, so a campaign team gains momentum as it closes in on the finishing line.

AB worked out the plan for the final five days of The Labour Party's 1997 General Election campaign. In the following story he provides a brief overview of the changes and range of integrated activities used during that time to gain momentum and mobilize the audience. He also reinforces the importance of scenario planning and the need for adaptability.

Lollipops, ponchos and a dynamic change of pace

With only five days to go before the polling day on 1 May 1997, the Labour campaign team knew that we had won the battle of the arguments. We also knew that we needed to keep and ideally increase the attention and support of the voters and, most importantly, encourage them to act on 1 May. To be sure of doing this we needed some newness, some extra energy, some clear, positive and very public ways of gaining momentum.

I began thinking about what we ought to do in those last five days some 10 months before, during the summer and early autumn of 1996. You always have to imagine certain possible scenarios and base your planning around these. I thought to myself, 'If we are in a really strong position at the start of the final week, how do we make the best use of it?' At that point I wasn't thinking that we were certain to win, only that I, like everyone else involved, was going to do everything I could to make it happen.

Early in 1997, when I had developed my plan sufficiently I shared it with Peter Mandelson. Although there was an agreement that it would work well, there was also a shared acceptance of the fact that it would only work if the conditions were right. And if the situation in the country leading into that final week had been different we certainly wouldn't have used it. As with every other type of campaign the people you are seeking permission from, in our case the voting public, are the guide. You always have to be close enough to listen to what your audience is telling you.

Thankfully, they were telling us that we were winning the arguments convincingly. We were convinced that if everyone voted we would win by a country mile. So now we had to increase our momentum, reinforce our messages in new, motivational ways, and encourage them to the polls. Even though General Elections are inevitably regarded as newsworthy, there is still always the need to be more newsworthy than your opposition and in ways that resonate powerfully and well with your supporters – both within the external audience and within the campaign itself.

So I introduced a significant number of changes and layers to our storytelling. During our by-election campaigning, John Braggins and myself had developed a way of demonstrating increased momentum by changing the visual media we used. I used this approach again. Lord Snowdon took an iconic photo of Tony Blair which we used widely on the campaign. I changed the colours on all the literature we used from red and yellow to red and purple. Most importantly, I supported this with a change of slogan. Throughout the campaign the slogan had been, 'Britain deserves better'. The new slogan read, 'Now vote because we deserve better'. I wanted to make it personal and encourage both the growing feeling of unity and the need to take action.

I prepared and distributed a range of our newly coloured media to over 90 of the most targeted seats. We had new billboards, sharing our slogan and the picture of Tony Blair. There were new window posters for homes and corex boards that could be placed on the street or on walls. The Tony Blair campaign bus always travelled in convoy with two other buses filled with journalists. The outside of all three buses was redecorated in our new design and colour scheme. And the journalists turned this into a news story! Talking of the journalists, I had blackcurrant and strawberry lollipops made for them with the words, 'Now vote, we deserve better' written on them.

I even had rain ponchos produced in the new colours with the slogan on for our local organizers and volunteers. I must admit, I wasn't really expecting them to be worn. I was using them to make a really serious point to those organizers and volunteers. And it was simply this, 'Even if it rains, we are not going to stop now. Nothing is going to prevent us from increasing our momentum.' And nothing did. Yet, wonderfully, on the Saturday that we launched the last five days it rained like mad and the rain ponchos were all used. The journalists had yet another story to write about the attention to detail of our campaign and the inevitability of our victory.

Beyond all the above, and of far more importance than the colour change, was the way I wanted to make every second count and to convey the sense that we cared about every voter. Tony Blair carried out three or four visits every day of those last five, meeting crowds of supporters in different parts of the country. The journalists were chasing just to keep up. Of everything I introduced for that week, this was the most physical and powerful sign of the increased pace we were setting as we approached polling day.

The grid demands a commitment of compliance from all in the campaign team. The grid can be as simple or as complex as is needed. It changes in the light of new information, ideas and feedback. Yet, despite its organic nature, the grid always shows precisely what we are going to do and are intending to do right now. AB states that there is 'Nowhere to hide' once the grid has been agreed. The operating principle is simple and powerful:

Until we know better, we do precisely what it says on the grid.

Two examples of a working grid are over leaf.

This grid for discussion – contains ideas only. Nothing agreed or signed off. This version last updated by AB 18/11.

Week 1 26/1 – 1/2	Story – Launch week a) Big Picture – What's it all about? b) Three is leading a wide campaign with partners					
	Mon 26th	Tues 27th	Weds 28th	Thurs 29th	Fri 30th	Weekend
PR – 3MC, GM, SP News – N Consumer – C Financial – F Trade – T **Events and Stunts**		Media event with 3rd parties A new kind of future, big picture, use overall costs, no price plan info Photo-op to support launch				Profile piece of KR??? Breaking the power of the big 4, David v Goliath, on behalf of the consumer
Regulatory/ third parties – GM, HD, JM Briefings Endorsements Speeches	Campaign flagged on Randalls/e-politix? Letters to MPs and MEPs introducing campaign + 3 Brief	Contact key political bloggers about campaign	Campaign flagged on APPG communication?	Position paper – the move to data-based pricing rather than time-based – *who is drafting?*	Post briefing pack on Terminate the Rate to MPs relevant Peers and MEPs	
Customer Management – RD				Promo graphics for Three.co.uk, Planet 3, My 3, landing page + microsite + text-yr-support		

Retail – TM	Feb Sales & Ops Pack includes TTR details	Portal overhaul and receipt messaging		Receipt wallets, Staff badges, Induction pack, Plasmas, Till point screen saver, Till receipt message, MTR button		
Call Centre – AM, JB		IVR 20 second announcement re launch				
ATL – AD			Tactical ads to drive PR story and support launch			
Online – AR, CM Three website TTR website Blogs Viral		Update 3.co.uk + Planet 3.org site hard launch iframes on first sponsors' sites.	Factual sites undated with launch info			
Internal – HD	Wall space in reception goes live – HD	Employee e-mail signatures re MTRs goes live – HD	Staff Briefing – HD			
Other Events		TelecomFinance conference London – Christian Salbaing speaking				
Decisions Reqd						

This grid for discussion – contains ideas only. Nothing agreed or signed off. This version last updated by AB 18/11.

Week 4 16/2 – 22/2	Story – The 3 future: a) Three's offer if there were no MTRs (tariffs and handsets) b) Three's Cast-iron Guarantees					
	Mon 16th	**Tues 17th**	**Weds 18th**	**Thurs 19th**	**Fri 20th**	**Weekend**
PR – 3MC, GM, SP News – N Consumer – C Financial – F Trade – T **Events and Stunts**	Press conference set in the future – as if MTRs scrapped – Three announce new price plans and offers – £25 'all you can eat' Three's cast-iron guarantees - No RPP – ever - Best network (from 2010) - Latest 3G handsets incl. in the £25 tariff - Low-user options	Postcard to journos – 'look at the phone and package you could get if we terminate the rate'	T – Media briefing – Three is developing new handsets to take advantage of 3G technology better, handsets will be cutting edge and incl. in the £25 all-inclusive tariff	T – Refresh story re Three's new network roll-out during 2009 – the deal with T Mobile		N – Letter to eg Times from Industry experts, or academics possibly – 'MTRs are outdated and are holding the UK back – they're stopping us from having a new mobile broadband future' N – Release academic research for the Sundays

Regulatory/third parties – GM, HD, JM Briefings Endorsements Speeches	Start preparations for Special Edition of 3 Brief	EU – Roaming Consideration of amendments made to IMCO & ITRE	Postcard to all Cabinet ministers – 'look at the phone and package you could get if we terminate the rate' Poss. over sized postcard to No 10?			
Customer Management – RD						E-newsletter
Retail – TM			MMS to retail team	MMS to retail team		
Call Centre – AM, JB						
ATL – AD						
Online – AR, CM Three website TTR website Blogs Viral	Update .org blog with Three's Cast-iron Guarantees + Three's offer					
Internal – HD						
Other Events	Mobile Challengers group to hold media event at GSMA World Congress					
Decisions Reqd						

Essentially, then, the grid provides a day-by-day overview of every activity that takes place, of the communications channels being used and the message and/or part of the narrative that is being shared at any given time. The grid is at the heart of the delivery of the campaign. It is the way the campaign team leader and team:

- Make sure that what is planned for today and tomorrow and the rest of the week is actually happening.
- Look to the short-term (next week).
- Keep their eyes on the medium-term (3–4 weeks ahead).
- Keep the longer term (the rest of the campaign) in perspective.

When using the grid to manage political campaigns AB held daily grid meetings. It was, he explains, a necessity because of the extremely fast moving nature of the campaigns. In the corporate and social worlds he has found that weekly meetings are usually sufficient and that sometimes one meeting every two weeks will suffice.

On a practical note, he advises addressing the grid contents in a different order at every meeting. Beginning always with the first line and working your way down brings with it the risk of never discussing the entire grid in the time available, and of ignoring the same details each time. Instead, he recommends beginning each meeting by focusing on a different line each time. This not only guarantees that all parts of the plan will receive attention, it also removes the sense of predictability and so increases the awareness, attention and energy levels of the team.

The two examples of Grids on pages 184–87 are taken from a bigger grid AB produced when he was working with Three on a campaign called 'Terminate the Rate'. They are early drafts with possible ideas for inclusion in the final grid. The grid went through many iterations before the campaign was launched. Note that the first column identifies the person responsible for implementation.

The first step in the formal creation of the grid is the shared agreement of the purpose, or ambition, of the campaign, the identification of the audience and creation of the messages that are to be shared.

ACTIVITY!

Remind yourself of your campaign ambition and the make-up of your audience.
List any messages you believe you will need to share.

There are two points to bear in mind relating to the creation and successful use of the grid. These are:

1 The creation of the grid reflects the non-linear nature of campaign development.

2 The grid needs to be managed well throughout the campaign.

Creating the grid

By the time we begin creating the grid there are lots of things happening. Through our audience analysis we are beginning to understand more about their needs, desires, doubt and fears, and the best communication channels to use to reach them. We are identifying key decision-makers and influencers and are getting a sense of what our audience needs to know, understand and believe in order for them to give us permission. This, in turn, is helping us with the development of the narrative, its sequencing and the associated messages. Our understanding of when and how polling day will be means that we are able to work backwards, week by week, day by day, planning our storytelling, messaging, activities and analysis. As AB says, 'There is a lot bubbling around'. And there needs to be, because the grid is the mechanism through which we bring everything together and plot a course that is deliberate, specific, measurable and manageable.

It takes time and a good deal of careful thinking to establish a detailed grid. The value of this investment in time and energy is that it speeds up the campaign process throughout and increases the chances that the campaign being experienced by the audience is precisely the same as the one being discussed and planned by the campaign team.

Managing the grid

According to John Braggins, the key to the successful adoption of the grid lies in ensuring that at least one person takes responsibility for its implementation and continued use.

He humorously refers to the grid manager and his or her dog-like pet, the campaign grid.

The grid manager

Grids are like dogs, they are great to have around, need feeding and sometimes leaving a mess in the corner.

Getting the concept of a campaign grid agreed by a client can be relatively easy. They can see how it can, and should, be populated by external events already planned, how it acts as a frame to enable them to put in their own internal events and then how it gives the opportunity to create stories, media highlights, press releases, conferences, seminars and all manner of activities to highlight their cause and key messages.

So a grid is great to have around.

The person given the task of managing the grid is often the person who has the skills to edit, colour, insert charts and so on. Inevitably, the cry will go out 'Send all your ideas to populate the grid with events as you plan them and send changes of dates to Holly.'

You see, the grid always needs feeding.

And then it is circulated and the key players look at it and gradually it becomes irrelevant as everyone gets on with their own priorities.

At which point it becomes a bit of a mess in the corner. And the reason is simply because a grid always needs an owner, someone to tickle its tummy and take it for walks.

The grid manager lives and breathes the grid, chases members of the team, checks that everyone and everything is on message, runs the campaign meetings, updates the grid content, demands explanations when events slide, gives praise for successful executions and plans and worries. The grid is the grid manager's living, breathing pet and it will never thrive if left alone.

Whether or not you like to think of the grid as a pet that needs looking after, the simple fact is that for a grid to be of value it has to be acted upon and that means that both it and the people in the campaign team need to be managed. A campaign grid, like a mission statement pinned on a hospital wall, or a commitment to customer service written on a supermarket's website, is worthless if it is not both directing and reflecting the behaviours and attitudes of all involved.[5] The difference between a grid and the other two examples offered is that an essential part of grid management is the willingness to adapt it throughout its lifespan in response to feedback. The grid is a means of progress chasing. It is a method of creating personal responsibility and ensuring that the desired actions are always happening as desired. The campaign team will always follow the grid unless the plan has to be adapted according to feedback. However, that adaptation will then be written up and, once again, every-one will do precisely what it says on the grid.

The grid itself marks repeated transitions from fantasy to reality. There is no fantasy, though, associated with successful management of the grid. This is a rigorous and repetitive requirement. John Braggins' so-called grid manager is the person with the responsibility for updating the grid and organizing a regular meeting at which everyone makes sure they understand what is happening during the period at hand, knows their individual responsibilities within that, and gains at least an overview of the plan for the following week or two. The grid manager ensures that the grid is at the heart of implementing the campaign, that it is current, specific and shared. Updating the grid in the light of feedback and creative input requires a mental flexibility, a willingness to adapt and change, which is another mark of the emotional intelligence needed to be a successful campaigner of communications.

Campaigns and, therefore, campaigners need to combine flexibility, analysis and creativity at the appropriate times and the best way to manage this is to be able to establish some emotional distance from the plan whenever the situation calls for it. This sense of detachment helps create the shift in perspective necessary to consider new information and ideas clearly, free from the blinkers created by the content of the current grid and the understanding and work that has led to that.

There are a number of ways this perspective-shift can be created. Firstly, it is important to remember that the grid is just a working tool, albeit a vital one, and that its purpose is to serve the cause. The grid is not an end in itself. It is created and managed to enable us to achieve our desired end outcome. Secondly, if the team has

---

[5] Actually they are worse than worthless; they are damaging because in each case time has been spent creating a public commitment that is not being honoured.

been built with care, the range of views and the balance of perspectives within it will encourage a sharing of ideas and, often, some lively debates about the best ways forward. This is all well and good, providing that those involved:

- are the most capable individuals for the given topic;
- understand that at some point a decision will be made that might not please everyone;
- know how to challenge and debate appropriately.

Finally, it is vital to spend some time imagining that you are in opposition to your plan and determining from that perspective where your weaknesses lie.

There is no point in gathering feedback from audience analysis without a willingness to act upon it if necessary. Again, the challenge on a personal and team level is to create and maintain a state of 'I love you, I love you not' when considering and managing the campaign plan. What we need to love most, though, is an ever-increasing momentum taking us towards polling day in the manner most likely to ensure success.

> *The grid is built on and grows out of Flexibility, Analysis, Creativity and Timeliness. That is FACT.*

The media story planner

In the *Campaign It!* approach media stories tell a part of the narrative in a newsworthy way. The actual delivery of the campaign, then, is made up of a number of stories delivered through a range of activities. The task essentially is to integrate a story with an activity and then find ways to make this worthy of media coverage. AB begins by asking:

- What is the basic content and point of the story?
- How does it fit into our overall narrative?
- How will we share it and what is the most appropriate event?
- What makes it newsworthy?
- What is the headline we would like to see?

Identifying the desired headline serves three purposes. It:

1 reinforces in the minds of the campaign team the way the particular story fits into the narrative and the message or key theme it is designed to share;

2 creates a higher-level desired outcome than just simply aiming to get media coverage.

3 helps you to consider the story from the perspective of news editors and so meet their needs for a story that has wiggle and is newsworthy.

Once these questions have been answered the rest of the story planning process deals with the practicalities of making the story happen successfully. Every new story must be factually accurate. If it is not, the story will unravel, our credibility will be undermined and our campaing will be damaged. There are a range of project management and planning tools that can be used to assist with this. Gantt charts would be one obvious example.

Decisions have to be made about both the nature of the media to be targeted and any degree of exclusivity that might be offered. Deciding whether or not to use online, national, regional, local, trade, print or digital media or, indeed, any combination of these is determined by their appropriateness for the audience and the campaign's ability to access them. Sometimes it is possible to make a story public through a specific form of media simply to encourage other forms to also run the story. For example, AB has placed stories in regional or even foreign media just so that he could encourage the interest and involvement of national media. This is another example of the need sometimes to take a circuitous route to create influence.

As we have mentioned in this chapter, it is essential that the campaign team are looking continually to add value to each storytelling event by considering what additional activities can be built around it. These value-added activities can happen both before and after the event itself. It is through this approach that the overall campaign looks more like an interconnected spiral, with smaller activities orbiting each main part of the storytelling process, rather than simply a series of individually connected chain links.

An example of a story planner pro forma is shown below.

Story title + Target date for use		Responsibilities and deadline
What's the headline we want?		
Story outline		
What makes it newsworthy		
How it fits to our narrative		
Target media		
Other media inc. regional, local, trade, specialist		
Event/pictures		
Online		
Research and supporting evidence needed		
Endorsements/stakeholders		
Notes/other		

Create your own media story planner, integrating activities with your stories.

The target individual plan

If there are significant individuals who have the power to influence the campaign either positively or negatively, the target individual plan underpins the creation of bespoke strategies for each of them. Analysis of these individuals is based on:

- their personal interests;
- their public statements and viewpoints;
- their aspirations;
- the people or groups who influence them.

Sometimes the purpose is to find ways to match these interests or aspirations, to find ways to gain their support whilst, if necessary, being able to negotiate an acceptable trade-off. Sometimes the purpose is to neutralize, or at least minimize, their effectiveness as opponents.

Whenever an individual bespoke strategy is created it, too, is placed on the grid and comes under the watchful eye of the grid manager.

LEARNING POINTS

- Third party endorsements can be a powerful way to develop audience support.
- The word *newsworthy* reminds us of the two things we need to ensure if our activities are to attract media attention.
- Trade-offs are an inevitable part of most campaigns.
- Use the campaign narrative over time to determine the most influential ways to layer your narrative and key themes throughout the duration of the campaign.
- Develop and manage a detailed and up-to-date campaign grid.
- Do exactly what it says on the grid.

ACTIVITY!

ACTIVITY!

Create your own campaign grid.

The magic of the web

When William Shakespeare wrote in Othello, 'Tis true, there's magic in the web', it is a pretty safe bet that he was not thinking about any form of technology. For us, though, the world wide web has changed the world. Or, at least, our ability to access information, make purchases, entertain ourselves and communicate with others. It has connected all aspects of our lives in a way that was unimaginable not too many decades, let alone centuries, ago. It has made things possible that once would have been thought of as flights of fancy. It is one of the great examples of what was once a fiction becoming such a commonplace part of our everyday existence that we now take it for granted.

The campaign grid is another web that turns fantasy into reality by making connections, drawing details together, connecting every aspect of the campaign in the most influential sequence and style possible. The grid reflects the individual nature and purpose of each campaign. It is, like every web, a bespoke creation based on and incorporating common key principles and content whilst being unique in its own right. It is, like the world wide web, a tool that we need to control and use appropriately. Unlike the world wide web, though, the grid has a limited lifespan. Every grid ends with polling day. In this sense the grid is like the eighteenth camel in our very first story. (Remember that?) The camel was the essential element that had to be introduced to achieve the desired outcome, just as the grid is the essential tool for running our campaign. When it has served its purpose, the grid, like the camel, just disappears with us. We are left only with the outcomes it has helped create and our final thoughts.

Final thoughts

'It's a test of ultimate will
The heartbreak climb uphill
Got to pick up the pace
If you want to stay in the race
More than just blind ambition
More than just simple greed
More than just a finish line
Must feed this burning need'
                    Neil Peart

We began by saying that this book is an introduction to a complex and extremely valuable process. And it is. Each chapter introduces a topic that is worthy of at least one book in its own right. We said that the application of the *Campaign It!* model will improve the way you create influence and that it can be applied to any and all aspects of our personal, professional and social lives. And in our experience, and the experience of those we work with, this is true. All that we have to do is care enough about something – anything! – and we can campaign for it, because we all have the right to.

However, just as Martha Graham said about the theatre, *campaign* is a verb, not a noun. In the opening to Chapter 1 we quoted John Powell when he said,

'Communication works for those who work at it.'

And therein lies the essential truth. To run a complex campaign well over an extended period of time is hard work. To share a narrative, messages and key themes through a deliberate sequence of well-planned, layered and detailed activities requires willpower not just skill. It requires courage and strength of mind and character, not just facts and figures. It requires the stamina to push your way uphill in search of the momentum that lies on the other side. And it requires the creativity, discipline and emotional flexibility needed to control and direct that momentum as you race towards polling day. In short, it requires the emotional compulsion that comes from having a cause.

In a media-rich Western society that makes it ever-more easy for people to gain their 15 minutes of fame, it is seductively easy to forget that we have to earn the right to be heard and, even more so, to be believed and trusted. To communicate effectively, efficiently and ethically and so influence the situations, communities or individuals we care about is one of the great challenges of our modern age and, we believe, one of our greatest responsibilities.

We made the point earlier that we influence others just because we exist. That isn't the entire truth. Our influence outlives us. When all is said and done, the things we have said and done will continue to shape the lives and attitudes of others and, sometimes, the environments they live in long after we have gone. This is our legacy. We might live for the 'here and now' and yet, inevitably, we influence the 'now and then'.

We can choose to campaign our communications in support of the causes that create the emotional power and passion in our life, or we can leave it to chance. At the core of our new paradigm is the belief that whenever you have a story to tell, you need to tell it as well as you possibly can. After all, only the best stories, told brilliantly, get heard and acted upon. And when they are, people gain new perspectives, change their behaviours, even draw new lines in their world because, as the following chapter explains, great stories can replace a question mark of doubt with an exclamation mark of achievement.

08 !

> We only live once, but once is enough if we do it right. Live your life with class, dignity, and style so that an exclamation, rather than a question mark signifies it! GARY RYAN BLAIR

> People often say that motivation doesn't last. Well, neither does bathing – that's why we recommend it daily. ZIG ZIGLAR

The purpose of this chapter is to:

1 Highlight the relationship between influence and motivation.
2 Reinforce the importance of cause in creating an emotional compulsion.
3 Explain the exclamation mark.

In this chapter we:

- Discuss the relationship between influence, motivation and cause.
- Tell the story of one campaign.
- Emphasize the importance of testing throughout the campaign.
- Consider the importance of willpower and determination in the face of apathy or opposition.

E-motion

The campaign narrative is designed and delivered in ways intended to persuade others to take action. Often this is an action they might not have taken had they not been influenced by the narrative. *To campaign* is a verb because someone has to take responsibility for creating and enacting a campaign, and because the campaign exists to encourage the audience to take action also. Novelists, poets, actors and film-makers tell stories just to engage the emotions of their audience for a period of time. Campaigners tell stories to engage and stir the emotions of their audience so that they go into motion. Campaign narratives motivate people and inform them how to act to make a difference, how they can turn their emotion into positive action. The equation looks like this:

Emotion + Direction + Opportunity = Motion

Campaigns aim to be e-motive, to give people a reason to act on their emotions. William James, the American philosopher and psychologist wrote:

'The emotions aren't always subject to reason, but they are always immediately subject to action.'

Great campaigns combine both emotion and reasons. They provide a complete motive for motion. If we are to influence others we have to understand how to motivate them, hence the need for audience analysis and an understanding of motivational traits.

That understanding has to be translated into action that inspires more action. And when the initial motivation has been created within the audience it has to be continually refuelled and developed by reminding them repeatedly of the narrative themes, the messages and the benefits on offer. It is unwise to presume that the person who is motivated by our story this week, will be equally, or more, motivated next week. In that time many other stories will have been told. Our audience has to be reminded. Our cause has to be shared in ways that inspire significant others, and often significant numbers of others, to join in and provide their support. As we develop momentum in our campaign, so we develop the motivation of our audience, day-by-day, week-by-week, until their enthusiasm for action is unstoppable.

The campaign narrative told through a range of integrated activities has to change the question mark of doubt, disagreement or ignorance into an exclamation mark of approval and commitment. For us, the exclamation mark in the *Campaign It!* model is a reminder of the fact that emotional commitment is the energy that fuels momentum. Even if, as the following story from AB demonstrates, that commitment comes at a cost.

Being in the zone

I used to live close to Finsbury Park station in London. It was a 15 minute tube ride from there to the very centre of London, and less than a 10-minute walk from our street to the station.

When my partner Sharon Macdonald and I moved there it was an area without residents' parking controls. As such our area was a magnet for commuters from outer London and the suburbs who would drive in, park up in our street and the surrounding ones, and catch a tube for the final part of the journey. At times, getting a parking slot anywhere close to our flat was a nightmare. Added to that, Highbury, home of Arsenal Football Club was less than a 20-minute walk away. On match days and nights parking became impossible.

Imagine how cheered we were when we heard that a Controlled Parking Zone (CPZ) was going to be introduced to our neighbourhood. Of course, there'd have to be a public consultation first, but we were confident of getting support from the community. After all, everyone suffered equally.

Signs went up on lampposts and other street furniture around and about advertising the consultation about the proposals. Strangely, nothing went up in the actual street in which we lived. I thought nothing of it, waiting instead for the consultation documents through my door. They never arrived. I started to get worried. I realized that I'd better look into it.

What I discovered horrified me. Of all the streets in the vicinity of Finsbury Park tube, one was excluded from the putative CPZ – ours! Our road was scheduled to be included in a different CPZ in 18 months' time. The implications were dreadful. Anybody could park in our road with impunity, and we couldn't purchase a permit to park in neighbouring streets that were within the CPZ because we weren't going to be part of it.

We had to intervene. We had to influence the local council to amend the CPZ to include our street. Someone had to take the lead to run a local campaign. The trouble was, we had to convince our neighbours that they should agree to pay the CPZ fee to park their car outside their home. Some, we guessed, would be relieved that they didn't have to pay out. We knew this was a short-sighted response and that the council would be unlikely to amend the CPZ once it was accepted.

There were about 75 houses in our street, many converted into two or three flats. Sharon drafted a letter explaining the situation that she delivered to every household, and then we started going door-to-door to get signatures on a petition. As we suspected, some were against it and we had to explain and persuade. We had a strong story to tell. Sharon was dogged in building support through a series of visits and making it easy for people to sign up.

I contacted the council officers to get more information. I had to find out what was going on, why we hadn't been included, what the timetable was and what possibilities there might now be. It took time and was frustrating. Most importantly I needed to know who the decision-makers were. It turned out to be the East Area committee, part of the devolved governance structure in Islington at the time. They were councillors who look after a particular part of the borough, and who discuss and decide on issues in that neighbourhood, who meet locally and who invite local residents to participate. Just the kind of community forum that would respond to emotionally delivered arguments and who would instinctively want to be on the side of the community. Of course, politics still would be at play. The committee would be a mixture of Labour and Liberal Democrat councillors with competing agendas.

Then I started contacting our local ward councillors and finding out what the process was to get the CPZ amended. I briefed my ward councillors, and explained the level of support we were building. I asked them to pass it on to specific other councillors. I had a lot of interactions with them throughout the whole campaign. As politicians, they realized the personal implications for themselves as well as the problems for the community. They agreed to put the issue on the agenda at the next meeting of the East Area committee. I contacted the two local papers to make sure they knew about the issue and to encourage them to come along to the meeting. And I made contact with the Chair of the committee to let him know what was coming – out of courtesy, of course, but I wanted to sound him out too and start to tell him our story.

Sharon had done a fantastic job at getting the support of the residents in our road, and she made sure there was a good turn-out at the meeting. She prepared briefing packs for the committee members so that we had our side of the story in a format that was easily understood and which demonstrated the strength of support in our favour.

I spoke at the meeting and used a lot of humour to chide the council officers who had drawn up their proposals 'by numbers' instead of by common sense. I'd worked out my story in advance, knew my beginning and ending, knew the interests of the various committee members so I could be specific to them, and used emotional arguments to build support and create common cause about council officers with those who were watching from the public. With laughter echoing around the room at the approach of the council officers I knew that the mood of the committee was turning in our favour.

I spoke to the journalist from the local paper as soon as my agenda item was over. I wanted to get to him quickly in case he had a train to catch. He told me that he was glad he'd turned up and that he'd had fun watching my speech and my discussions with the councillors and the officers. I was able to give him some nice quotes that he used.

It worked. The councillors on the East Area committee voted in favour of the good folk of Birnam Road – although there was a twist in the tale. Politics were at play, as ever, and the councillors knew that they simply couldn't overturn their officers just like that. They ordered a second consultation, just of our road. If the residents agreed, they could be included. We had to influence our neighbours all over again. We had to get them to take action a second time, and this time we had to get them to complete and return a third-party consultation form, a task that is much harder than getting signatures on a petition we controlled.

However, having got so far we were determined to win.

We wrote a letter to our neighbours immediately and I delivered it the next day. We wanted to say thank you, give an update and, crucially, get our neighbours ready for the consultation.

We also prepared a letter to be delivered to everyone in our street just as soon as the consultation mailing arrived. And once it did, we went door-to-door to reinforce the need to take the time and trouble to fill in and return the forms, leaving letters behind for all those who weren't in. We kept records of everyone who had signed our petition and targeted them, as well as going back to everyone a second time if we hadn't met them the first time.

I realized that we were asking people for some big things. We were asking:

- councillors to go against their officers;

- councillors and officers to open up a 'done deal' and therefore delay its implementation;

- neighours to take action twice in order to be forced to spend money!

There was a bigger turn-out in our special consultation than in the council's original, with an overwhelming majority in favour of joining the CPZ. I was disappointed that it wasn't unanimous, but Sharon was more pragmatic. 'We won,' she said, 'Although I'm not sure how many thanks we will get when everyone realizes it's going to cost them nearly a hundred pounds a year just to park their car!'

From the *Campaign It!* perspective the above story can be summarized as follows:

- **Cause:** Avoiding the mayhem that would have been the inevitable result of not having parking restrictions on the street.
- **Audience:** Neighbours, councillors, council officers, media, neighbouring groups.
- **Analysis:** Of the number of neighbours on the street and their attitudes and likely interest in the issue; of council procedures and schedules; of decision-makers (councillors) and their advisers (their officers); of environmental

factors; of the accepted rationale for creating parking zones in other areas and streets; of the most useful media to engage.

- **Mapping:** Worked out the sequence of the story, found out the procedures for influencing the decision, planned the communications to fit the process and its timetable, brought it together for the committee. A second plan was then developed based around the arrival of the consultation pack.

- **Narrative:** The themes were: We have to prevent this mayhem; this is how it will affect you; this is the solution; and this is the action you need to take.

- **Integrated activities:** Door-to-door visits; letters; communications with councillors; briefing pack for committee members; contacts with local press; a speech; record keeping of neighbour's responses.

- **Grid (plan of activities):** Communications were sequenced and timed to meet external milestones (committee meeting and consultation pack arrival).

- **Influencing conversations:** Between councillors and their officers, between neighbours and between local residents and their elected representatives through the activities outlined above.

- **Testing:** Through discussion, Q&A, and gaining feedback from key elements of the audience, especially the decision-makers and neighbours.

Learning points

For AB the cause was clear. It was to avoid the inevitable mayhem that would have been created and, of course, to maintain parking space for himself and his neighbours. By making it a shared cause, by highlighting through his narrative the dangers of inactivity and the benefits of supporting his campaign, he was able to effectively engage and mobilize his audience. This was especially important given that the neighbours were required to act on two separate occasions.

The neighbours were only one of the audiences AB had to understand and influence. Without the support of his neighbours the campaign would almost certainly have failed, however they were not the decision-makers. AB's analysis of the council's procedures and meeting schedules, and of the priorities and strategies of the councillors and their officers, enabled him to match both their processes and their thinking. It made it easier for him to create an argument and deliver it in ways that would appeal to those who had the power to change the plan. His involvement of the media added an extra pressure on the councillors and, by doing everything he could to control the way the story was reported in the local paper, AB shared it with a wider audience and reinforced it with his neighbours. His use of humour in his presentation helped to give the story the required wiggle.

The requirement to go through a consultation process, meant that the original plan had to be adapted and updated, and that the neighbours had to be reminded of the benefits of action. Throughout the campaign AB was fully aware that he was asking people to make some significant commitment and changes. His neighbours had to give up their time to provide their support and the councillors and their officers had to undo a decision already made. The conversations he sought to influence, then, were amongst these groups.

The activities in the campaign were limited in number, which made integration relatively simple. AB's communications were planned to fit in with the external milestones set by the council's schedule and feedback was gained mainly through informal means.

The parking zone story reminds us of the likelihood of managing simultaneous campaigns as it was not the only campaign AB was involved in at that time. It also reminds us of the fact that we can campaign any type of cause in any part of our life.

Be-cause

Sometimes, in the most emotive of campaigns, the cause reflects a personal principle, belief or value, some essential part of our own identity and associated world-view, which connects us to the campaign so strongly that we become at one with it. Sometimes, in the most challenging of campaigns, we are tested to our limit by those events we cannot prevent. Irrespective of the gradation of cause or the degree of difficulty of the campaign, the process by which we develop momentum and gain support has to be planned, organized and flexible. The determination to continue is not enough. What is required is the determination to continue in a strategic, adaptive and disciplined manner.

It is important to distinguish here between strategic thinking and strategic planning. Strategic thinking determines the creation and, later, the adaptation of the plan in the light of feedback. A military maxim states that no plan survives the first point of contact intact. Whether or not that is true for all communications campaigns is open to debate. However, the ability to think strategically, to be able to analyse environments and the current and likely behaviours of others, to think creatively and systemically, to shift between observing the big picture and giving attention to detail, to gather and interpret feedback accurately, is an essential prerequisite of creating and managing a plan. It underpins the creation and ongoing development of the campaign grid.

The details shown on the campaign grid are only changed when the feedback and test results indicate the need for change. The ways that the campaign is influencing the audience can be tested both formally and informally. In the parking zone campaign, AB used conversations and the number of signatures on a petition as primary methods of testing the outcomes that were being created and getting an insight into the level of progress being made.

Feedback feeds the forward development of the plan. Testing needs to be as free from bias as it is possible to be. It is not a mechanism for seeking justification for what is being done. Rather, the purpose is to find out precisely where the campaign is at and where, and how, it needs to go next. Once again, genuine curiosity needs to drive the process. Alone, though, curiosity is often not enough. It needs to be supported and surrounded by a range of other traits, many of which we have discussed already, all of which combine to create a special kind of strength.

Final thoughts

'Strength does not come from physical capacity. It comes from an indomitable will.'

Mahatma Gandhi

As we move towards the end of this introduction to campaigning communications, we find ourselves returning inevitably to the beginning, to the power of cause.

It is the emotional compulsion created by the fact that we care about our cause that, in turn, grows and strengthens our willpower. In this context, strength is not just the capability to remove obstacles or to force our way forwards. It is equally the willingness to take knocks, to accept setbacks, and to regroup, to learn from the experience and continue on. Without a cause to motivate us, without a purpose we find e-motive, there is no need to campaign. There is no need for willpower and determination. However, once we commit to a campaign, particularly over an extended period of time, it is almost certain that we will need to find and exercise our will. We might not be strong to begin with and we might not need to be. Strength can be developed throughout the process and as we build momentum. To begin, we just need to care.

That's all.

Being a campaigner

> "Campaigning is communication fuelled by a cause and an emotional compulsion, crafted by a range of attributes and skills, bound by values and time. **ALAN BARNARD**

> "Whatever course you decide upon, there is always someone to tell you that you are wrong. There are always difficulties arising which tempt you to believe that your critics are right. To map out a course of action and follow it to an end requires courage.
>
> **RALPH WALDO EMERSON**

We began by offering our new definition of campaigning and showing its place within the framework we called *Thinking inside the box*. The decision to include our philosophy of campaigning along with the attributes of a campaigner was made because we feel that campaigning is more than a clinical, technical process. Through our communication we share far more than just information and data. Ultimately we share ourself. And through that process of sharing we engage in an interactive feedback loop that influences everyone directly involved and, often, others who are not.

We know the costs we can pay for miscommunication. We know, too, the positive and powerful impacts we can have when our communication is based on insight, understanding, care and respect and is then delivered with eloquence and skill.

Communication is both a right and a responsibility. Caring about, and being willing to commit to, a cause creates a feeling of purpose, reinforces a sense of identity and belonging, and often brings with it a number of challenges. Whenever we campaign our communications we are not only showing what we believe in, we are also showing at least a part of who we are and of what we are striving for.

Campaigning always has a purpose. It needs a philosophy and ethics because through our communications we affect peoples' lives and, therefore, we need acceptable boundaries within which we operate. We need to develop our emotional intelligence to ensure that we balance our commitment to the cause with our personal values and respect for others. We have to know what we will not do to win, as clearly as we know what we will do. We also have to accept the right of others to disagree or oppose us, and even to just not care.

Importantly, as individuals we do not have to be brilliant at every aspect of campaigning. It is a discipline that invites collaborative working and it encourages team building and sharing. We can engage the support of those with complimentary skills and attitudes. We can work with, and learn from, them as we analyse our audience, create our narrative, map out our campaign, put it into action and then respond to feedback.

Finally, no matter how important, knowledgeable or powerful we think we are, there are always people from whom we need to gain permission for us to succeed. *Campaign It!* is just a way of becoming better at that.

Now, in this concluding chapter, AB shares some stories about how he got involved with campaigning and how campaigning became a central part of his life. He charts his development as a campaigner and discusses what it means to campaign communications. As you read these stories, think about the *Campaign It!* model, and about the skills, attitudes, approaches, techniques and philosophy of being a campaigner.

Identity

AB: 'I've always been a campaigner, and over the years I've learnt to become better at it.

'I know that now, but I didn't start describing myself as a campaigner until the summer of 2001, when I started a company with a friend, Dorian Jabri, which we called Silent Wave. Our premise was new. We wanted to make better use of corporate social responsibility to build a company's image. A few others were already in the field but we thought we knew how to do it better and that the time was right. And after all, I knew about building brands, I thought, as I had been doing it successfully for the Labour Party and for Labour politicians for years. Now we had to add meaning to it. We already had that meaning, cause and sense of identity for Labour; we had to find it for the brands we anticipated helping.

'As part of setting ourselves up we had to decide how we would explain ourselves to our potential clients. And that was when I knew what I was. I was a campaigner. I realized that my approach to using communications was to use them to achieve a particular outcome, that there was always a purpose to them. I put communications together as a sequence, coordinating the various channels around the same story that would deliver the outcome I was after. It was always a campaign.

'It is exactly what I had been doing at Labour on behalf of the various politicians I had been helping. And, I have since understood, it is what I had been doing for years and years beforehand in order to influence the outcomes I was after.'

A beginning, an ending

'I joined the Labour Party in late 1983 because I was fed up putting the world to rights from the comfort of my local pub. Mrs Thatcher was just starting her second term in office, the miners' strike was dividing the nation, the much loved NHS was judged to be in decline, gas, water, electricity were being privatized and the Tory Government was split over Europe. Labour were at their lowest point, Michael Foot had given way to Neil Kinnock and fights with the Militant Tendency were fresh in people's minds. There was a sense that voters were looking for reasons to vote Labour and Labour was doing its best not to give them one. Labour needed people prepared to look to the future and not gaze back wistfully at the past. It was time to stop just talking about what I believed and to start actually doing something about it.

'But reality is never as easy as discussions in a pub. It took me another five years before I got my first chance to show what I could do for Labour. A few months after I joined Labour I started work for Stonham Housing Association, a provider of hostel-type accommodation mostly for young (ex) offenders, in their Slough project. I did my Labour Party leafleting in my spare time, whilst honing my ideas in the pub.

'In 1985 I moved from Slough to become Deputy Project Leader of a new type of Stonham project in the five north east London Boroughs of Waltham Forest, Newham, Redbridge, Havering and Barking & Dagenham. It was a dispersed project, with our residents living in two-person shared flats remote from our office, unlike the traditional residential hostels with a live-in warden. It required a whole new mindset and approach to helping our residents, all of whom were aged 18–25 and had to be referred to us by the North East London Probation Service. The goal of the project was to help prevent them from re-offending by stabilizing their housing needs, preparing them for independent living and then moving them on into their own, permanent accommodation.

'This dispersed hostel was at the cutting edge of hostel accommodation for offenders and it wasn't to everybody's taste. The existing management committee that we had inherited from the tenanted project were not cut out for this new approach. Nor was the project leader who was very soon on his way. I was promoted, becoming Stonham's youngest project leader. For the first time, I could influence a project how I wanted.

'My first task was to get new colleagues to help me mould it as I wanted. The second was to change the management committee and find new entrepreneurial thinkers who could make the most of the project. Looking back, I now know that I ran a campaign to make the changes happen. I analysed the needs and the gaps, found the right people and started to interact with them so that eventually they couldn't say no. I had to explain the benefits of their involvement with the project and map out a vision of the future that they could share in. And I had to get them to agree to volunteer a huge amount of their spare time to help me realize it.

'I had become part of local steering groups running campaigns against the impacts being caused to our sector by government policies of the day. Eventually I decided that I had to campaign on a bigger stage and wanted to work for a housing campaign group. I left Stonham in late '87 and worked as a freelance trainer for NACRO, running short courses and developing new ones, working in conjunction with Janet Maitland and my deputy from Stonham, Deb Jenkins. I wanted to make contact with the likes of Shelter and SHAC. At the time I was motivated by the fact that 1.1 million houses were standing empty, many of them owned by government departments, which could have been used to ease the homelessness problem of the time.

'However I never got started! Events conspired to propel me on to a different course.

'I had moved to live in Islington with my old mate from school, Roy. I volunteered in the '86 local elections and for Chris Smith at the 1987 General Election. Afterwards I started to become more active in the local Labour Party. During the General Election campaign I had observed lots of ways in which I thought the campaign could have been improved. I reasoned that if I could help Labour get into government the housing campaigning that I was committed to would be so much easier.'

Politics, pounds and a lesson from a Sea Monster

'I lived in Canonbury East ward of Islington South and Finsbury constituency so that was the obvious place to start and to establish myself. Both of my councillors were SDP and the local Labour Party branch had a membership of just 25 people, of whom around 6 would turn up for the monthly meetings. We were lucky to get a dozen people volunteering for us.

'Fortunately many of the membership were recently joined, young and enthusiastic. Unfortunately they all had demanding jobs. They needed somebody to coordinate and organize them. I had time to volunteer and a determination to make my local party better. In my local ward our coffers were bare. We had to raise money to communicate our ideas and plans with the local electorate.

'We used to meet in an upstairs room of the Rosemary Branch pub. It was a pub theatre. The alternative comedy cabaret circuit was becoming established in London at the time, and I used often to go to the Meccano Club at the Camden Head in Islington on a Friday or Saturday night. All the acts were radical and I reasoned that they were bound to support Labour. I planned to set up a regular fundraising comedy club at the Rosemary Branch to bring money into the local party. My favourite acts at the time were John Hegley and Otiz Cannelloni. I resolved to seek them out at their next gig and ask for their help, reasoning that if I was going to put on a gig I might as well book the acts I liked.

'There were lots of big fundraising events around at the time – the Secret Policeman's Ball on behalf of Amnesty International, for example – but none for the Labour Party and certainly none for such a local branch as Canonbury East. I was worried that John and Otiz would say "No" simply because they were being asked all the time for pro-bono gigs, and mine was quite small beer by comparison. So I decided to offer them a small payment to cover costs, and to organize my gig around their other commitments on the evening. The Rosemary Branch theatre could seat about 50 people. I thought I could squeeze a few more in, so I decided to offer each of the four acts enough money for taxis and drinks rather than expect them to do it as a favour. With a full house, I would still make a tidy profit for the local party.

'On that basis John and Otiz both said "Yes". They also put me in contact with a cabaret organizer, Ivor Dembina, who agreed to help and to act as compere for the next few gigs to help me get started. Now all I needed was one more act and when Ivor put me in touch with an up-and-coming performer called The Sea Monster I had my first line-up sorted.

'We marketed it with flyers in the Rosemary Branch, through other Labour Party branches and in *Time Out*. On the night of the show we had people queuing to get in.

'At the end of the first show, I sat at the top of the stairs leading to the Rosemary Branch theatre feeling good about what I had achieved and sharing a beer with the Sea Monster. She was relatively new on the circuit and asked me what I thought about her act.

'"Very funny," I told her, "although I'm not sure about the self-deprecating humour. Shouldn't the alternative circuit be challenging some of those stereotypes about women rather than celebrating them as part of an act?" Luckily for us all, Jo Brand ignored the pompous musings of a wannabe Islington new man.

'Raising money for my local Labour Party was a campaign in itself, part of a bigger campaign to be able to communicate with the electorate. The money raised was put to good use. Desktop publishing had just come on the scene giving the ability for anybody to produce the artwork for printed literature easily. I've still got copies of the newsletters I produced with the money we raised. I wouldn't do them that way now. The content was written by us and for us, rather than for the voters we sought to influence. They were written in our language, about the things that we thought were important and which we thought the voters should care about. At no point back then did we consider asking the voters what was top of their list of priorities so that we could let them know our position on whatever it was.

'It was a few years before Phillip Gould introduced me to political research and even then I was sceptical in the first instance. "What, we're going to base our entire strategy on what just eight people in a room have told you?" I asked him incredulously. It was just another part of my education.'

Margate, Margaret and May

'Two things happened in the autumn of 1988 that were important for me, and set me on the track of becoming a professional campaigner. A vacancy occurred on the council in the south of the constituency. I became the assistant agent and, although I was only a volunteer, I took over the day-to-day running of the campaign. It was my first experience of being responsible for a discrete campaign.

'We won, against expectations. The campaign was hard work, filled with long evenings and late nights, motivating volunteers to do more, and building camaraderie around our shared cause. Finally, too, we had started listening to voters and had begun tailoring our communications around their priorities. We worked every day for six weeks. It was both exhausting and exhilarating. I knew that the outcome had been influenced by my activities on the campaign. Excitingly, others had also become aware of what I was doing, including the MP and his staff.

'The second thing was a residential training weekend a few weeks later, run by the London regional Labour Party in a Margate hotel. Activists from all over London attended, including some people who worked full time as constituency organizers. I didn't know before then that you could be paid to work for the Labour Party at a local level. The direction of my campaigning career was now set. I was going to become a full-time, paid constituency agent.

'Most importantly, at the Margate weekend I met Margaret McDonagh, one of the London Labour Party staff members, who became a great friend. Back then she was clearly someone that I had to learn from. And she still is. It was obvious to me that she wanted to improve the ways in which Labour campaigned and communicated. She understood, too, that successful campaigns needed money behind them. Margaret was driven, determined to succeed and was going to let nothing get in the way of her cause to make Labour in London fit for purpose.

'That weekend I was introduced to campaigning ideas, techniques and concepts that I was determined to apply back in Islington. I had an open mind and was willing to learn. I always wanted to find ways of doing things better. I wasn't scared of new approaches. In fact I welcomed them. I always have.

'My involvement in the local Labour Party grew during 1989. There were plans, promoted by Margaret McDonagh and supported by the MP Chris Smith and the local party lay officers, to establish a paid constituency agent role in Islington South and Finsbury constituency. I was determined to make the job mine and was successful, starting early in 1990.

'My immediate task was to be the formal election agent for 26 council candidates in May. We won 23 of the 26 seats including gaining 13 from the opposition. Our messaging was tighter than ever before, our literature was innovative, our organization and coordination was improved. There were lots of cameos that indicated things were changing and that our campaigning was different.'

Learning and leading

'I had a lot of work to do before the General Election. Chris Smith was defending a majority of only 805 and I had to make use of every day. I was still learning, although I had plenty of ideas of my own to test and develop.

'At the time a traditional election campaign consisted of:

- an "introductory" leaflet, delivered at the start of the four-week campaign to introduce the candidates;
- an election address, setting out policies and what the candidates would do for local people, usually delivered towards the end of the period;
- canvassing, calling on doors to ask people if they were for or against so that they could be called on polling day to go out and vote;
- supporters being asked to put a poster up.

'Everyone had two pieces of paper pushed through their letterbox. Everyone had someone on the doorstep once, although we didn't ever manage to speak to everyone. Those who had told us they were voting Labour were harassed three or four times on polling day to get them to go and vote. To my mind it was very simplistic. I was never even certain that those we encouraged out to vote on polling day were all Labour voters. More importantly, we included few opportunities to deliver a political message, or provide reasons to vote for us to those who were undecided. We needed people to change their minds and that needed regular communications over a much longer period than the final four weeks.

'I realized that we couldn't afford to deliver repeated communications to every voter. I could target our work much more effectively if I could focus on the people who were undecided. And the sooner I knew who they were, the more time we had to communicate a reason for them to choose Labour.

'This meant changing the culture of the way the local party operated. We had to turn our attention away from those who always voted Labour and towards those who had either previously voted for other parties or who hadn't yet made up their minds. And we had to do it for longer than just the four weeks of an election campaign in a much more deliberate way. I had to get more work out of our volunteers and get them working far in advance of the election being called. Even more importantly, I had to find more volunteers. I was determined to handpick the volunteers I wanted to help me lead the campaign. I also wanted to professionalize the activities of those volunteer ward organizers as best I could. After all, although I was still learning myself, I was now a professional campaigner. I was obliged to lead the way.

'I started passing on everything I had learnt from Margaret and her team whilst adding a few tweaks of my own. As well as reviewing the past month's activities so we could learn from the successes and failures, and planning the next month's activities, I introduced a training element to our monthly ward organizer meetings. The things I had just learnt I was teaching my team. We were growing and developing together, but I made sure that as their leader it was never obvious that some of the things I was teaching I had only learnt myself a few days before!

'Out of all the things I have done, building this team over two years, remains my single most satisfying achievement. One of them, Edna Griffiths, a stalwart of the local party, asked me if she could continue to come to the meetings even though she became too ill to be active, because, she told me, that over her many long years as a member and activist, they were the most enjoyable, most informative and most useful of all the meetings she had ever been to.

'Another ward organizer, Chris Farley, sent me a postcard on the eve of the 1992 General Election to wish me luck and to thank me for my work. He addressed it to "Il capo dei capi", which means "the boss of bosses". It did make me very proud that people were recognizing and valuing the changes we were making. That was thanks in no small part to the work of Margaret McDonagh and her team in the London region, although I like to think that I had played my role too.

'It was also thanks to another giant of political campaigning, John Braggins. I had met John a few times, at the Margate training weekends. He was – still is – an unassuming man who is also a great raconteur. John was Labour's by-election guru. Whenever there was a parliamentary by-election, John went to assist. He was the one who set the strategy and the day-to-day tactics.

'Parliamentary by-elections were where the new thinking took place. They were held under the glare of the country's political media spotlight. Mistakes were magnified. Successes were building blocks to future electoral success. They were very important. Labour had to take them seriously and run them very professionally. The party invested a lot of resource in them, calling on professional staff from around the country for the four- or five-week period of the campaign. I soon got my chance to be one of them.

'In November 1990 I went to work in the Bradford North by-election. I worked alongside Margaret to coordinate the activities of the Eccleshill ward of around 10,000 voters. This was heaven. Not only was I playing an important role in an intense election campaign I was also getting the benefit of Margaret's experience directly. And I was able to interact with John Braggins, the by-election supremo. I was wide-eyed with delight. When the others wanted to go and have a bite to eat and a beer before a well-earned rest in their hotel I was pestering John. "Why have you done that?" I would ask. "What about doing this?" "What does that mean?" "Can I have a go at...?" This was a sweet shop and all my Christmases rolled into one.

'John and I clicked straight away. His sense of humour was fabulous. His abilities were more so. I wanted to be able to do what he could. John became my hero. He still is. He's my great friend too, and, fantastically, now he is my business partner.

'When I got back to Islington I would call him regularly and explain my latest bit of thinking. John's initial answer would always be the same. "Why?" he would say. It used to infuriate me. I thought that I had come up with the best idea ever, and now I had to explain and justify it. Of course, through doing that we improved every idea I had that could work and disregarded those that couldn't.

'On General Election polling day, 9 April 1992, we had a fantastic operation. Everything came together as it should. Over two years of preparation and campaigning communications proved its worth. John Braggins designed a strategy for the first 48 hours of the campaign. We implemented it and we blew the opposition away. We never looked back and, even though we were a marginal to which resources were directed, I sent volunteers to help in neighbouring seats.

'Our majority was 10,652 – a massive increase. Chris got 52 per cent of the vote. Our strategy of targeting voters, in particular former Liberal Democrat voters, had paid off. The Lib Dems were pushed into third place. Our campaign had been a spectacular success.

'Unfortunately that wasn't the case across the country. The Conservatives were back in power with a slim majority. All our efforts had come to nothing nationally. We weren't going to fix the housing and homelessness problem. I remembered the campaign advice that had been coming out of head office during the campaign. It was different to the ideas and advice that I had got from Margaret and her team in London; if only the rest of the country could have had that same advice. The results in London's key seats were significantly better than those in the rest of the country. Targeting resources in key seats is an insurance policy in case the national messaging was wrong. In 1992 we got both our insurance policy wrong in much of the country and our national message wrong in all of it. We were simply not wanted by the voters.'

Head office, America, 92 seats and a question about vets

'I knew that my next step would have to be to get a job at Labour's head office if I wanted to make improvements happen more widely. I had to wait another

18 months before I got to apply for the next job of my dreams – Labour's national Targeting and Key Seats Officer.

'I started on 1 November 1993. On my first day I tore up Labour's policy on targeting and wrote my own. It was based on what I had done in Islington. I remember being very nervous about this but I had the courage of my convictions. And I had to do what I believed to be right. That would mean transforming the culture of the party nationally in the way that I had in Islington.

'And it would mean changing the content of our targeted messaging too. No longer should we target nurses, for example, and tell them about the appalling state of the NHS under the Tories. They of all people knew that to be the case, they worked in it everyday. If we were going to encourage them to vote Labour we needed to explain about our economic policy, about our tax plans and how they were going to be able to get on the housing ladder.

'The previous year Margaret McDonagh and I volunteered for the first Clinton– Gore campaign. We went to California because the Democrats there had the reputation of being at the cutting edge of American campaigning. John Braggins went on a different trip, a wider tour of America to observe the election from both the Republican and Democrat perspectives as a guest of the US Information Agency.

'On our return the three of us wrote a pamphlet about the lessons that Labour could learn from the US Presidential election and presented it to the party nationally. The report was largely ignored because there was a lot of nervousness about the "Clintonization" of the Labour Party at the time. It was felt by many senior politicians that Bill Clinton had won by altering his policies and becoming more "right-wing". That sentiment ignored the central learning from our pamphlet that being "on-message" was paramount. In other words, we had to explain our policies and plans in ways that the voters would accept and focus on a few core themes including, crucially, our economic position. We also learnt about the importance of defining the opposition on our terms – "attack" – and about defending ourselves from opposition attacks – "rapid rebuttal". Fundraising was on another level in the USA, but Margaret and I knew that already. Our pamphlet allowed us to stress its importance.

'Margaret had brought back with her a small, credit-card-sized plastic "leaflet" for want of a better description. It was exactly the same as a credit card in shape, size and material. We hadn't seen this device before. It was a simple thing to keep in a wallet or purse and was in favour of Proposition 186, a measure about access to healthcare that was also on the ballot in California that year. It contained a simple summary of the benefits that would flow from voting "Yes". We thought it was very clever. Margaret still has it in her purse.

'My work in Islington, and my experiences in America influenced my work at head office. I started to work on parliamentary by-elections alongside John Braggins and we were given free rein to conduct the campaigns as we saw fit. We implemented our new ideas from America and had great success. We knew that once they had become accepted as legitimate by-election techniques we could roll them out across the country as standard practice.

'Once Tony Blair became leader, and he appointed Margaret as General Election Coordinator (and subsequently as Labour's youngest and first-ever female General Secretary) John and I were encouraged to develop and implement our ideas and thinking. Finally we could do the things we knew were right. It turned out that the three of us had two-and-a-half years working together at head office in the run-up to the General Election of 1997. It was just long enough to effect the changes we needed. We transformed campaigning in the 92 key seats that we targeted – those we had to win on a swing of 6 per cent or less. Our member mobilization, and the use of phone banks, both run by Carol Linforth as part of the Key Seats Task Force, were on a scale never seen before in a political campaign in the UK. The phone banks were so good that they were giving the campaign message advice before it came through in the research. It kept us ahead of the game.

'From our American trip we introduced message discipline. At a very senior General Election planning meeting in 1996 Margaret produced from her purse the credit card "leaflet" on Proposition 186 she had kept from our trip to California. It was the genesis of the most important element of the 1997 campaign, the new Labour pledge card. In its final form this gave five pledges to the British people. These pledges showed a difference between the values of the two parties and the benefits on offer if people voted for us. They were brilliant examples of the flagship policies that high-lighted the themes of our narrative. They became the biggest symbol of new Labour. Yet they came about out of a desire to instil message discipline into our politicians and spokespeople, and to prevent them from wandering off along other policy lines and promises and confusing the voter. We had a story to tell, and we had to be co-ordinated and disciplined to do it. The pledge card was the device we used.

'Most importantly we knew that we had to reach out to voters we called "switch-ers" (those who had voted Tory in previous elections) because the electoral mathe-matics showed there were just not enough natural Labour supporters for us to win. This was a mistake that Labour had made time after time, thinking that if only we could explain our "Labour-ness" better, voters would see the light and come flooding to us. Tony Blair helped us to change all that.

'Taking this message out to our volunteers and activists around the party was tough going. They wanted to do the things they always had done. They were resist-ant to change, especially to reaching out to former Conservative voters and to new campaigning techniques. Politics is one of two areas[1] where it is easy for everyone to be an expert. And the Labour Party had plenty of 'experts' amongst its members.

'As part of our campaign to change the culture of campaigning we had a massive training programme for our candidates, our professional organizers and for the lead-ing lay activists. We had put a lot of resource into developing our professional staff and I wanted them to be accepted as the leading campaigners in each constituency.

'I developed a routine for the inevitable opposition from long-standing party activists. I would ask if there was a vet in the room. I would then proceed to explain how I, as a completely untrained person, would go about neutering a cat. Of course a vet undertakes years of training before they operate on a cat, and not everyone could become a vet. I wanted to explain that whilst everyone could become a campaigner, and that many in the room with me were indeed campaigners, we could all learn to become better at it, that there were new and improved techniques that we all could adopt, and that some people were professional at it, just as some people

---

[1] Football is the other, and, for my sins, changing public perceptions of that was to be my next job after Labour. Perhaps I'm just a masochist at heart!

are professional vets. For me, as a professional, campaigning is always an evolving process and just because it has been done a certain way in the past it doesn't mean that it always will be or always should be. We need to be open-minded and learn to become better.

'We were successful, though. We did indeed change the culture. And we won many more seats than we had targeted, even those where much of the campaigning was done in the old-fashioned way. That was because our national messaging, delivered by Tony Blair through the media, especially the broadcast media, captured the mood of the time. In all honesty, to encourage the extra 15 per cent of undecided voters we needed to make it to 43 per cent, we probably didn't need to campaign at all on the ground, our national messaging in 1997 was that good. (Although intense activity on the ground can fuel a national mood.) But we weren't to know that when we started. In order to increase our chances of winning we had to work hard to win those 92 seats to give us a working majority. And in order to win those seats we had to change the way we campaigned.

'I stayed at Labour for another two years but I wanted a new challenge. It was clear to me that we were going to win at least the next two General Elections. It would be the one after that we would have to plan and organize for, but the nature of politics and the people involved meant that planning that far in advance was anathema. The Welsh referendum was a great experience. However, being the National Election Agent for all 84 Labour candidates in the first European elections under the list system, when we couldn't do anything but lose seats and few voters cared one way or the other, wasn't. As ever, working on by-elections with John was inspirational, but even they had lost their edge because we were in government. It was time for something new.'

The beautiful game and location, location, location

'I was determined to make sure that my next job would be fun, interesting, challenging and worthwhile. It would take a campaign to get it. I have been a life-long Chelsea fan, and had finally been able to spend time going to matches again after the 1997 General Election. By the start of the 1998 season I had season tickets along with my partner, Sharon Macdonald. She had worked for Labour too from 1994 until 1998 in charge of direct marketing recruitment and fundraising and she'd been part of the Labour team that had revolutionized our communications. I used to complain to her regularly about the paucity of Chelsea's communications off the field; and how they got it all so badly wrong when they tried to use their communications to build their image, recruit new fans, upgrade fans to have a deeper relationship with the club, influence other clubs, players and regulators. It drove me mad. They missed so many opportunities. They didn't have a consistent narrative. They weren't nimble and flexible enough.

' "I think I could help Chelsea out," I told Sharon in early 1998. "I'm going to see if I can create a job for myself there."

'I wrote to the Chairman, Ken Bates, a man who had a reputation, carefully cultivated, as irascible and independent. I spent five weeks crafting a letter to him, reworking it, considering each sentence, thinking through how I could best influence him. Finally I sent it. A couple of weeks later I got a message on my pager.

' "If you call Ken Bates on xxx xxx xxxx he will tell you why you can't have a job at Chelsea," it said.

' "Fantastic," I thought. "He just couldn't resist. At least I can talk to him on the phone now. The next step is to get to meet him."

'The upshot, as I knew it would be, was that he invited me in to meet him. I thought through my approach. I knew that I had to match him like for like. He had to think that I was someone he could do business with, who was prepared to call a spade a spade and who would stand up against idiocy. I knew that my Achilles heel was that we didn't know each other at all. At least Tony Blair had known Alastair Campbell before taking him on, and he had also had a long-standing relationship with Peter Mandelson. I knew the importance of trust in making change happen from the top. Bates had to feel that I could be "one of them", whatever his "one of them" was.

'I went to the Chelsea Megastore on the way to the meeting and bought two books, one about Chelsea and the other about Ken Bates' role in rebuilding a club that was teetering on bankruptcy. I thought they might come in handy. I went up to his office and waited outside. He came out and called me inside, wearing his trademark light grey suit, looking like Father Christmas with his white hair and beard. We sat on his sofa, half twisted round facing each other.

'He came straight out fighting. "I see you've got Chris Smith as one of your referees, are you gay or straight?" was his opening gambit.

' "Nothing to do with you, mate," I countered. "What you need to know is that I've just been part of changing history, helping to overhaul and modernize a political party so that it won a landslide election. And I can do the same for Chelsea."

'The interview continued in the same vein. Bates put the boot into Tony Blair and Labour and I argued back. We were getting on like a house on fire. Eventually we talked football and football communications. And at the end of it he offered me a job. Only it wasn't the one I was expecting nor hoping it to be.

'Bates was in charge of the redevelopment of the new Wembley Stadium. "I'm just about to appoint someone to be the Marketing Director for Wembley," he told me. "But I'll put it on hold. Go and see my Chief Executive there, Bob Stubbs. If you get on and can do a deal, the job's yours."

'I asked him to sign the two books I had bought. In the biography he wrote that it was unauthorized and that I shouldn't believe a word of it. In the other he wrote something rude about Tony Blair. I guess he was used to having the last word, so I let him, shook his hand and went off to make arrangements to meet Bob Stubbs.

'I knew that the job at Wembley wasn't the job for me and so did Stubbs. When I met him we passed a pleasant half-hour in his office chatting over coffee out of courtesy to Bates. We then agreed the lines that we would take to explain why I wasn't taking the job.

'Just after that I got a call from a friend of mine, Jason Hughes, who had worked with me at Labour and had since gone to work on the 2006 World Cup bid for

The Football Association. Jason tipped me off that David Davies, the FA Executive Director, was creating a new job in his department. Jason suggested that I apply for it, which I duly did. I met David, had the interview and got on very well with him. He was very interested in the work I had done at Labour in helping to modernize their communications. He told me that it was exactly what he needed to help him make the big changes he knew were necessary at The Football Association.

'David asked me to do two things. Firstly to write him a paper about "Football as a power for good in society". Secondly to meet one of his team, Mark Sudbury. When I did, Mark explained that the job I was applying for had been his idea and that he had been hoping to be appointed. He told me that David had changed his thinking about the role since meeting me. Consequently, Mark would be moving to a different new job. Mark was one of the people who impressed me at the FA and was one of my few allies for change. Another was Kelly Simmons, the FA's Head of Football Development.

'My job title was Head of Campaigns and Research. It was clear to me before I began that the FA had little experience of running any kind of credible campaign. It had no idea what it wanted to achieve, nor even what it was really there for. It just sort of existed, dangling at the whim of the football media and the Premier League. I needed to help it get a narrative. Then I could help it communicate and bring that narrative to life, and start to use its new image to make the internal changes that had to happen if the FA was to maintain its legitimacy to run football into the twenty-first century. I had to concentrate on the research part of my job title initially. Campaigning would have to wait.

'First I had to research internally. I chatted to and interviewed as many people as I could inside the organization. I was dismayed to find out that, amongst many other basic things, the FA didn't even know how many people played the game of football in England. It was clearly going to be an uphill struggle. With that done, I turned my attentions outward.

'I started with qualitative research, focus groups, using a fabulous research company called TW Research. Initially I had a budget for just six groups. The trouble was that I didn't know whom to start talking and listening to. Whose views mattered? Football was so pervasive that it was hard to know where to start. I decided that one group had to be 12–16 year-old boys and another had to be women. The others were men of varying age groupings. As well as the required demographics to make the groups homogenous enough to enable all participants to contribute to the discussion I decided on a screening questionnaire of 10 questions. The respondents had to agree that football was important to them and a main topic of conversation for them. They had to answer some basic questions about the game and they had to have watched the whole of a live game of football during the preceding month, although I did not mind what level of game nor how they watched it.

'I reported the findings in January 2000. It made gloomy reading. However, I could see brightness ahead already. It most certainly was a communications issue. The groups had given me plenty of ideas as to how we could match FA activity with consumer desires. We needed purpose, a narrative and a set of simple things we could communicate to become symbols of a changing FA in touch with its audiences.

'One of my major early recommendations was that the FA had to move out of its offices in an old converted hotel in Lancaster Gate near Paddington. There, the individual offices, in former bedrooms, were more like monastic cells than somewhere that encouraged modern, collegiate working. We needed a symbol of change as well as the reality of change.

'Ken Bates wanted the FA to move to the new Wembley Stadium, but I knew this would be crazy. If we wanted to be at the heart of influencing opinion we had to be in central London, where the political and media action was. Lancaster Gate epitomized all that the public thought was old-fashioned, stuffy and out of touch.

'I lobbied David continually that we should move, and eventually the appointment of Adam Crozier, a former advertising executive, as Chief Executive unlocked the door for me. We moved in 2000 to open-plan offices in Soho Square. Our new offices were great. People in the same teams and departments could sit in the same room. We even had LCD screens in reception playing clips of exciting football from all levels. We really were moving straight from the nineteenth century into the twenty-first in one fell swoop!

'I wanted to make our move to Soho Square a symbol of a changing Football Association.

'The trouble was that we weren't used to blowing our own trumpet. The FA was always on the back foot, defending something that had gone wrong, or a decision made that wasn't understood by the media or football fans. We moved under cover of darkness one weekend. There was no fanfare, no official opening, nothing that would draw attention to ourselves. And so we lost one piece of initiative that we could have made use of in our modernization process.

'My initial research allowed me to get a preliminary understanding of perceptions of the FA. I then set up what I called my series of "News Monitor and FA Performance Tracker" polls. These were all qualitative. I didn't have enough knowledge to start measuring numbers through quantitative polling until later in 2000. I secured the budget for two evenings a month, four groups, to learn how the FA was perceived. My theory was that, based on these, we could develop strategies to influence that perception. I also used these groups for particular sub-projects too on anything that we specifically wanted to learn about.

'I was starting as well to use research as a tool more widely around the organization in order to help with thinking, planning and decision-making. I also wanted to validate other information I was learning from my News Monitor series. The first quantitative poll I commissioned was a survey of England Members Club in March 2000 to get their views on the relative merits of the various professional competitions. I preceded this with qualitative research to test the questions.

'I did the first modelling and general opinion of the FA in August 2000 and followed that with a survey of the FA's handling of Eriksson's appointment in November 2000.

'In 2001 I started to include Omnibus polling, where I bought space on a larger quantitative poll being carried out for many different clients. Omnibuses are eclectic polls, including questions about consumer behaviour and opinion for all manner of companies. I wanted to start to validate specific things I had learnt from the qualitative research and also to start segmenting the English population into their various involvements with football. I wanted to build a statistically valid model of the football public. Such a model would help us to target our communications and would help me to prepare a benchmark quantitative poll as a starting point to tracking opinion about our success or otherwise.

'I also started a large-scale survey of grassroots players, referees and administrators in March 2001. I worked closely with Kelly Simmons in the Football Development department to make sure this would help her in her role.

'By March 2001 I was ready to present my findings and my suggested plan for building a new image for the FA to the senior management team. I had worked out the FA's narrative, how that should be broken down into key themes, the policies that would appeal to the public to be used as "flagships" and make it easier for the public to understand our story. I knew the top-line and supporting messages that could be interwoven into everything we said or did, how to integrate all consumer touch-points to deliver our message and keep everything we did consistent and focused and I had fitted it all into the Chief Executive's vision and purpose for the organization. I even had a slogan: *The Football Association – a new set of goals*, to encapsulate everything about a changing and improving FA.

'It was the culmination of 18 months of research, learning, thinking and planning. I had learnt what the public and the various stakeholders wanted and I had matched it to our day-to-day work so that everything we did built our image using our key themes consistently. I tested it out with a trial presentation to Kelly Simmons' team of Football Development Officers. They were delighted. It was everything they wanted, a framework around which to organize their work within a confident FA that was becoming fit for purpose in the twenty-first century world of fast-moving and instantaneous communications.

'My trouble was that when I presented this to the senior management team, nobody in the room really wanted to implement my plan. I hadn't done my "political" preparations well, which was odd given my background. David Davies was my lone supporter in the room, and he was aware enough to realize when he was batting on a sticky wicket.

'I left the meeting dejected. I couldn't imagine how I could be influential at the FA following that reception for my ideas. I'd got the politics badly wrong. I knew that I had to think about another job, even though I'm certain that the content of what I was proposing was sound. I'd give the same presentation today; much of it is still relevant. I'm sharing this story because it proves the point that suits don't sell themselves. You can do the best research ever and have the latest facts and figures to support your argument and yet if you have not campaigned your cause appropriately the chances are you will not gain support. I knew this, of course. Somehow I forgot it at the FA and failed to create and run an internal campaign prior to my presentation.

'I left work at The Football Association at the end of July and started Silent Wave with Dorian. I regard my time at the FA as one of the most significant learning experiences in my life. They're often tough lessons, but it always seems that you learn the most from failures. It gave me the confidence to set up in business on my own. And that was when I learnt I was a campaigner.'

bbm

'After a couple of years Dorian and I went our separate ways. We just wanted our work to go in slightly different directions, and we remain friends. At the same time, a number of Labour MPs had been asking me for advice about their communications.

'I carried out some research for one of them. The main insight from the research was that hardly anyone understood what the role was of a Member of Parliament. I told her that I would help her only if she agreed to go out knocking on doors and chatting to residents in her constituency at least once a week, preferably more, and contact them just as regularly on the phone. She agreed.

'I developed three themes for her activities and communications. They were:

- to become the local community champion, working tirelessly to improve and build strong local communities;
- to use her office as a hub for making change happen (there is power and authority invested in the Office of MP which few MPs actually use deliberately to make local improvements);
- to act as an educator in all her communications and interactions, explaining her behaviours to her constituents and making clear how it would benefit them and involving them in the solutions as much as possible.

'All the time she was explaining the role of a Member of Parliament and what it meant for local people.

'I helped a number of MPs out in this way, developing my thinking and learning and sharing best practice and ideas amongst them all. In all my work, for my commercial clients and my pro-bono work, I was now deliberately thinking about building a sequence of communications designed to achieve all my clients' outcomes. Of course, a prerequisite for that was to know exactly what those outcomes were, and understanding that became the first thing I defined with every client.

'Within a year I was ready to take my thinking and ideas out more widely and in August 2005 my company, *bbm*, was created.

'Our first problem was that no one other than us had any idea what a campaign of communications was. Most people thought that a campaign was only connected to politics, marketing or the military. No one understood that it was of value to an organization or a community. We had to be educational in our approach, growing the knowledge of what it means to campaign communications to achieve specific outcomes, of the power of integrating channels around a compelling narrative linked to a cause. That education continues. This book is part of it.'

Very final thoughts

'The future is not an inheritance; it is an opportunity and an obligation.'
Bill Clinton

A campaign of communications can be applied to achieve any outcome.

For campaigners the desire to improve is a fundamental part of their identity. There is no space for a vet in the room. Unless, of course, they really are a vet and you happen to have a sick pet with you. The costs of miscommunication, especially when you really care about your cause, are too significant for complacency or arrogance. The challenge of being heard, trusted and remembered in our modern age is so great that we have to work at it with flair, skill, determination, consistency and rigour. And we have to keep getting better. We have to keep learning.

Campaigns start from nothing other than an emotional compulsion to achieve a desired outcome, an empty whiteboard, and the willingness to close the gap between the two. It takes courage to begin and willpower and determination to finish. When you choose to campaign you are choosing to be a pioneer and a leader. You are choosing to go first because somebody has to and because you care. No two campaigns are ever the same, and that means that you have to do things differently each time. It means you have to be creative, curious and willing to adapt in response to feedback. It means you have to be comfortable at least, and excited at best, with uncertainty.

Most of all, it means that you have to take responsibility for shaping the future.

INDEX

NB page references in *italic* indicate tables